Also by Dorothy and Thomas Hoobler

The Crimes of Paris

The Monsters: Mary Shelley and the Curse of Frankenstein

Vietnam: Why We Fought

Samurai Detective Series

American Family Album Series

Century Kids Series

Her Story Series

Images Across the Ages Series

Mandela

Showa: The Age of Hirohito

An Album of World War I

that the Bearer
you last night
to give him, as
as many Hours
after 9 O'Clock
to Dennis and an
my Account: This
call it which

Are You Prepared for the Storm of Love Making?

LETTERS OF LOVE AND LUST FROM THE WHITE HOUSE

Dorothy
and
Thomas
Hoobler

Simon & Schuster

NEW YORK LONDON TORONTO
SYDNEY NEW DELHI

100 YEARS

SIMON &
SCHUSTER

1230 Avenue of the Americas
New York, NY 10020

First Simon & Schuster hardcover edition February 2024

SIMON & SCHUSTER and colophon are registered trademarks
of Simon & Schuster, LLC

Simon & Schuster: Celebrating 100 Years of Publishing in 2024

For information about special discounts for bulk purchases,
please contact Simon & Schuster Special Sales at 1-866-506-1949
or business@simonandschuster.com.

The Simon & Schuster Speakers Bureau can bring authors to your
live event. For more information or to book an event, contact
the Simon & Schuster Speakers Bureau at 1-866-248-3049
or visit our website at www.simonspeakers.com.

Interior design by Paul Dippolito

Manufactured in the United States of America

1   3   5   7   9   10   8   6   4   2

Library of Congress Cataloging-in-Publication Data has been applied for.

ISBN 978-1-6680-1484-4
ISBN 978-1-6680-1486-8 (ebook)

For Our Daughter, Ellen

Contents

Introduction

This is a book of love stories. Every one of them involved a president of the United States, and we will tell their stories through letters they wrote. Through this collection of carefully chosen letters, we reveal the writers at their most vulnerable, providing a surprisingly intimate and deeply personal portrait that is often obscured by the public persona. The private face of presidents, as with other men, was not always the side they showed to the public. These letters reveal the tender romantics among the men who occupied the White House as well as those who were inept in matters of the heart. The letters also show the presidents who were surprisingly sexy and expose those who were consummate philanderers.

When these men wooed the women they wanted to marry or seduce, they could be playful, passionate, tender, consumed by desire. No president of the twentieth century appeared more straitlaced than Woodrow Wilson. Yet after ten years of married life, Wilson, about to return home after a long absence, wrote to his first wife, Ellen, "Do you think you can stand the innumerable kisses and the passionate embraces you will receive? Are you prepared for the storm of love making with which you will be assailed?"

The letters, too, often reveal the character of the writer. Lyndon B. Johnson, who wrote courtship letters to Lady Bird Taylor on House of Representatives stationery, jotted anxious little notes above the letterhead, such as "Question—Attention: Who do you love?"

The correspondence between the presidents and their wives also says much about their relationships and offers an unexpected window into the quiet but undeniable power that many of the early First Ladies were able to wield in the background.

John and Abigail Adams were remarkable for the respect they showed each other. The first time John met her, when she was only fifteen, he called her a "wit." She had no hesitation in cautioning him to "remember the ladies" when he was helping to write the Constitution. (His reply showed that he was something of a wit himself.) Their more than two thousand letters are full of clever sparring matches.

John and Abigail's son John Quincy had a very different marriage with his wife. Imperious by nature, he excluded his wife, Louisa Catherine, from his diplomatic and political careers as much as possible. Louisa once wrote, "I have nothing to do with the disposal of affairs and have never but once been consulted."

The marriage of James K. Polk and his wife, Sarah Childress, was quite the opposite. One of his relatives commented after meeting her that she displayed "a great deal of spice and more independence of judgment than was fitting in any one woman." Polk was fortunate in his choice of a mate; she played an active role in his career, clipping and even writing articles in newspapers, giving advice (which he took), and taking care of their plantation while he was elsewhere campaigning. All of their letters are more concerned with politics than romance.

As married people know, marriages are not all smooth sailing. Some of the letters are poignant and heartbreaking, reflecting times of loss, such as the death of a child. A great many reveal the hardships of separation, for many times letter writers were away on the battlefield. The weight of the office and the difficult decisions these men confronted also comes across in the correspondence.

Harry S. Truman wrote the following to his wife, Bess, after feeling she was unsympathetic to the problems he faced as president: "You can never appreciate what it means to come home as I did the other evening after doing at least one hundred things I didn't want to do and have the only person in the world whose approval and good opinion I value look at me like I'm something the cat dragged in." But Truman, a wise man who had been in love with Bess since he was five years old, put the letter aside. His daughter found it in his desk after he died. Several presidents also had extramarital affairs. It is not surprising that fewer of these letters have been preserved. In fact, the provocative letters written by Warren G. Harding to Carrie Phillips were later used to blackmail him. Nevertheless, his letters to Phillips are among the most passionate, and explicit, of presidential letters. Writing to Phillips, Harding re-called their dalliance the year before when "our hearts sang the rapture without words and we greeted the New Year from the hallowed heights of heaven . . ."

While we strived to include letters by every president, not all are rep-resented in this book. Some letters were destroyed, such as those of Thomas Jefferson, whose wife's dying wish was that he not only burn the letters he had written to her but that he not marry again. (She had been raised by a stepmother who treated her cruelly and she didn't want her two daughters by Jefferson to suffer the same fate.)

Other letters were lost or forgotten. Martin Van Buren's wife died eighteen years before he became president and is not even mentioned in his autobiography. Zachary Taylor wrote many letters during his ser-vice in the Mexican War, but none that he wrote to his wife were sal-vaged. This doesn't mean that Van Buren or Taylor wrote no letters; it reflects the attitude of their times that such intimate letters were pri-vate, and to be kept that way.

Although Herbert and Lou Hoover were together for most of their adult lives, the Hoover Presidential Library assured us that they have no letters. Laura Bush, wife of George W. Bush, wrote in her autobiog-raphy that she and George only spent one day apart from the moment they met as adults until the day of their wedding. Hence, no court-ship letters. (He had spent that one day with his extended family in Maine, where he missed Laura so much that he immediately flew back to Texas.) We contacted every other living former president but their letters were not available. In a digital era of tweets, texts, and emails, we are unlikely to ever get such an intimate look at our modern presidents through records of private, handwritten letters.

The letters in this book are divided into four sections: Romancing, Separation, Adversity, and Lovers. Before each letter, we note the name of the president who wrote the letter, and to whom he sent it. You may find letters from a single president in different sections. While many presidents weren't great at spelling or grammar, we've left the letters just as they were written to provide the most authentic reading experience, except where we deleted a few unnecessary commas. The letters also reflect the writing conventions of the time, which we have also left intact, adding a bracketed note in the text for clarity when needed.

Lastly, in writing about our presidents, we realize that history has revealed their many strengths but also their flaws—from misogyny and racism to ineptitude and misconduct. With rare exceptions, those who held office in the early years of the republic were enslavers.

So we stress that in this book, we write about the presidents as men who fell in love and expressed their feelings as other men did. That was one aspect of their lives, not the only one. Through this lens, we hope to understand them as we never have before.

PART 1

Romancing

Introduction

When a man writes a letter to a woman he is in love with, he generally has one purpose: to persuade her to love him. There are many ways to do this. Some are clever; some are not. Perhaps the clumsiest in this section is in Ulysses S. Grant's letter to Julia Dent. He drew twenty-one long dashes on the paper and wrote, *"Read these blank lines just as I intend them, and they will express more than words."*

Well, of course Julia wanted words more than dashes, but she had to specifically ask him to express his affections—and, eventually, she received them. You'll find those in this section, too.

At the other extreme might be John Tyler, who expressed himself in language as flowery as any Southern gentleman of the 1810s would: *"From the first moment of my acquaintance with you, I felt the influence of genuine affection; but now, when I reflect upon the sacrifice which you make to virtue and to feeling, by conferring your hand upon me, who have nothing to boast of but an honest and upright soul, and a heart of purest love, I feel gratitude superadded to affection by you."*

It worked for Tyler. In fact, it worked twice, because after his first wife passed away, he wooed and won another. His second wife, Julia Gardiner, was thirty years younger than Tyler, and in time they had seven children. Closer to our own time is the courtship of Claudia Alta "Lady Bird" Taylor by Lyndon B. Johnson. As a congressman later, Johnson was known for winning votes through sheer persistence—what some called "twisting arms." That was the way he won Lady Bird, too. He met her in Texas in September 1934, and after he returned to Washington, DC, wrote her every day with sentiments like this: *"Again I repeat—I love you—only you—Want to always love—only you . . ."* He demanded that she write him just as often. After more than two months of this, she agreed to marry him, and they wed in November 1934. They remained together for the rest of his life.

In the end, maybe the best approach is for the lover to convince his beloved that the one thing above all others that he'd rather do is write to her; as John Adams expressed it to Abigail Smith: *"Now Letter-Writing is, to me, the most agreeable Amusement, and Writing to you, the most entertaining and Agreeable of all Letter-Writing."*

Reading the letters is entertaining, too, as we hope you'll discover.

George Washington to Martha Dandridge Custis Washington

At the end of her life, Martha Washington tried to burn all the letters she had ever received from her husband. Fortunately for us, she missed a few. Scholars disagree on which of the remaining ones are genuine. Only two are generally accepted as coming from Washington's hand. Here is one, and you will find the other in Part 2.

Neither of these was written during their courtship, but George's feelings toward Martha are evident from the letter below. We do know that their courtship began in the spring of 1758 when Colonel and Mrs. Richard Chamberlayne invited their neighbor, Martha Custis, to pay a visit to their plantation on the Pamunkey River in Virginia. While she was there, Chamberlayne was out for a stroll when he encountered his friend George Washington and invited him to stay for dinner.

Chamberlayne may not have known it, but he was playing Cupid. Martha's husband, Daniel Parke Custis, had died the year before, leaving his widow a fortune and a grand home named, coincidentally, the White House. Martha was only twenty-six and beautiful. She also had two children and was doubtless looking for someone to be a father to them.

Washington tried to beg off from the invitation. He was the commander of the Virginia militia and was headed for Williamsburg, the colony's capital, to meet with the governor. However, after Chamberlayne pointed out the desirability of his houseguest, Washington accepted the invitation.

Although called the "Father of the Country," George Washington had no known biological children. The two young children in this picture are Martha's grandchildren. The boy was named after George Washington.

The dinner was a success, and Washington stayed the night. He finally did leave to keep his appointment with the governor, but it wasn't long before he called on Martha again. They were married on January 6, 1759, at Martha's home.

Neither could have guessed that more than sixteen years later, Washington would be chosen to lead the colonies in rebellion against Britain. He was the logical man for the job, because no one else had as much military experience as he did. But it carried obvious personal risks. He would assume command immediately and did not even have the time to return to Virginia to say goodbye to his wife. He wrote the following note without knowing when, or if, he would meet her again.

Phila. June 23d 1775.

My dearest,

As I am within a few Minutes of leaving this City, I could not think of departing from it without dropping you a line; especially as I do not know whether it may be in my power to write again until I get to the Camp at Boston—I go fully trusting in that Providence, which has been more bountiful to me than I deserve, & in full confidence of a happy meeting with you sometime in the Fall—I have not time to add more, as I am surrounded with company to take Leave of me—I retain an unalterable affection for you, which neither time or distance can change, my best love to Jack & Nelly [her children] *& regard for the rest of the Family concludes me with the utmost truth & sincerity.*

Yr entire,

Go: Washington

Actually, Martha was able to visit him, and the troops he commanded, each winter for the next eight years when the fighting halted. The soldiers were impressed by Martha's visits, for she knitted socks and other things for them and offered encouragement. The Marquis de Lafayette, the French nobleman who had joined Washington's army, recalled that she "loved her husband madly."

John Adams to Abigail Smith

John Adams and Abigail Smith Adams more than made up for Martha Washington's reluctance to make her husband's letters public. The second president and his wife were separated so often that there are about eleven hundred letters between them. They first met when John was a struggling twenty-four-year-old lawyer and Abigail was only fifteen. Both were strong-willed and it was not a case of love at first sight.

Over time, a mutual attraction grew between the two and they married after a three-year courtship. Abigail's mother tried to discourage the union because she didn't think John could earn enough to support a wife. But he persisted and before long he developed a pet name for her, which he used on the following "bill."

Octr. 4th, 1762

Miss Adorable
*   By the same Token that the Bearer hereof satt up with you last night I hereby order you to give him, as many Kisses, and as many Hours of your Company after 9 OClock as he shall please to Demand and charge them to my Account. . . . I presume I have good Right to draw upon you for the Kisses as I have given two or three Millions at least, when one has been recd, [received] and of Consequence the Account between us is immensely in favour of yours*
*   John Adams*

Abigail saw beneath the surface of the homely young lawyer. He had what she most respected: a good education. The daughter of a minister, she had been taught the basics by her mother and through reading whichever books she found in her father's library. She was thirsty for more.

Against the advice of her parents, she and John became engaged in 1764, when she was nineteen. Evidently she encouraged John's advice on how she could improve herself, leading to the next letter, an unusual one for a fiancé to write. Even more unusual—to our modern eyes—are the supposed "faults" he found in her. Across the centuries, we might discern a twinkle in the young man's eye as he responds to her request, for his suggestions have a wry tone that implies that Abigail's imperfections were really very trivial.

Boston May 7th. 1764

I promised you, Sometime agone, a Catalogue of your Faults, Imperfections, Defects—or whatever you please to call them . . . But I must caution you, before I proceed to recollect yourself, [that] instead of being vexed or fretted or thrown into a Passion, to resolve upon a Reformation—for this is my sincere Aim, in laying before you, this Picture of yourself.

In the first Place, then, give me leave to say, you have been extreamly negligent, in attending so little to Cards. You have very little Inclination, to that noble and elegant Diversion, and whenever you have taken a Hand you have held it but awkwardly and played it, with a very uncourtly, and indifferent, Air . . .

Another Thing, which ought to be mentioned, and by all means amended, is, the Effect of a Country Life and Education, I mean, a certain Modesty, sensibility, Bashfulness, call it by which of these Names you will, that enkindles Blushes forsooth at every Violation of Decency, in Company, and lays a most insupportable Constraint on the freedom of Behavior . . .

In the Third Place, you could never yet be prevail'd on to learn to sing. This I take very soberly to be an Imperfection of the most

*moment of any. An Ear for Musick would be a source of much
Pleasure . . .*

*In the Fourth Place you very often hang your Head like a
Bulrush. You do not sit, erected as you ought [and so] it happens
that you appear too short for a Beauty, and the Company looses
the sweet smiles of that Countenance and the bright sparkles of
those Eyes. This Fault is the Effect and Consequence of another,
still more inexcusable in a Lady, I mean the Habit of Reading,
Writing and Thinking. But both the Cause and the Effect ought to
be repented and amended as soon as possible.*

*Another Fault, which seems to have been obstinately persisted
in, after frequent Remonstrances, Advices and Admonitions of
your Friends, is that of sitting with the Leggs across. This ruins
the figure and . . . injures the Health. And springs I fear from the
former source, vizt [such as] too much Thinking. These Things
ought not to be!*

*A sixth Imperfection is that of Walking, with the Toes bending
inward. This Imperfection is commonly called Parrot-toed, I
think, I know not for what Reason. . . .*

*Thus have I given a faithful Portraiture of all the Spotts, I have
hitherto discerned . . . Nearly Three Weeks have I conned and
studied for more, but more are not to be discovered. All the rest is
bright and luminous. . . .*

Lysander

John signed the letter with the pet name Abigail had given him. Lysander was a Trojan military hero. This held a tinge of irony since John
was not a military man and never took up arms in the Revolution. Abigail responded to this letter in the same spirit, writing, "I thank you
for your Catalogue, but must confess I was so hardened as to read over
most of my Faults with as much pleasure, as an other person would have
read their perfections. And Lysander must excuse me if I still persist
in some of them, at least till I am convinced that an alteration would
contribute to his happiness . . . but you know I think that a gentleman
has no business to concern himself about the Leggs of a Lady. For my

part I do not apprehend any bad effects from the practice, yet since you desire it, and that you may not for the future trouble yourself so much about it, will reform."

Thirty-five years after they met, John would become the second president of a nation that didn't exist when he and Abigail first met each other. He served from 1797 to 1801.

Theirs would be a marriage of equals, unusual for the times.

James Madison to Dolley Payne Todd

At age forty-six, James Madison had never been married. He had once fallen in love with Kitty Floyd, a fifteen-year-old girl, and proposed to her—by letter. She accepted, but he wanted to wait until Congress adjourned for the year. This proved to be a mistake, for she accepted another man's offer and sent Madison a rejection—by letter.

So, when he became aware of a young widow whose mother ran a boardinghouse, he didn't tarry. He asked Aaron Burr, who had stayed in the boardinghouse, to make an introduction.

Dolley Payne grew up in a Quaker family and married a Quaker lawyer in 1790, when she was twenty-two. Soon she was the mother of two sons, but then tragedy struck. An epidemic of yellow fever swept through Philadelphia, home to many of the Quaker faith. Dolley's husband, John Todd, succumbed to the disease and so did one of their sons. Widows seldom had a way to earn a living in those days, unless they inherited a fortune from their husbands, which wasn't the case with Dolley.

Physically, James Madison must not have seemed a good catch. Shy and short (at five feet, four inches, he was the shortest president). But he had a brilliant mind and was the principal author of the Constitution and the Bill of Rights. George Washington, not a lawyer, often consulted Madison and asked him to write his inaugural address. (The House of Representatives then asked him to write the official reply to Washington's address.)

When Madison asked for Dolley's hand, once again the courtship began by letter. This time, Madison used allies. He asked Dolley's cousin, the wife of a congressman, to tell Dolley how much in love with her he was: "To begin, he thinks so much of you in the day that he has Lost his Tongue, at night he Dreames of you . . . Calling on you to relieve his Flame for he Burns to such an excess that he will be shortly consumed & he hopes that your Heart will be calous to every other swain but himself." Dolley finally consented to his proposal, although the letter she sent has been lost. Here is Madison's reply to the happy news.

Orange, NJ
Aug 18, [1794]

I read some days ago your precious favor [letter] *from Fredg.*
[Fredericksburg, PA, where she had gone to escape the epidemic]
but hope you will conceive the joy it gave me. The delay in
hearing of your leaving . . . which I regarded as the only satis-
factory proof of your recovery had filled me with extreme
disquietude, and the communication of the welcome event was
endeared to me by the stile in which it was conveyed. I hope you
will never have another deliberation [in other words, change her
mind] *on that subject. If the sentiments of my heart can guarantee*
those of yours, they assure me there can never be a cause for it.
[The letter has been damaged, making its contents difficult to read.]

Dolley and James were married on September 15, 1794. The following day, she wrote her best friend "to tell you in short, that in the course of this day I give my Hand to the Man who of all other's I most admire. . . . In this Union I have everything that is soothing and greatful in prospect—& my little Payne *[her surviving son]* will have a generous & tender protector." She signed the letter Dolley Payne Todd, and then, realizing her mistake, wrote, "Dolley Madison! Alass!" In time, however, she would fall deeply in love with Madison. Because she married an Episcopalian, Dolley was expelled from the Quakers. It was just as well, because she later became known for her fashionable clothing and the weekly parties she gave while First Lady. Serving as hostess for Jefferson, the third president (whose wife had died), and as the wife of Madison, the fourth president, she set the standard for presidential wives.

The Madisons' marriage was by all accounts a happy one. In an 1877 article in *Lippincott's Monthly Magazine*, a woman who claimed to have visited the Madisons in 1835, when James was over eighty years old, recounted this giddy scene:

"Mr. and Mrs. Madison would in private sometimes romp and tease each other like two children, and engage in antics that would astonish the muse of history. Mrs. Madison was stronger as well as larger than he. She could—and did—seize his hands, draw him upon her back and go round the room with him whenever she particularly wished to impress him with a due sense of man's inferiority."

When Dolley Madison died, thirteen years after her husband, Congress adjourned for a day in her honor.

John Quincy Adams to Louisa Catherine Johnson

Twenty-seven-year-old John Quincy Adams could not have known that he was destined to become the United States' sixth president when he arrived in Europe in 1794. President George Washington had just appointed him the US ambassador to the Netherlands, a job John Quincy was well suited for, because his father, John Adams, now vice president, had served in the same post earlier.

John Quincy, at that time only eleven, had accompanied him, spending much of his childhood in Europe.

His new assignment did not keep John Quincy in the Netherlands for long. He was ordered to go to London to take over the duties of the American ambassador, who was busy negotiating a treaty in Spain. On this trip John Quincy met Joshua Johnson, the American consul in London, and became smitten with twenty-one-year-old Louisa Catherine, one of Johnson's daughters—enough so that John Quincy had a miniature portrait of himself painted and sent to her.

June 2, 1796

I [spent] *about an hour devoted to a last sitting to Mr: Hull.* [The artist who was painting a miniature of John.] *He has I think as good a likeness as has yet been taken of that original, and you I think will like it better than the large portrait because it is not so much flattered. As soon as it is finished, he will send or carry it to your Pappa, who will doubtless know that it is destined for you. Accept it as a token of an affection which will cease only with the last pulse of the heart of him whose image it is, and may it often meet your eye, with one half the delight which at this instant he derives from a look at the precious corresponding pledge of your regard* [a similar portrait of Louisa], *which now lies on the table before him. . . .*

I am indeed desirous to hear from you, and I am sure a detail of the minutest and most trivial circumstances in which you have any concern would give me pleasure. Six days have elapsed since I last enjoyed the happiness of seeing you, and in every hour of the time there have been many days [meaning that each hour without her seemed like a day]. *I shall take the earliest opportunity of writing to my friends in America, and if I can procure any prospect that will enable me to indulge the wishes of my heart, I shall cheerfully resign a career of public life which can offer nothing satisfactory to Ambition, and which forbids the possession of that private happiness, the first object of my hopes and which you only can confer.*

Your ever faithful and affectionate friend
John Q. Adams

Despite these affectionate sentiments, the courtship between John Quincy and Louisa Catherine did not go smoothly. John Quincy felt

Louisa Adams, wife of John Quincy Adams. Both she and her husband had strong personalities that often clashed. Louisa adapted to John's coldness by binging on chocolates and writing political satires.

himself intellectually superior to Louisa, and frequently lectured her about what he felt her conduct should be. On at least one occasion, she resisted his attempts to improve her, and he complained about her "rebellious quality." Evidently, he had not benefited from observing his parents' more equal relationship.

Louisa, in turn, complained that his devotion to "his books" took precedence over their relationship. She wrote: ". . . you are I think too young a man to devote all your time to your books, and solitude . . . indeed my beloved friend it is a dangerous indulgence, you know I think it prejudicial to your health, excuse me when I say hurtful to your temper."

His reply followed:

The Hague, April 13 [1797]

. . . I should not think it necessary to renew the discussion between us with regard to my books; but you tell me that my attachment to them is hurtful to my temper. I receive the intimation with thanks, because it is not flattering, but it does not meet with the assent of my own mind.—I believe that my temper never was and never will be hurt by my devotion to study or to solitude—There is another thing which never fails to hurt it . . . and that is, any attempt by those whom I love, to cross the current of my character, or control my sentiments or manners . . . I believe all my friends will find it, saving trouble to themselves, and they will certainly consult my happiness, by considering them as articles upon which I am incorrigible. . . .

But you intimate a suspicion, that this attachment, unless I should check it, may even interfere with that which I bear to you, and may render even your society irksome to me. No—I can never believe that possible. Instead of weakening, the ardent love of literature tends to confirm, to increase to exalt every virtuous and laudable affection.—I shall love you the more, in proportion to my degree of application. . . .

My lovely friend, reprove me for every day of my time that I lose in indolence: persuade yourself, that no man in my condition of life, ever hurt his health, by too much application to his duties, but that thousands have ruined themselves by neglecting them. Cheer my Industry, instead of dissuading me from it. Encourage me to persevere, instead of endeavouring to divert me from such purposes, and be assured that every exhortation of that kind will be more worthy of yourself, and more useful to me, than any intimation that either my health or my temper suffer by my application to books or my solitude.

Remember me affectionately to all the family, and believe me ever faithfully yours,

A.

Louisa's parents, who had seven daughters to find husbands for, were eager to have John Quincy take the next step in the relationship. Adams had resumed his diplomatic duties in the Netherlands, and the courtship was conducted primarily through letters. There was another problem: in 1797, John Quincy's father had taken office as the second president of the United States, and it might prove an embarrassment if his son married a woman who was born in Britain—even though Louisa's father was born in the United States, giving his children American citizenship as well.

Matters came to a head when the Johnson family prepared to return to the United States, and John Quincy received orders to relocate to Portugal. The young couple seemed destined to be separated for the foreseeable future. Then John Quincy wrote what was both a warning and a definite proposal:

May 12, 1797

You know the man you have chosen for the friend of your life—You know him the better for that absence which has at once shown you a trial of his affection and of his temper. He has disguised to you none of his feelings and weaknesses. You know the chances of hardship, inconvenience and danger which you may be called to share with him. You know the inviolable attachment to his Country and his resolute determination not to continue long his absence from it. You know that upon his retirement the state of his fortune will require privations [financial sacrifices] which will be painful to him only as they may affect you. Choose, Louisa, choose for yourself, and be assured that his Heart will ratify your choice.

Louisa lost no time in replying. She wrote, "Why my beloved friend did you tell me to choose, what I have always declared, requires not a moments hesitation to determine, no my Adams, I have long ardently wished you might be enabled to return, and I have repeatedly assured you, that no personal inconvenience, would prevent my accompanying you, if possible—need I then say more to convince you, that your return would make me happy, and that I anticipate it with the utmost pleasure—I only fear my friend, that you will find me a troublesome companion—

"In regard to your temper &c:, *[the eighteenth-century equivalent of etc.]* I can only say, that the more I know you, the more I admire, esteem, and love you, and the greater is my inclination, to do every thing in my power, to promote your happiness, and welfare—

". . . I would say a great deal if I knew how to express it. but it is impossible, and I must simply stile myself, yours unalterably,

   Louisa C. Johnson"

They were married in London on July 26, 1797. Until the presidency of Donald Trump brought his wife Melanija Knavs Trump to the White House, Louisa was the only First Lady to be born abroad.

Andrew Jackson to
Rachel Donelson Jackson

Andrew Jackson became the seventh president of the United States in 1829 and served until 1837. He was the first president since Washington to become popular as a war hero, winning the Battle of New Orleans to keep the British from gaining control of the Mississippi in the War of 1812. He was also the first president whose forebears came from Ireland.

The relationship between Jackson and his wife, Rachel Donelson, is one of the great presidential love stories. Rachel was a beautiful young woman, described as having "lustrous black eyes, dark glossy hair, full red lips, brunette complexion, though of brilliant coloring, *[and]* a sweet oval face rippling with smiles and dimples." She had many admirers, but in her early twenties married a man named Lewis Robards who was apparently abusive to her. She left him and returned to her home in Nashville, which was then a small frontier community.

By the time she met twenty-one-year-old Andrew Jackson in 1788, she assumed that her first husband had divorced her, and she wed Jackson in 1791. Robards, hearing of this, sued her for desertion and adultery, leading to a legal dissolution of her first marriage. Rachel and Jackson remarried in a quiet ceremony. Nevertheless, Jackson's political opponents used the incident to spread the tale that Rachel was a bigamist.

Jackson was eager for a political career and after Tennessee became a state, he was elected as its first representative to the US Congress. Rachel didn't enjoy political life, in part because of the scurrilous stories about her. Ironically, in the following letter, written early in their marriage, Jackson promises to retire from politics, but he never did. Years later, after Rachel died just before his inauguration as president, he blamed people who defamed his wife for her early death.

Knoxville, May 9 1796

My Dearest Heart,

It is with the greatest pleasure I sit down to write you. Tho I am absent My heart rests with you. With what pleasing hopes I view the future period when I shall be restored to your arms there to spend My days in Domestic Sweetness with you the Dear Companion of my life, never to be separated from you again during this Transitory and fluctuating life.

I mean to retire from the Buss of publick life, and Spend My Time with you alone in Sweet Retirement, which is My only ambition and ultimate wish.

I have this moment finished My business here . . . and tho it is now half after ten o'clock, could not think of going to bed without writing you. May it give you pleasure to Receive it. May it add to your Contentment until I return. May you be blessed with health. May the Goddess of Slumber every evening light on your eyebrows and gently lull you to sleep, and conduct you through the night with pleasing thoughts and pleasant dreams. Could I only know you were contented and enjoyed Peace of Mind, what satisfaction it would afford me whilst travelling the

*loanly and tiresome road. It would relieve My anxious breast
and shorten the way—May the great "I am" bless and protect
you until that happy and wished for moment arrives when I get
restored to your sweet embrace which is the Nightly prayer of
your affectionate husband,*
   Andrew Jackson

*P.S. My compliments to my good old Mother Mrs. Donelson,
[Rachel's mother] that best of friends. Tell her with what pain I
reflect upon leaving home without shaking her by the hand and
asking her blessing.*

John Tyler to Letitia Christian Tyler

John Tyler, the son of a governor of Virginia, met Letitia Christian
at a party in 1809. Her parents owned a large plantation near Richmond, the capital of Virginia, and Tyler was soon a frequent visitor.
The following letter, which contains the most flowery language in
this book, was said to be the first he ever wrote to her, even though it
appears she had already accepted his proposal of marriage. Despite
his passionate words, he was strictly the Southern gentleman in his
conduct. He later told his daughter that it wasn't until a few weeks
before their wedding that he kissed Letitia—on the hand. They were
married on his twenty-third birthday, March 29, 1813. She would turn
twenty-three later that year.

Richmond, December 5th 1812

*Although I could not entirely obtain your permission to write to
you, yet I am well aware that you will not be displeased at my
exercising a privilege so valuable to one standing in the relation that I do to you. To think of you and to write to you, are
the only sources from whence I can derive any real satisfaction*

during my residence in this place. [Young John was already a member of the Virginia House of Delegates.] *The prerogative of thinking of those we love, and from whom we are separated, seems to be guaranteed to us by nature, because we cannot be deprived of it either by the bustle and confusion of a town, or by the important duties that attach to our existence. Believe me, my L., that this observation has been completely verified by me since I last saw you, for although deafened by noise, and attentive to the duties of my station, yet you are the subject of my serious meditations and the object of my fervent prayers to heaven. From the first moment of my acquaintance with you, I felt the influence of genuine affection; but now, when I reflect upon the sacrifice which you make to virtue and to feeling, by conferring your hand upon me, who have nothing to boast of but an honest and upright soul, and a heart of purest love, I feel gratitude superadded to affection by you. Indeed, I do esteem myself most rich in possessing you. The mean and sordid wretch who yields the unspeakable bliss of possessing her whom he ardently loves, may boast of his ill-acquired wealth, and display his treasures in all the pride of ostentation to the world, but who shall administer to him comfort in the hour of affliction? Whose seraph smile shall chase away the fiends which torment him? The partner of his bosom he neither esteems nor regards, and he knows nothing of the balm which tender affection can bestow. . . .*

You express some degree of astonishment, my L., at an observation I once made to you, "that I would not have been willingly wealthy at the time that I addressed you." Suffer me to repeat it. If I had been wealthy, the idea of your being actuated by prudential considerations [money] *in accepting my suit, would have eternally tortured me. But I exposed to you frankly and unblushingly my situation in life—my hopes and my fears, my prospects and my dependencies—and you nobly responded. To ensure your happiness is now my only object, and whether I float or sink in the stream of fortune, you may be assured of this, that I shall never cease to love you. Forgive me for these remarks, which I have been irresistibly led to make. . . .*

Again suffer me to assure you of my constant esteem and affection, and believe me to be most faithfully,
John Tyler
To Miss Letitia Christian
New Kent.

Letitia's daughter-in-law praised Letitia's skill at managing large households, which was fortunate, for she had eight children with Tyler, seven of whom lived to adulthood.

For Tyler's letters to his second wife, see Part 3.

Abraham Lincoln to Two Women

Even though more books have been written about Lincoln than any other president, there are still mysteries about his love life. His first serious romantic relationship may have been with a woman named Ann Rutledge, whom he supposedly met while living in New Salem, Illinois. Historians have found no evidence that they were engaged, but the two of them reportedly developed a close bond before she died, probably of typhoid fever. As a result, romantic stories about the two of them have been invented—but no letters.

There is a second, better documented, romance between Lincoln and a woman named Mary Owens. But it's not often retold, because its outcome reflects somewhat badly on Lincoln. But there is a letter. Three letters in fact, and the first one we are including was written by Lincoln to a woman who was married to a friend of his. Here, he gives his side of the failed romance. Lincoln was well-known for spinning a good yarn, and his talent is very much on display here:

Abraham Lincoln to
Eliza Browning "Mrs. Orville H."

Springfield, [Illinois] *April 1, 1838*

Dear Madam:

. . . I shall make the history of so much of my own life, as has elapsed since I saw you, the subject of this letter. . . .

It was then, in the autumn of 1836, that a married lady of my acquaintance [Mrs. Bennett Abell], *and who was a great friend of mine, being about to pay a visit to her father and other relatives residing in Kentucky, proposed to me, that on her return she could bring a sister* [Mary S. Owens] *of hers with her, upon condition that I would engage to become her brother-in-law. . . . I, of course, accepted the proposal, for . . . I was most confoundedly pleased with the project. I had seen the said sister some three years before, thought her inteligent and agreeable, and saw no good objection to plodding life through hand in hand with her. Time passed on, the lady took her journey and in due time returned, sister in company sure enough. . . . All this occured upon my hearing of her arrival in the neighbourhood, for, be it remembered, I had not yet seen her, except about three years previous, as before mentioned.*

In a few days we had an interview, and although I had seen her before, she did not look as my imagination had pictured her. I knew she was over-size, but she now appeared a fair match for Falstaff. [She was reportedly five feet five, 150 pounds.] *I knew she was called an "old maid", and I felt no doubt of at least half of the appelation; but now, when I beheld her, I could not for my life avoid thinking of my mother, and this, not from withered features, for her skin was too full of fat, to permit its contracting in wrinkles, but from her want of teeth, weather-beaten appear-ance in general, and from a kind of notion that ran in my head that nothing could have commenced at the size of infancy, and reached her present bulk in less than thirtyfive or forty years, and, in short, I was not all pleased with her. But what could I do? I had told her sister that I would take her for better or for worse, and I made a point of honor and conscience in all things, to stick to my word, especially if others had been induced to act on it, which in this case, I doubted not they had, for I was now fairly convinced, that no other man on earth would have her, and hence the conclusion that they were bent on holding me to my bargain. Well, thought I, I have said it, and . . . it shall not be my fault if I fail to do it. And once I determined to consider her my wife; and this done, all my powers of discovery were put to the rack, in search of perfections in her, which might be fairly set-off against her defects. I tried to imagine she was handsome, which, but for her unfortunate corpulency, was actually true. Exclusive of this, no woman that I have seen, has a finer face. I also tried to convince myself that the mind was much more to be valued than the person, and in this, she was not inferior. . . .*

All this while, although I was fixed . . . in my resolution, I found I was continually repenting the rashness, which had led me to make it. Through life I have been in no bondage, either real or immaginary from the thraldom of which I so much desired to be free. . . . After all my suffering upon this deeply interesting subject, here I am, wholly unexpectedly, completely out of the "scraps"; and I now want to know, if you can guess how I got out of it. Out clear in every sense of the term, no violation of word, honor or conscience. I dont believe you can guess, and so I may as well tell you at once. . . . After I had delayed the matter as long as I thought I could in honor do, which by the way had brought me round into the last fall . . . I mustered my resolution, and made the proposal to her direct; but, shocking to relate, she answered, No. At first I supposed she did it through an affectation of modesty, which I thought but ill became her, under the peculiar circumstances of her case, but on my renewal of the charge, I found she [repeated it] with greater firmness than before. I tried it again and again, but with the same success, or rather with the same want of success. I finally was forced to give it up, at which I verry unexpectedly found myself mortified almost beyond endurance. I was mortified, it seemed to me, in a hundred different ways. My vanity was deeply wounded by the reflection, that I had so long been too stupid to discover her intentions, and at the same time never doubting that I understood them perfectly; and also, that she whom I had taught myself to believe no body else would have, had actually rejected me with all my fancied greatness; and to cap the whole, I then, for the first time, began to suspect that I was really a little in love with her. But let it all go. I'll try and out live it. Others have been made fools of by the girls; but this can never be with truth said of me. I most emphatically, in this instance, made a fool of myself. I have now come to the conclusion never again to think of marrying; and for this reason; I can never be satisfied with any one who would be block-head enough to have me.

When you receive this, write me a long yarn about something to amuse me. Give my respects to Mr. Browning. Your sincere friend
    A. Lincoln

Abraham Lincoln to Mary S. Owens

As you see, Lincoln was a good storyteller, and like many who have this gift, he would never let the truth stand in the way of an entertaining tale. Fortunately, there is a second letter—one that he wrote to Mary Owens eleven months before he wrote the above to Eliza Browning. And it throws a different light on why Mary Owens "rejected" him.

Springfield, May 7, 1837

Friend Mary
    . . . . This thing of living in Springfield is rather a dull business after all, at least it is so to me. I am quite as lonesome here as [I] ever was anywhere in my life. . . . I am often thinking about what we said of your coming to live at Springfield. I am afraid you would not be satisfied. There is a great deal of flourishing about in carriages here, which it would be your doom to see without

shareing in it. You would have to be poor without the means of hiding your poverty. Do you believe you could bear that patiently? Whatever woman may cast her lot with mine, should any ever do so, it is my intention to do all in my power to make her happy and contented, and there is nothing I can immagine, that would make me more unhappy than to fail in the effort. I know I should be much happier with you than the way I am, provided I saw no signs of discontent in you. What you have said to me may have been in jest, or I may have misunderstood it. If so, then let it be forgotten; if otherwise, I much wish you would think seriously before you decide. For my part I have already decided. What I have said I will most positively abide by, provided you wish it. My opinion is that you had better not do it. You have not been accustomed to hardship, and it may be more severe than you now immagine. I know you are capable of thinking correctly on any subject, and if you deliberate maturely upon this, before you decide, then I am willing to abide your decision.

You must write me a good long letter after you get this. You have nothing else to do, and though it might not seem inter- esting to you, after you had written it, it would be a good deal of company to me . . . Tell your sister I dont want to hear any more about selling out and moving. That gives me the hypo [hypochon- dria] whenever I think of it. Yours, &c.

Lincoln

When Lincoln retold the story of his broken "engagement" he made it seem as though he had made a fool of himself. But it is clear from this second letter that he had engineered his role as a jilted lover. There was a third letter, in which Lincoln wrote to Mary and acknowl- edged her decision to turn him down. As far as is known, Mary Owens never replied to Lincoln's last letter. She did, however, marry another man and have four children.

Because there are no extant letters that Lincoln wrote during his courtship of Mary Todd, we have decided to give a brief summation of their romance here.

On December 16, 1839, when Lincoln was thirty, he attended a cotillion. There he met Mary Todd, who would one day be his wife. She did not lack suitors; her father was wealthy, and she lived in Springfield with her sisters and brother-in-law, in what was one of the largest houses in town. But she and Lincoln hit it off because they both had a talent for mimicking people they knew. Lincoln's sense of humor appealed to her. Within a year they were engaged to be married. Headstrong Mary overcame any objections her family might have had.

Then, out of the blue, Lincoln arrived to tell her the planned marriage could not take place. Pressed for a reason, he told Mary he was no longer in love with her. Supposedly he did not think he could earn enough to support a wife.

But there was a darker reason that Lincoln confided only to a close friend, his future law partner and biographer, William Herndon. When Lincoln was young, he had patronized a prostitute in another town. Now he thought he was showing symptoms of syphilis and could not in good conscience spread it to his new wife. (Some of today's scholars doubt that Lincoln had contracted syphilis, even though he feared it.) Herndon did not include this story in his book but revealed it in a note to Jesse Weik, who had helped him write the biography.

Not knowing the truth, Mary Todd decided to redouble her efforts to attract Lincoln. Meanwhile, he was taking some mercury pills, then an antidote for the disease, and his symptoms seemed to fade. The wedding was again scheduled, nearly two years later, though Lincoln still had misgivings. He was thirty-three and his bride ten years younger. (Stephen Douglas, who would become Lincoln's opponent in the presidential election, also proposed to Mary Todd but she turned him down.)

On the morning of the ceremony, Lincoln was dressing in his boardinghouse room. He answered a knock at the door to find his friend Elizabeth Butler, clad in her best dress and no doubt dispatched to see that Lincoln showed up. She brought along her two children, a nine-year-old girl named Salome and a five-year-old boy named Speed. As their mother tied Lincoln's tie for him, Speed asked, "Where are you going, Mr. Lincoln?"

He considered the falling rain outside his window and said, "To Hell, I suppose."

Ulysses S. Grant to Julia Dent

Ulysses S. Grant, who would become the eighteenth president of the United States, graduated from West Point in 1843 but did not enjoy military life and planned to resign his commission after the required four years. His roommate at the Military Academy was Frederick Dent, who introduced Grant to his sister, Julia. Grant became a frequent visitor to the Dent home, and the young couple fell in love. He won Julia's affection when her canary died; he built a tiny yellow coffin and persuaded some of his fellow officers to serve as an honor guard at the bird's "funeral."

Julia was sensitive about her crossed eyes, but he found them endearing. Later, when she wanted to have the condition surgically corrected, he talked her out of it—but all the photographs of her show her in profile.

When Grant proposed, however, Julia demurred. She was only eighteen and knew her father would oppose the marriage because the twenty-two-year-old Grant was still in the army, which at that time was not a lucrative career. Even so Grant persuaded her to accept his West Point ring as a pledge of his love.

Their affection would endure many separations, so the courtship continued by letter. The first of these came in 1844, when Grant was stationed at Camp Salubrity in Louisiana. His letter shows his innate shyness, as when he wrote:

June 4th, 1844

. . . Julia! I cannot express the regrets that I feel at having to leave Jeff. Bks. [Jefferson Barracks, his first post, which was near Julia's home in Missouri] *at the time that I did. I was just learning how to*

enjoy the place and the Society, at least a part of it. Blank [twenty-one long dashes follow this word]. *Read these blank lines just as I intend them and they will express more than words—You must not forget to write soon and what to seal with* [a kiss?]. *Until I hear from you I shall be,—I don't know what I was going to say, but I recon it was your most humble and Obt.* [obedient] *Friend.*
    Ulysses S Grant

Evidently Julia wanted a more specific declaration of affection than dashes, because three months later, Grant wrote:

> *Camp Necessity La.*
> *Grand Ecore & Texas Road*
> *August 31st 1844*

. . . You say you were at a loss to ascribe a meaning to the blank lines in my first letter! Nothing is easier, they were only intended to express an attachment which words would fail to express. Julia do not keep anything a secret from me with persons standing in the relation that we do to each other there should be no backwardness about making any request—You commenced to make a request of me and checked yourself—Do not be afraid that any thing you may request will not be granted, and just think too the good you might do by giving good advice—No one is so capable of giving good advice as a lady, for they always practice just what they would preach. . . . You say Julia that you often dream of me! Do tell me some of your good ones; don't tell me any more of the bad ones; but it is an old saying that dreams go by contraries so I shall hope you will never find me in the condition you drempt I was in—And to think too that while I am writing this the ring I used to wear is on your hand—Parting with that ring Julia was the strongest evidence I could have given you (that is—in the way of a present) of the depth and sincerity of my love for you—Write to me soon, much [sooner?] *than the last time and . . . take a little ride and put your letter in the Post*

Office—On the road think of some of the conversations we used
to have when we rode out together
  Most Truly and Devotedly Your Lover
  Ulysses

Grant and Julia Dent became engaged in 1845, but he still had two years
remaining in his required army service. He was transferred to a post in
Texas, as war with Mexico threatened. Mail service was erratic, and like
most couples separated by war, he and Julia were troubled by the long
time it took to receive letters from each other.

Corpus Christi, Texas
Sept. 14th 1845

My Dear Julia
  I have just received your letter of the 21st . . . in which you
reproach me so heavily for not writing to you oftener. You know
my Dear Julia that I never let two days pass over after receiving a
letter from you without answering it. But we are so far separated
now that we should not be concerned with writing a letter and
waiting an answer before we write again. Hereafter I will write
evry two or three weeks at farthest, and wont you do the same
Julia? I received your letter before the last only about three weeks
ago and answered it immediately. Your letters always afford me
a great deal of happiness because they assure me again that you
love me still; I never doubted your love Julia for one instant but it
is so pleasant to hear it repeated, for my own part I would sacri-
fice everything Earthly to make my Dear Julia my own forever.
All that I would ask would be that my Regiment should be at a
healthy post and you be with me, then I would be content. . . .
  U S Grant

There is no date on this next letter, but the contents indicate that Grant
was still in Texas, which was not yet part of the United States. It is clear
that, having not seen any military action, he was hoping that he and
Julia would soon be married. One obstacle had always been that her

parents didn't think Grant could afford to provide for their daughter on a military man's salary. Grant proposed a drastic step.

My Dear Julia . . .

Now my Dear Julia . . . don't you think it time for us to begin to settle upon some plan for consummating what we believe is for our mutual happiness? After an engagement of sixteen or seventeen months ought we not to think of bringing that engagement to an end, in the way that all true and constant lovers should? I have always expressed myself willing you know my Dear Julia to resign my appointment in the army for the sake of overcomeing the objections of your parents, and I would still do so, at the same time I think they mistake an army life very much. No set of ladies that I ever saw are better contented . . . than those in the Army [as wives of officers]; *and you Julia would be contented knowing how much and how dearly devoted I am to you—I cannot help writing thus affectionately since you told me that no one but yourself reads my letters.*

Your Pa asks what I could do out of the Army? I can tell you: I have at this time the offer of a professorship of mathematics at a tolerably well endowed College in Hillsboro, Ohio, a large and flourishing town, where my salary would probably equal or exceed my present pay. The Principle of the Institution . . . says I can have until next spring to think of this matter. . . .

Yours most affectionately,
Ulysses

Rutherford B. Hayes to Lucy Webb

Rutherford B. Hayes—destined to become the nineteenth president—wrote to Lucy Webb in 1851 about the first time he met her, when he was twenty-five and she was only fourteen. He quoted from his diary entry for July 8, 1847: "Visited Delaware *[a town in Ohio]* with Mother and Laura. Attended a Sons of Temperance celebration; saw Miss L. Webb and left for home next morning."

   He continued his letter:

> *Nothing very much like love in that. Still, it wouldn't have been written if I hadn't heard a good deal about you . . . I remember I thought you a bright, sunny-hearted little girl, not quite old enough to fall in love with, and so I didn't. After this I saw you no more for over three years. I occasionally heard of you and thought I would manage to see you sometime . . . Heard it conjectured that you were engaged and all that, but made up my mind to see you.*

He did see her, more and more often. Then they met at a wedding. It was a custom to conceal a gold ring inside a cake, and the person who received that slice would supposedly be the next to marry. As it happened, Rutherford found the ring in his slice of cake, but he was already smitten with Lucy and gave the ring to her. That was the beginning of their courtship.

   Finally, on June 14, 1851, Hayes wrote in his diary that he had impulsively grasped the hand of Lucy Webb and told her, "I love you." At first he wrote, *"she did not comprehend it; really, no sham,"* but when Rutherford repeated it *"more deliberately,"* then *"a puzzled expression of pleasure and surprise stole over her fine features. She grew more lovely every breath,* [and] *returned the pressure of my hand. I knew it was as I wished, but I waited, perhaps repeated* [my declaration] *again, until she said, 'I must confess, I like you very well.'"*

A week later, he wrote Lucy the following letter, even though it was a Sunday and they both were very religious.

Columbus, June 22, 1851

Dearest Lucy:

I know it is very wicked to spend this holy Sabbath morning writing sweet nonsense to my lady-love, instead of piously preparing to go to church with mother, as a dutiful son ought to do, but then I'm hardly responsible. This love is, indeed, an awful thing; as Byron said, "it interferes with all a man's projects for good and glory." Besides, I am only fulfilling my scriptural destiny in "forsaking father and mother"—and all that—and—and—I can't quote any farther. But the pith of it is—leaving your mother to go alone to church, and stealing off up into a quiet chamber to spoil good paper with wretched scribbling to puzzle the eye of the dearest girl of all the world. Well, you'll forgive the sin I hope. I know you will if you have thought a tithe as much about me—but you haven't—as I have about you, the five or six days past,—and with a pardon beaming from your—I was going to say deep, and then sweet, but no one adjective can describe it—eye, I shall feel a heathenish indifference as to any other forgiveness. For "at this present," that eye has become to me, and I trust will ever continue, "like a star in the mariner's heaven"—an eye which is to give color, shape, and character to all my future hopes, fancies, and "reveries." . . .

To think that that lovely vision is an actual, living, breathing being, and is loved by me, and loves in return, and will one day be my bride—my abiding, forgiving, trustful, loving wife—then make my happy home blessed indeed with her cheerful smile and silver voice and warm true heart! . . .

I can not be vain enough to think that love will blind you to my deficiencies and faults; but doubtless there are many which I might remove or remedy if I could but fully know your thoughts and tastes in regard to them. Some faults and imperfections we all have which cannot be got rid of; and with such, sensible people will always cheerfully bear in those they love. Within certain limits the formation of character and manners, tastes and disposition, is within our own control. If we do but try—try heartily and cheerfully—we can be, for all the purposes of every-day happiness, precisely what we would wish to be. But I have sermonized too long even for a Sunday. If you don't like such preaching, you must adopt my theory, and endeavor to break me of the habit. In future I am your pupil, and if you do not form me to such character, tastes, and disposition, as will be congenial to your own, and make your life happy with me, remember you must share in the responsibility. . . .

So, Lucy, good-bye for a week or ten days longer. I think of you constantly, and the more I think of you the deeper I am in love with you . . .

Believe me, faithfully yours,
Rutherford

When the two of them became engaged, Lucy returned to Rutherford the ring he had found in the piece of wedding cake. He wore it all his life. Rutherford wrote her this letter before they were married:

Cincinnati, August 4, 1851

My Dear Lucy—

I feel very lonesome without you. Such glorious moonlit evenings as we are now having only serve to aggravate the feeling by constantly reminding me of the happiness your absence deprives me of. But I suppose I must philosophize, as Mother always does in such circumstance: "It is probably all for the best." I shall be the better able to appreciate your society by being for a time "all alone by myself." . . . I have spent several hours of the night meditating about you, and about your many and manifold perfections, the happiness already enjoyed, and the still greater happiness which Providence has in store for us . . . Thinking in this way led of course to a review in my own mind of all I could recollect of you from the time I saw you in Delaware until now . . .

I have noticed a number of heresies as to matters of love which I propose to discuss with you. I think between us we can get at the true orthodox doctrines on this subject. Emerson says: "The accepted lover has lost the wildest charm of his maiden in her acceptance of him. She was heaven whilst he pursued her as a star: she cannot be heaven if she stoops to such a one as he." This to me is rank heresy. Instead of losing, the "accepted" lover gains the wildest charm. Before, the star was distant, cold, its heaven unappreciated and not understood—distance lends no enchantment but coldness rather. Mr. Emerson don't know anything. Talk about stars in heaven when your sweetheart is leaning on your arm and her hand clasped lovingly in yours!—A man in love sees no stars at all comparable to his maiden's eyes. He knows no heaven more blissful than the certainty of her affection. Old

This daguerreotype was made on the wedding day of Rutherford B. Hayes and Lucy Webb on December 30, 1852. Lucy was the first First Lady to be a college graduate.

*Mr. Gregory, in his wisdom, lectures his daughters, and tells
them never to show as much feeling as they have towards their
lovers—no, nor even towards their husbands when married.
Pshaw! I should fear that the feeling didn't exist if not shown. It is
the people who warm towards one in manner and words who are
usually ardent in reality.*

R.

Lucy and Rutherford were married December 30, 1852. Two months
later, he wrote in his diary:

February 27, 1853

*Almost two months married. The great step of life which makes
or mars the whole after journey, has been happily taken. The
dear friend who is to share with me the joys and life of our earthly
being grows steadily nearer and dearer to me. A better wife I
never hoped to have. . . . I do not see how our tender and affectionate relations can be disturbed. . . . She . . . is, in short, so true
a wife that I cannot think it possible that any shadow of disappointment will ever cloud the prospect—save only such calamities
as are the common allotment of Providence to all. Let me strive
to be as true to her as she is to me. . . . Blessings on his head who
first invented marriage!*

James A. Garfield to
Lucretia "Crete" Rudolph

James Abram Garfield, the last president to be born in a log cabin, grew
up in poverty. The youngest of four children, he helped work the family's small farm in northeastern Ohio after his father died. When he was
old enough, he got a job on a canal boat but contracted malaria after
falling into the water some sixteen times.

His mother encouraged him to get an education, and he enrolled in a secondary school (later called Hiram College) operated by the Disciples of Christ. After a year, the school engaged him as a teacher, and he fell in love with a student, Lucretia Rudolph. She was seventeen, and he a year older. They apparently reached an agreement to marry, and to improve himself he enrolled as a junior at Williams College in Massachusetts. His degree from Williams brought him an offer to become president of Hiram College in 1857, at the tender age of twenty-six. The following year, he married Lucretia, who had become a teacher herself.

Garfield was much in demand as a public speaker, and along with his political career, that meant the couple spent much of their mar-

James and Lucretia Garfield had a troubled relationship because of James's frequent infidelity. Lucretia called it being burned by "the fire of lawless passion." Still, they stayed together, and after an assassin shot James, she was constantly by his bedside.

ried life apart. They wrote each other more than twelve hundred letters during their courtship and marriage. Garfield was particularly adept at writing. He was said to be able to simultaneously write with both hands—and in fact to write in both Latin and Greek at the same time.

Excerpts below are from a letter recalling the first "anniversary" of the day he declared his love. Garfield recalls his feelings when Lucretia responded.

Williams College, Nov. 16, 1854

My Dear Lucretia,

. . . . I cannot tell you how strangely I felt when I found your first letter, recognizing the receipt of mine, and speaking words of kindness. I cannot trace my heart's history from its first faint beginnings when the first little tendrils of my heart began to cling to yours. How frail were those tendrils then! They might easily have been broken, turned away, and forbidden to twine. But as time rolled on, they grew in strength and numbers till they have intertwined themselves around your whole being. My mind follows along through that correspondence in all the different features and recounts my secret heart-throbbings at those happy little interviews. You remember them all—the midnight return from the New Year's sleigh ride, the visiting Perintha's [a friend of theirs] school, that lower chapel consecrated by the evening farewells of the . . . students, when alternating between hope and doubt, I ventured to tell you what you knew already, and with a soul full of agitation waited to hear from your own lips a response to my affection. Never, while reason sits on the throne of my being, can I forget the fullness of joy that filled my heart, when in that tone of earnestness that spoke all your soul, you told me I was loved. Then came the spring, its studies and duties, and its thousand little spots of joy and sunshine, when we watched the opening peach blossoms at your window, while the sun all bright and golden was sinking below the western forests, [and] walked

upon our lengthened shadow as we descended the hill that slopes eastward from your home. . . .

The hour of departure came and with beloved friends behind, and the cold world of strangers before, I left the scene of all those happy hours. Since that hour, Dearest One, your loved letters, those Souvenirs of the heart, have cheered and blessed me and here they lie before me with that likeness of your own dear self. And now in the silence of the night, your spirit seems to be with me here, and whisper words of tenderest affection, and I cannot tell you the gratitude of my heart to God, that I have found a treasure so dear to me. Dear loved one, I would not be too hopeful and expect too much—I trust I am not. I have long ago determined to let sober judgment and not impulse rule my head. But I am cheered by the hope that our hearts may someday be united without an intervening distance. Is it too much to hope that we may yet enjoy each other's society in that holiest and closest of unions? I would fain write more—My mind leads on to the days when life advances and to that scene where life broadens and deepens into eternal life, and my Soul rises up in strong desire that we may there meet, freed from this clay of mortality, and drink together of the water of life that flows from the Throne of God. . . .

May Good Angels guard your slumbers and our Father save you is the prayer of

Your own

James

Despite these pious blessings, the courtship and marriage between James and Lucretia was a rocky one. He could not resist other women. See Part 3 for those letters.

Grover Cleveland to
Frances "Frank" Folsom

Grover Cleveland became the twenty-second president in 1885. He was only the second bachelor to enter the White House. (James Buchanan was the first.) Though Cleveland's personal honesty as mayor of Buffalo and governor of New York State had not been questioned, a story appeared in a newspaper that disclosed Cleveland had paid for the upbringing of a child born to an unmarried woman who asserted Cleveland was her child's father. The child's paternity was never proven.

That was not the only child Cleveland was supporting. Frances Folsom, who acquired the nickname "Frank," was the daughter of Grover Cleveland's former law partner. Upon the partner's death in 1875 when Frances was eleven, Cleveland became the girl's guardian. Over the next ten years, their relationship grew from stepfather/daughter until Cleveland confessed his love for her.

Frances accepted his proposal of marriage but planned to finish her education at Wells College in upstate New York. Her first visit to the White House was during spring break, 1885. They kept their plans to wed a secret for as long as they could. Here the forty-eight-year-old president writes a letter in which he sounds more like a paternal figure than a husband-to-be, warning her about the problems she would face as the "Lady of the White House." (She was twenty-one.) Today's Americans will find Cleveland's estimates of the prospects for raising money after his presidency quite amusing.

December 13, 1885

. . . While I love you Frank as dearly as I can, it pleases me very much to read what you write about your improvements and all that. I am glad to believe that you appreciate something that is before you as the wife of the President and Lady of the White House. I guess there never was anyone so young and so unused to such responsibilities, who occupied the place before; and my

anxiety is my darling Child, that you should be as well prepared as it is possible . . . Of course the more other people admire and praise you the more proud I should be, but I love you just exactly as you are and for just what you are; and that Darling you must never doubt . . .

. . . Lizzie [Rose Elizabeth Cleveland, the president's sister, who served as his White House hostess before he married] *and I have been walking in the East Room and have talked a good deal about you and the marriage . . . She thinks it would be wise to have no one at the wedding but relatives, but that it would be a wonderful thing to invite the Cabinet. Perhaps they* [the Cabinet] *could well come after the ceremony. But I'll tell you what I think . . . we will find some way to get married so that we can't get away from each other very easy . . . I've warned you "time and time again" and as nearly as I can make out you seemed bound to rush to your fate . . . I am glad you contemplate paying a little attention to the science of hen raising—for I don't know what else we can do when we quit here . . . We must be very frugal and saving because I suppose there is no way for an Ex-President to earn money . . .*

Write me all the time Darling and tell me just exactly how much you love me and if you love me better and better or less and less . . .
G.C.

To avoid publicity, "Frank" Folsom took an overseas trip before her wedding, which was scheduled for June 1886. Cleveland wrote her this letter, which his secretary delivered on her return. Her grandfather had just died, and Cleveland fretted that she might wish to change the date of the wedding. It's clear that he was as involved in the planning as her own father (or mother!) might have been.

May 23, 1886

My Darling Frank
I feel to night that you are almost here. It seems a dreadfully long time since I have written to you . . . I feel dreadfully to think that the first news you receive as you arrive will be of death

*among your relations . . . I know that you will be glad to hear
that I have made arrangements for us two to go away immediately after the ceremony and be together for a week . . . But
why do I talk of all these things when I have no idea of how you
will feel about the date of the ceremony when you know of your
Grandfather[']s death? . . . Everything will be as you desire . . .
I have thought that perhaps after all you would prefer to have
the ceremony on the 2nd as contemplated and reduce it to a very
quick affair indeed, though we planned to have it quick in any
event. If there is a postponement there will be all sorts of . . . talk
and the propriety of the situation will furnish material for . . .
the gossips . . . to tell you the truth my Love I mean to leave
this to you . . . only adding that Col Lamont* [Cleveland's private
secretary] *who starts to-morrow morning to meet you and who
will hand you this can tell you all you want to know. I want you
to talk to him just exactly as freely as you would to me . . . He
knows all my thoughts in connection with the matter except he
cannot know how much I love you. Its rather strange to do such
things by proxy but in this case it is the only way . . . and I am sure
no one outside of ourselves is more interested or has our welfare
and comfort more at heart . . . I've been awfully good and patient
[. . .] but God knows how much I want to take you in my arms . . .
I cannot think of any more to nite for the Colonel will say all for
me except to express my tender and everlasting love. He will even
talk to you about the ring and learn from you whether you will let
me put it on your finger just before we stand before the minister.
If you would like it just as well we have thought it might be better
than to try and introduce it into a Presbyterian ceremony. Don't
fail to tell him how you desire to have even this matter arranged.
You see we have thought of all the slightest detail . . .*
   God bless my Darling
   G.C.

On June 2, 1886, Grover Cleveland became the first and only president to be married at the White House, and "Frank," at age twenty-one,

President Cleveland.

President Cleveland's Bride.

"TWO HEARTS THAT BEAT AS ONE."

Twenty-one-year-old Frances Folsom, a recent graduate of Wells College, married Grover Cleveland in the first White House wedding of a president. The nation was fascinated—pictures of the couple appeared in many forms, such as the commercial card shown here.

became the youngest First Lady. To Cleveland's annoyance, reporters found the Maryland cottage where the newlyweds were honeymooning and watched them day and night with telescopes. They even stopped deliverymen taking food to the cottage so the newspapers could report what Grover and Frank were eating.

Even though the president's wife was popular with the public, Cleveland lost the next presidential election, despite winning the popular vote. By that time, however, his wife had decided being hostess at the White House was preferable to raising chickens. As the Clevelands were moving out, she told a White House staff member to take good care of everything because she and her husband would be back in four years. They were, too, making Cleveland the only president to serve two nonconsecutive terms, serving both as the twenty-second and twenty-fourth president.

His marriage to "Frank" Folsom was exceptionally happy and lasted twenty-two years, until his death in 1908. During the years between his presidencies, Frank gave birth to a daughter they named Ruth. The Clevelands didn't need to support themselves by raising chickens; Grover found a job with a prestigious New York law firm.

After Grover's death, Mrs. Cleveland married again, this time to a professor of archaeology at Princeton; she would outlive her first husband by thirty-nine years. Toward the end of her life, she was invited to a dinner hosted by President Harry S. Truman in honor of General Dwight D. Eisenhower. She struck up a conversation with "Ike," who asked her where she had lived in Washington before. He was startled by her answer: "The White House."

Theodore Roosevelt to Alice Hathaway Lee

In 1878, when Theodore Roosevelt was a student at Harvard, he visited the family of a classmate, Richard Saltonstall. Right next door lived the Lee family, who had an eighteen-year-old daughter named Alice. Everyone called her "Sunshine" because she was perpetually cheerful. Roosevelt fell in love at once, later writing, "As long as I live, I shall never forget how sweetly she looked." He proposed the following year, but Alice waited eight months before saying yes.

During their engagement, Theodore wrote her the following letter. Note that the ever-active Roosevelt advises his fiancée to engage in strenuous activities.

Oyster Bay, Long Island
August 15, 1880

Darling Queenie,
　I am going to church in a few minutes, but I can't resist writing you a line or two. . . .
　Little Sunshine, I have been missing you more than I can tell; I perfectly long to hold you in my arms and kiss your sweet, bright face; you are never absent from my thoughts.

I have just received your dear little letter, which Elliott [his brother, who would become the father of Eleanor Roosevelt] *has brought out of town (he has arrived a minute ago); it is the sweetest little note I have ever read, and makes me long to be with you even more, if possible. Sweet, blue-eyed queen, I prize your letters so! Do write me often.*

Get plenty of sleep, and as much exercise and lawn tennis as you want; and remember that the more good times you have— dancing, visiting, or anything else you like—the happier I am. The more attention you have the better pleased I'll be. Mother and Elliott have just come in from feeding the horses with sugar, and send their best to my darling with the wavy brown hair and beautiful, sweet mouth. I do love you so, and I have complete trust in your love for me; I know that you love me so that you will like to get married to me—for you will always be your own mistress, and mine too. Be sure and write me soon again, just such a letter as the last one; it was so lovely, and so characteristic of you. Give my love to all.

Your lover,
Thee

As the time grew near for their wedding day, the couple continued to write each other amorous letters, such as the following:

> *Oyster Bay, L.I.* [The Roosevelt family home on Long Island]
> *October 17, 1880* [two weeks before their wedding]

My Dearest Love,
You are too good to write me so often when you have so much to do. I hope you are not all tired out with the work. But at any rate you will have two weeks complete rest at Oyster Bay, and then you shall do just as you please in everything. Oh my darling, I do so hope and pray I can make you happy. I shall try very hard to be as unselfish and sunny tempered as you are, and I shall save

you from everything I can. My own true love, you have made my happiness almost too great, and I feel I can do so little for you in return. I worship you so that it seems almost desecration to touch you, and yet when I am with you I can hardly let you a moment out of my arms. My dearest queen, no man was worthy of your love, but I shall try very hard to deserve it, at least in part.

Goodbye, my own heart's darling.
Your loving
Thee

Theodore Roosevelt to Alice Lee Roosevelt

Even after they were married, Roosevelt's tireless activities and projects continued to occupy him. He entered politics and was running for the New York State Assembly when he wrote to Alice, who was only about thirty miles away. Apparently she never tired of receiving his passionate declarations of love. Who would?

New York City
November 5, 1881

My purest and sweetest little wife,
I so longed for you when I received your darling little letter that I could hardly contain my desire to see you. Oh, my sweetest true love, pray for nothing but that I may be worthy of you; you are the light and sunshine of my life and I can never cease thanking the good God who gave you to me, I could not live without you, my sweet mouthed, fair haired darling, and I care for nothing whatever else but you. I wish for nothing but to have you to love and cherish all the days of my life, and you have been more to me than any other wife could be to any other husband. You are all in all, my hearts darling, and I care for nothing else; and you have given me more than I can ever repay.

Alice Lee and Theodore Roosevelt were engaged on Valentine's Day, 1884, and married seven months later on Theodore's birthday. When Alice died of complications from childbirth, her inconsolable husband wanted no one to use her name afterward.

The canvass [his election campaign] *is getting on superbly, there seems to me a good chance of my election, but I don't care, anyway. I enclose a piece from the Evening Post; Be sure and keep all the newspaper scraps for me.*

My book is all entirely finished, except the remodelling of the first chapter, so everything is getting along well except financially. I confess am in by no means a good condition from a monetary point of view, and in awfully bad odour with Uncle Jim. Uncle

Jimmie is standing by me like a perfect old trump. With best love to the darling little motherling, pretty Pussie, dearest Bysie, and above all for your sweet self, I am your ever loving,
   Thee

A little more than three years after their marriage, Alice gave birth to a daughter. Two days later, Alice died at the age of twenty-two. Theodore's mother died the same day. (It was ironically Valentine's Day, which had been celebrated in the United States since early in the nineteenth century.) Roosevelt was grief-stricken and seldom spoke about his wife afterward, not even to their daughter, also named Alice. In a tribute to his wife, he later wrote, "When my heart's dearest died, the light went from my life forever." Afterward, he never let anyone call him by the nickname "Thee," which he'd used when writing to Alice.

William Howard Taft to Helen "Nellie" Herron

William Howard Taft was born into the ruling class. His father was a founder of Skull and Bones, the prestigious Yale University society, and served as the US attorney general and secretary of war. A native of Cincinnati, the younger Taft started a law firm and was appointed to a judgeship while he was still in his twenties.

Helen (Nellie) Herron's family also traveled in high political circles. Her father was a classmate of President Benjamin Harrison and a law partner of President Rutherford B. Hayes. Her mother was the daughter and sister of US congressmen. According to the editor of a volume of Taft's letters, the Herron family spent Christmas 1877 with the Hayes family in the White House, and seventeen-year-old Nellie Herron said she wanted to return one day as First Lady. It seemed only natural that she and Taft would become attracted to each other.

Here is the earliest surviving letter that Taft wrote Nellie Herron, not previously published. At this time, she was twenty-one and he was twenty-five. She evidently did not want to go to a dance with him if "fancy dress" was required. Taft's early letters are stiffly formal.

[Stationery: Collector's Office, United States Internal Revenue Service, where Taft was working at the time.]

Cincinnati, April 19th, 1882

My Dear Miss Herron,

I hope you have not given up going to the Clifton German [a dance in the Cincinnati German neighborhood of Clifton] *now that the objectionable feature of the ball, the fancy dress, has been given up. The pleasure of a dance in that beautiful Clifton Hall we ought not to forego. At what time this evening should I call for you? Will you kindly let me know by the bearer.*

Sincerely yours,

Wm H Taft

The courtship moved slowly. Taft continued to write other letters in the same vein. Here are three of them.

May 15th, 1883

My Dear Miss Herron,

I hope that you are going to Miss Donahue's this evening and that I may have the pleasure of escorting you thither. Will you kindly let me know by bearer your pleasure in the matter?

Very sincerely,

Wm H Taft

Saturday, November 3rd [1883?]

My Dear Miss Herron,

Will you make a pedestrian excursion with one tomorrow (Sunday) afternoon to Miss Keyes'? If I tire out before we reach our destination, we can take a car. I shall be indebted to you

if you can make the sacrifice. I shall call at three o'clock if the
weather permits. Will you kindly let me know by bearer whether
you can go?
   Very sincerely yours,
   Wm H Taft

[Written on stationery of Lloyd and Taft, Attorneys and Counselors.
By this time Taft and a friend had opened their own law firm. He
was moving up in the world.]

                                 Cincinnati, Feb. 19th, 1884
My dear Miss Herron,
   Will you please let the boy who brings this note have the Public
Library book which I left at your house last Saturday evening?
The book was the essay on Culture and Anarchy by Matthew
Arnold. I shall try to finish both that and the essay on criticism
this week. This is my day for a letter from Ninna but I have been
disappointed. When there is much to write about, there is little
time to write. This is a consolation, but it does not fill entirely the
aching void. If the boy [messenger] does not find you at home, I'll
call for the book just after supper.
   Sincerely yours,
   Wm H Taft

In the next letter, the formality of Taft's earlier notes gives way to the
giddy, near-incoherence of a young man in love, even though he has not
yet declared it openly. Here he is making an excuse for being unable
to attend Nellie's "Salon," a discussion group that met on Sundays to
consider intellectual issues. The excuse was accompanied by a bouquet
of white roses. And "Miss Herron" has become "Nellie." No one could
have guessed from the evidence of this letter that the author would go
on to be the only American to hold the offices of both president and
chief justice of the Supreme Court.

March 12, 1884

Dear Nellie,

The excuse for the roses is the note and the excuse for the note is the roses. Each phenomenon finds its reason for being in the other. If there is excuse for neither and they are both suspended in midair . . . so much the worse for the sender. Circumstances over which my control [was] *extremely limited prevent me from enjoying a tete a tete with the mistress of the art. I could not, however, forego the pleasure of sending her some roses of Yorkish hue.* [In the Wars of the Roses, the York forces used white roses as their symbol.] *The House of York was left lamenting and so am I . . . If these roses serve but to remind you of a man who is left behind you once or twice during the evening while you are making six other men happy, they will have accomplished the purpose of the sender. I can go to* [Columbus, Ohio] *on no other day but Saturday. Horace* [his brother] *and I then shall have to lose* [miss] *the Salon. Aunt Delia can not realize what sacrifice we make* [for] *her. Still less can she appreciate my individual sacrifice in missing that sweet school of Peripatetic philosophy in which I am an humble but enthusiastic disciple each Sunday afternoon. If in your search for the story of that successful reformer Cavour* [Camillo Benso, Count of Cavour, a reformer, one of the architects of the unification of Italy] *you should be delving into the treasures of your friend Newton about the hour of noon on Saturday, it would give an unsuccessful reformer* [the author of the letter: himself] *great pleasure to protect you from the library at your door, upon that day when he can explain in person his absence from the Salon. If, however, you have exhausted Brother Newton on Cavour, then I shall pursue my walk dinnerwards alone, relying on this note to sufficiently express my regret. I am not sure whether I will tell Aunt Delia what was in my first letter or not. On the whole I think I shall save it for another person. If, Nellie, in this note you detect signs of mental aberration in the writer, give him the benefit of the doubt and believe him.*

Always sincerely yours,
Wm H Taft

Over the course of a year, friendship developed into love, and sometime around May 1885, Taft proposed and Nellie accepted. Afterward, he sent her this poem he had more or less copied from Robert Burns. They were married a year later.

If my love's like a red, red rose
That's newly sprung in June
If my love's like the melodie
That's sweetly played in tune
As fair art thou my bonnie lass
So deep in love am I
And I will have thee still, my dear
Till a' the seas gang dry
May 10th—June 20th, 1885

Woodrow Wilson to Ellen Louise Axson

In April 1883, twenty-six-year-old Thomas Woodrow Wilson, a budding scholar, paid a visit to Rome, Georgia. There he met Ellen Axson, the twenty-two-year-old daughter of a local minister. Wilson intended to pursue an academic career, specializing in American history and government.

Ellen was attracted by Wilson's mind. Even growing up in a small town, she had taken advantage of every educational opportunity open to women. She had read all the classics and was an accomplished painter. The young couple hit it off at once—so much so that Ellen was disappointed when Wilson did not propose by the time he left Rome a month later. He hesitated to pop the question because he knew his teaching salary was not enough to support a wife.

Nevertheless, he and Ellen expressed their feelings for each other in letters they wrote, and the next time they met, in September, he proposed just as he was about to board a train for his home in Baltimore. She said yes immediately, and they kissed—in public, no doubt raising eyebrows among those who might have witnessed the occasion.

The couple was in fact unusually open with each other about what kinds of premarital love making pleased them. In May 1885, a month before they would finally wed, Wilson wrote her the following letter.

Baltimore, May 31, 1885

My own darling,

. . . You did not tell me till just the other day, precious, that you are fond of being petted. You had several times said, in Rome and in Wilmington last summer, that you liked me to kiss and caress you: but you said that only at my earnest and persistent solicitation, and I had a sort of lingering uneasiness lest you had

Here, Woodrow Wilson and his first wife, Ellen Axson, are relaxing during his campaign for governor of New Jersey. Woodrow fell in love on first meeting Ellen and his passion never waned.

said it . . . for fear of hurting my feelings. But if you now volun-
tarily base your promise of letting your love for me come out in
whatever expression it will—if you call your right to pet me—a
"sweet privilege"—on the express ground that you are too fond
of being petted yourself to neglect such 'instructions' as mine.
I have clear title to feel the delight with which I read that sweet
statement. You didn't think—did you, sweetheart,—that that
would be a part of your letter of which my heart would take
special hold. Ah, my little queen, you don't know what a precious
privilege it is in my eyes to be free to use every language of love
to you. If you love to be petted, you are going to marry some one
who dearly loves to pet you. His past conduct must have already
satisfied you on that point! . . .

   Your own Woodrow

Ellen was instrumental in opening Wilson to a world in which women were taking a more equal place. She would attend lectures unescorted, raised money to provide women's rooms at the school infirmary, and was a talented artist who sketched nude models. On a trip to Europe, she wrote to Wilson, "This is certainly the woman's century! They have taken possession of the earth!"

   Additional letters from Woodrow Wilson to his wife Ellen Axson can be found in Part 2.

Woodrow Wilson to Edith Bolling Galt

In August 1914, less than two years into Wilson's first term as president, Woodrow Wilson's beloved wife, Ellen, died suddenly at fifty-four. He was distraught. In the room where his wife had just passed, Wilson burst into tears and said, "Oh my God, what am I going to do?"

   Fortunately for him, his wife knew him well and in her last illness had made her physician, Dr. Cary Grayson, promise to take good care of her husband. Dr. Grayson understood her: the president needed a woman. It was a request that was important to the nation, for Wilson immediately sank into a deep depression that kept him from giving full attention to his work. This came just as World War I had broken out in Europe, and Wilson was under pressure to determine what role the United States should play in the conflict. He needed all the help he could get.

Dr. Grayson, as the White House Cupid, knew Wilson's character and realized that the next First Lady should not be a young girl who would have to be wooed and won over by the fifty-seven-year-old president. He approached Edith Galt, a forty-three-year-old widow who, like the president, was from Virginia. After her husband died in 1908, she had managed the fashionable jewelry store they owned in Washington, DC.

By all accounts, the president was smitten from the beginning. Wilson's cousin Helen Bones, who sipped tea with Wilson, Edith, and Dr. Grayson at the first private meeting of the couple, said, "I can't say that I foresaw in the first minute what was going to happen. It may have taken ten minutes."

That began a round of dinners, teas, and automobile rides that were designed to sweep Edith off her feet. Wilson also wrote her frequently, despite the time-consuming duties he had as president. On May 7, 1915, a crisis arose that threatened to draw the United States into the war in Europe. A German submarine sank the *Lusitania*, a passenger ship that had embarked from New York carrying nearly 1,200 passengers, including 128 Americans. Wilson felt pressure to make a strong response.

In the hot months of summer, members of the government fled Washington for cooler places. In July, despite the crisis, Wilson and Edith traveled to his summer house in Cornish, New Hampshire. However, many Americans, including former president Theodore Roosevelt, felt that Wilson should take military action and even enter the war. He was compelled to return to Washington to deal with the crisis.

But as he indicates in the following letter, his thoughts were on other things.

The White House
Tuesday
20 July, 1915 5 p.m.

My adorable Sweetheart,

How perfectly and altogether lovely you are! Your letter, written Sunday night, has filled my heart with overflowing. It is so perfect a love letter, and the joy and comfort and strength with which it has blessed me spring from so many sources of loveliness and womanly insight and tenderness, of ineffable charm and dearness, that I do not know which I feel the more keenly, the joy that you love me so, or the pain that, loving me so you cannot come to me and never, never leave my side again! I do indeed need you, my precious Darling. . . . It was cruelly hard to drive away from the house [in Cornish] on Sunday and leave you standing there in the doorway as if

Less than a year after the death of his first wife, Woodrow met a widow named Edith Bolling Galt. He was smitten and soon proposed. Edith thrived on the allure of power, and after Wilson's stroke, she took over the government.

you were not a part of me and I were not leaving my inspiration and real life behind me. I did not lift my hat to my home: I lifted it to you and did not cover my head again until the turn of the drive hid you from sight and I was no longer in the presence of the sweet, the incomparable lady without whose presence no place can be my home. You are everything to me. Without you I am maimed and imperfect. For I have learned what you are and my heart is wholly enthralled. You are my ideal companion, the close and delightful chum of my mind. You are my perfect playmate, with whom everything that is gay and mirthful and imaginative in me is at its best. You are the sweetest lover in the world, full of delicacy and charm and tenderness and all the wonders of self-revelation which only makes you the more lovely the more complete it is. You match and satisfy every part of me, grave or gay, of the mind or of the heart,—the man of letters, the man of affairs, the boy, the poet, the lover. When you are mine for every day I shall be complete and strong and happy indeed.

Do you wonder what I am doing in the study at 5 o'clock in the afternoon, writing to you? I simply must write to you every minute I am free to. It is just as instinctive with me, and just as necessary to me, as if you were here in the house and I were free for a little while to go and hold you in my arms and pour out to you everything that was in my mind and heart. . . .

What thoughts of you fill and gladden my heart, my Sweetheart! How deep I have drunk of the sweet fountains of love that are in you—and how pure and wholesome and refreshing they are, how full of life and every sweet perfection! I have seen so many lovely things that make me feel as if I had been in a sanctuary, and yet in a place where there was welcome for everything that was human and natural and unaffected and intimate, and I have learned to love you, my Sweetheart, more and more and more, with each day and hour, with each experience and revelation of your very heart. It seems to me now as if you were indeed a very part of me. Those wonderful mornings when our minds grew to be intimate friends . . . those afternoons of mere irresponsible companionship in the simple pleasures of a drive or a game of pool; those never-to-be-forgotten evenings when our hearts were opened to one another without reserve and with the joy of young lovers, as you say in this priceless letter that came to me to-day, there was no one else in the world for us,—they have made me feel, not only that you were mine and I was yours as it has seldom been given to two lovers to be united but also that I had come into a world of joy and intimate happiness wholly created by one lovely, one incomparably lovely woman to whom my heart must always bow down with a new sense of privilege, a new knowledge of love. My love for you is deeper than all words, my precious One, and I enjoy you so! Everything in me enjoys you so,—and misses you so intolerably when you are away from me! Thank God for work! I do not know how I could endure the longing if I were not obliged to keep my brains busy all the while. Ah, how I need you! How empty the hours are without you! I can make shift while the working hours last, but when they are over, when there is time and opportunity for a touch of home,—when bed-time comes and you are not here to crown the day with your sweet sympathy and tenderness and comprehension of my need, how I get by these crises I do not know . . .

Your own Woodrow

Remember, this is not even the entirety of one letter, and there are countless such letters that Wilson wrote to Edith during the eight months of their courtship. Also, he did not dictate these to a secretary, but wrote them out in longhand himself, still finding time to perform the duties of president at a time of crisis, when he was trying to prevent the United States from being drawn into the war.

After Edith returned to Washington, her romance with Wilson continued. It was irregular for a president to visit a private home, yet Wilson was frequently seen at Edith's house till late at night. Rumors went around Washington that they were sleeping together. But he wanted her to join him in the White House and asked her to marry him. The following letter tells of his feelings when she said yes.

[The White House] *Monday,*
7:30 a.m. 4 Oct., 1915

My own precious Darling,

Good morning! I hope you had a lovely, restful sleep and that you felt my arms about you, my heart close to yours. It is five months to-day, my Sweetheart since I told you of the great love for you that had come into my heart and asked you to be my wife,—only five months, and yet I seem to have known and loved you always. I cannot think of happiness apart from you. You fill my thoughts and my life. My spirits rise and fall with yours. Your thoughts and your love govern the whole day for me. And, as these crowded months have gone by, filled with experiences that seemed to search our hearts to their very depths—to depths to which no plummet had ever reached before—how steadily we have struggled towards the light—with what joy we have seen it broaden about us, until now we stand, hand in hand, where it shines warm and life-giving in all its full and vital splendor! We have not loved lightly, my Darling. With a great price we have bought this supreme happiness. It has been tested by fire, and has come out refined and purged. We know ourselves and we know one another better than it would have been possible to learn them by the experiences of any ordinary five years, or any commonplace lifetime, and we know that it was inevitable that we should love one another and utterly give our hearts up to one another. Out of the fire has come to me, little by little revealed and made perfect, the woman I perfectly love and adore, the lovely lovely woman who, at each stage of the strange struggle, seemed to me to grow more lovely and

*more desirable. I loved you, my precious Edith, ah, how tenderly
and deeply, that May evening when I first opened my heart to
you, but I now know that that was but the beginning of my love.
It has grown like a great tide of life and joy, until now I know
that my whole destiny is centred in you, my sweet, sweet Love,
my incomparable Darling!*

    Your own Woodrow

Though Edith accepted his proposal, Wilson's advisors didn't want him
to tie the knot until after the 1916 presidential election, fearing that
taking a new wife so soon after his first wife had died would bring public
disapproval. Nevertheless, at Wilson's insistence, the couple wed on December 18, 1915. A secret service agent reported that when the couple
departed on their honeymoon, Wilson danced down the aisle of their
railroad car, singing, "Oh, you beautiful doll."

    She was to become more than that, for the United States did
in fact enter the war and tipped the scales in favor of the Allies—
England, France, and Italy. Wilson and his wife went to Europe for
the peace conference that was supposed to draw up a treaty. The
president wanted to establish an international League of Nations
that would settle disputes among nations without warfare. However,
the US Congress balked at the idea and refused to ratify the treaty.
Wilson embarked on a speaking tour to whip up enthusiasm for the
League. Fatigued and strained, he suffered a stroke from which he
would never fully recover.

    For the rest of Wilson's term, he mostly stayed in his bedroom, hid-
den from all but a few people. Edith served as gatekeeper and inter-
preter of the president's wishes. She did not make decisions that were
uninformed. Early in their relationship she had told him, "Much as I
enjoy your delicious love letters, I enjoy even more the ones in which
you tell me . . . of what you are working on . . . for then I feel I am
sharing your work and being taken into partnership as it were." After
Wilson's stroke, Edith assumed many of his powers, sending out letters
with his signature and relaying commands that she said he had given
her. The vice president was never permitted to see him, and he met with

the cabinet only once. As one member of the Senate proclaimed: "We have petticoat government. Mrs. Wilson is president!" True or not, the situation resulted in Wilson's refusing to compromise on the League of Nations, and the Senate voted it down.

Calvin Coolidge to Grace Goodhue

Calvin Coolidge was born in 1872 on the Fourth of July (the only president to have been so) in Vermont. After graduating from Amherst College, he moved to Northampton, Massachusetts, where he apprenticed at a law firm partnered by two other Amherst graduates. After passing the bar exam, he opened his own firm, and because he frequently settled his clients' cases without going to court, his practice had grown.

Coolidge lived in an apartment building across the street from the Clarke School for the Deaf. One day, as he was shaving, a teacher at the school saw him through an open window and was struck by the fact that he was wearing a "union suit" (combined undershirt and shorts) while wearing a derby.

The woman was Grace Goodhue, who grew up in Burlington, Vermont, the only child of a steamboat inspector and his wife. She received a good education in local schools and then enrolled in the University of Vermont, where she was active in a theater group and the glee club. After graduation, she obtained a teaching position at the Clarke School for the Deaf.

Her first glimpse of Calvin made her laugh, and he looked out his window. Grace turned away in embarrassment but was determined to meet the man. She enlisted the help of a janitor, who presented a potted plant to the man with Grace's compliments. A meeting was soon arranged, and the subject of the derby came up. Calvin explained that the derby prevented his hair from falling into his face while he shaved. Perfectly logical.

Calvin responded to his new acquaintance by bombarding her with letters—as often as every other day. No matter that they lived across the street from each other; he would notify her by letter what time he would drop in, take her for a walk, go skating together, and frequently attend plays or concerts, for he, too, was a devotee of the arts. These can't strictly be called "love letters," for in none of them does he actually declare his love, though he often compliments her and says she makes him happy. He approached familiarity carefully; it took him months to stop addressing the letters "My dear Miss Donahue" and change to "My dear Grace." The letters that follow are previously unpublished.

[2-10-1905]

My dear Grace—

When I came in from that banquet last night your light made me think you might be up again with your malady [she had suffered from a bad cold]. *I hope not. I'm so sorry it is troubling you, do get some treatment for it. . . . I didn't enjoy the banquet. I don't know why; it seemed as though I never dreaded speaking so, but when I got through I didn't mind Doctor Dennis so very much.*

It is so pleasant today. I would like to take you driving. Can't you swap school for a sleigh? Or may I ask you to come after tea—about 7-20? Please telephone me between 4 and 4:30 if you do not decide to come—otherwise be on the watch for me so I needn't ring for you. I know I am always wanting something of you—perhaps you are so used to it now you don't mind. Just think what a temptation you are and try to forgive me if I seem to want too much.

Sincerely,

Calvin

Friday

[2-14-1905]

My dear Grace,

I suppose you are on duty tonight in the third story—I wish you much joy.

I have been rather busy this week getting ready for Court which convenes Monday morning. How did your party go off? From the way you were prancing around when I looked over after the guests were gone I imagine it was a great success.

My candy I enjoyed eating . . . very, very much. You were so good [to share it with me]. I hope I may have the pleasure of being with you soon, and want you [to] tell me what you are thinking and doing.

Sincerely,

Calvin

Friday

Presumably Coolidge is here responding to a student's essay Grace sent him. Evidently, she was not the only one who looked at people through their windows.

[2/27/1905]

My dear Grace—

The little essay you sent me—isn't it almost pathetic to see the boy struggle to learn? If you will only keep on looking as you did last evening I won't complain if you never taste steak. I'm so glad you are better.

I really didn't mean to call on you last night, but when I saw you sitting in the window, I couldn't help it. If you don't want to tempt me you best keep out of sight. You were so nice to entertain me—often you have a way of making me so happy and make me wonder whatever you can get one half so precious as the things you give.

Sincerely,

Calvin

Monday

Eating ice cream during the hot Washington summer, Calvin and Grace Coolidge enjoy a garden party held to honor veterans of World War I. The Coolidges loved pet animals and even kept a raccoon in the White House.

When their families became aware of the budding romance, reactions were mixed. Calvin's grandmother told him he should marry her, but Grace's mother was dead set against the marriage. Calvin was not what anyone could call romantic. When he finally proposed, he only announced, "I am going to be married to you." Years later, after he became the thirtieth president, Grace's mother declared he could never have succeeded without Grace.

She was not the only one who thought so. Whenever Grace was away, he became so depressed that she had to write him every day. In the White House, he would go to the mail room, look through the new arrivals, pull her letter out, and read it on the spot.

Harry S. Truman to
Elizabeth Virginia "Bess" Wallace

Harry S. Truman, the thirty-third president of the United States, served from the death of President Franklin D. Roosevelt in 1945 until 1953—a period when the United States took the leadership of what was then called the "free world." Yet the man who led this exercise of power was relatively unschooled; Truman's only higher education was in a Kansas City "commercial college." He was, however, an avid reader and well informed about the events of the day. His greatest virtue was persistence, as his love letters show.

Born the son of a farmer in Independence, Missouri, Harry was only six years old when he met Bess Wallace, age five, in Sunday school at the Presbyterian church. They also attended the same grade school. The first time Harry proposed, twenty-one years after they met, he remembered the feelings he had for her even in Sunday school.

Harry came from a Democratic family and had been a page at the National Democratic Convention in Kansas City in 1900. After attending business school for a year, he returned to his family's farm.

Bess's family was socially above his, but her father had committed suicide when Bess was very young, a source of shame at the time. Her mother was the daughter of a wealthy flour miller and had enough money to raise her daughter, the eldest child, and three sons. Bess had even gone to a finishing school in Kansas City. Harry was always aware of the differences in their backgrounds when he wrote to her. He made attempts to show that he, too, was educated, and apparently gave her a book by Sir Walter Scott as a Christmas present.

Grandview, Mo.
December 31, 1910

My Dear Bessie,
I am very glad you liked the book. I liked it so well myself I nearly kept it. I saw it advertised in Life and remembered that you were fond of Scott when we went to school.

Nothing would please me better than to come to see you
during the holidays or any other time for the matter of that, but
Papa broke his leg the other day and I am chief nurse, next to my
mother, besides being farm boss now. So you see I'll be somewhat
closely confined for some time to come. I hope you'll let the invi-
tation be a standing one though and I shall avail myself of it at the
very first opportunity. . . .

If you see fit to let me hear from you sometimes, I shall certainly
appreciate it. Farm life as an everyday affair is not generally excit-
ing. Wishing you and all of you the very happiest New Year, I am
  Very sincerely,
  Harry S. Truman

Truman did not always use the S middle initial, but he did so here (with
a period), apparently to impress Bess. He explained later that it was a
family compromise between the names of his two grandfathers, Ander-
son Shipp Truman and Solomon Young.

Harry also showed his appreciation of the fine arts by obtaining
tickets to a Shakespeare play.

Grandview, Mo.
April 12, 1911

Dear Bessie:
  I got your good letter yesterday and will answer it later. I have
some tickets to Sothern-Marlow [a theater presentation featuring
Edward H. Sothern and Julia Marlow, Shakespearean actors]
Saturday night and if you will help me use them I shall be very
glad. I tried for Macbeth for Saturday matinee but everything was
gone. It is Taming of the Shrew and I think is as good as Mac.
  If you can't go, why my phone number is Hickman No. 6 and it
costs ten cents. So you'd better save the dime [by not calling him]
and go. . . . If I don't hear from you, I shall be around at 7:00 p.m.
Saturday.
  Sincerely,
  Harry

His first proposal came after seven and a half years:

Grandview, Mo.
June 22, 1911

Dear Bessie:

[He begins with a reference to the drought that was then afflicting the farmers of Missouri.] *From all appearances I am not such a very pious person am I? The elements evidently mistook one of my wishes for dry instead of wet. I guess we'll all have to go to drinking whiskey if it doesn't rain very soon. Water and potatoes will soon be as much of a luxury as pineapples and diamonds.*

Speaking of diamonds, would you wear a solitaire on your left hand should I get it? Now that is a rather personal or pointed question provided you take it for all it means. You know, were I an Italian or a poet I would commence and use all the luscious language of two continents. I am not either but only a kind of good-for-nothing American farmer. I've always had a sneakin' notion that some day maybe I'd amount to something. I doubt it now though like everything, it is a family failing of ours to be poor financiers. I am blest that way. Still that doesn't keep me from having always thought that you were all that a girl could be possibly and impossibly. You may not have guessed it but I've been crazy about you ever since we went to Sunday school together. But I never had the nerve to think you'd even look at me. I don't think so now but I can't keep from telling you what I think of you. . . .

Still if you turn me down, I'll not be thoroughly disappointed for it's no more than I expect. . . .

Please write as soon as you feel that way. The sooner, the better pleased I am.

More than sincerely,
Harry

Bess did turn down Harry's offer, but he made it clear he wasn't giving up. In fact, it took him another eight years before he succeeded in marrying her.

Grandview, MO.
July 12, 1911

Dear Bessie:

You know that you turned me down so easy that I am almost happy anyway. I never was fool enough to think that a girl like you could ever care for a fellow like me but I couldn't help telling you how I felt. I have always wanted you to have some fine, rich, good-looking man, but I knew that if ever I got the chance I'd tell you how I felt even if I didn't even get to say another word to you. What makes me feel real good is that you were good enough to answer me seriously and not make fun of me anyway. You know when a fellow tells a girl all his heart and she makes a joke of it I suppose it would be the awfulest feeling in the world. You know I never had any desire to say such things to anyone else. All my girl friends think I am a cheerful idiot and a confirmed old bach. [bachelor] They really don't know the reason nor ever will. I have been so afraid you were not even going to let me be your good friend. To be even in that class is something.

You may think I'll get over it as all boys do. I guess I am something of a freak myself. I really never had any desire to make love to a girl just for the fun of it, and you have always been the reason. I have never met a girl in my life that you were not the first to be compared with her, to see wherein she was lacking and she always was.

Please don't think I am talking nonsense or bosh, for if ever I told the truth I am telling it now and I'll never tell such things to anyone else or bother you with them again. I have always been more idealist than practical anyway, so I really never expected any reward for loving you. I shall always hope though.

As I said before I am more than glad to be your good friend for that is more than I expected. So when I come down there Saturday (which I'll do if I don't hear from you) I'll not put on any hangdog airs but will try to be the same old Harry. . . .

I hope you will continue your good letters as I really enjoy them and will try to answer them to the best of my ability, and although

I may sometimes remind you of how I feel toward you I'll try and not bore you to death with it.
    Very sincerely,
    Harry

    Grandview, Mo.
    July 21, 1913

Dear Bess:
    Did you ever see the Madonna in the moon? I imagined I saw her. The proper directions are to think of your girl's countenance and then you can see it. I don't know how the girls are supposed to see it. Probably imagine they are gazing into a mirror. I'd rather look at the real thing, than to hurt my eyes and pain my head gazing into the moon's face. Not that I'd ever have to put forth any effort whatever to conjure up your face because it's always in plain sight. I never see a pretty girl or the picture of one that I don't think, well if she didn't have this imperfection or that one why she'd look like Bess. You know perfection can only be reached once. You're it. So what's the use of imagining you in the moon when I can see yourself at Independence [the town where Bess lived].
    Sincerely,
    Harry

At some point before the next letter was written, Bess evidently told Harry she loved him, and that she would someday marry him.

    Grandview, Mo.
    November 4, 1913

Dear Bess,
    Your letter has made a confirmed optimist out of me sure enough. I know now that everything is good and grand . . . I have been all up in the air, clear above earth ever since it came. I guess you thought I didn't have much sense Sunday [when he apparently visited her], *but I just couldn't say anything—only hoped you would but some way feared very much you wouldn't. You know, I've always thought that*

the best man in the world is hardly good enough for any woman. But when it comes to the best girl in all the universe caring for an ordinary gink like me—well, you'll have to let me get used to it. . . .

[Harry had been planning to stake a claim to some land in Montana and had high hopes for making himself a success there.] *You may be sure I'm not going to wait till I'm Montana's chief executive to ask you to be Mrs. Governor, but I sure want to have some decent place to ask you to. I'm hoping it won't be long. I wish it was tomorrow. Let's get engaged anyway to see how it feels. No one need know it but you and me until we get ready to tell it anyway. If you see a man you think more of in the meantime, engagements are easy enough broken. I'd always said I'd have you or no one and that's what I mean to do.*

Most sincerely,
Harry

She agreed.

John F. Kennedy to Jacqueline Bouvier

At their wedding reception on September 12, 1953, the couple toasted each other playfully. Jacqueline said Jack had never sent her a single love letter during their courtship. She read aloud a postcard he had sent her from Bermuda. Here it is, in its entirety:

"Wish you were here, Jack."

Despite the many stories about John F. Kennedy's affairs (see Part 4), the affection between him and his wife endured. J. B. West, who was chief usher at the White House, related in his memoirs that after a swim, Kennedy had lunch upstairs with Jacqueline. Afterward, "he closed the door, firmly. Mrs. Kennedy dropped everything, no matter how important, to join her husband. . . . During these hours . . . No telephone calls were allowed, no folders sent up, no interruptions from the staff. Nobody went upstairs, for any reason."

Jack and Jacqueline Kennedy made a beautiful couple at their wedding in September 1953. The union of a "Debutante of the Year" and Washington's most eligible bachelor brought crowds of people to St. Mary's Church in Newport.

The Kennedys shared sorrows as well. In August 1963, Jackie gave birth to a boy they named Patrick Bouvier. He died two days later. A person who was with the Kennedys at that time said, "She hung onto him and he held her in his arms, something nobody ever saw at any other time because they were very private people." Reportedly, Jackie told her husband that, as great as this loss was, "the one blow I could not bear would be to lose you."

Lyndon B. Johnson to
Claudia Alta "Lady Bird" Taylor

Lyndon B. Johnson, thirty-sixth president of the United States, did not start out to pursue a career in politics. The son of a farmer, he graduated from high school at age fifteen. After enrolling in a teachers college, he began teaching at local schools. When a friend of Johnson's father won an election to the US House of Representatives, he hired Lyndon as his assistant. The young man (he was twenty-three) thrived in the heady atmosphere of Washington. When Franklin D. Roosevelt became president in 1933, Johnson enthusiastically supported FDR's New Deal social programs. One day far in the future, President Lyndon B. Johnson's Great Society programs would mirror and expand FDR's.

On a trip back to Texas, Johnson met Claudia Alta Taylor, who had acquired the nickname Lady Bird as an infant. She was the only daughter of a wealthy Texas property owner. Her mother had died when Lady Bird was five, and she was raised by an aunt. She enjoyed studying and obtained degrees in history and journalism from the University of Texas by the time she was twenty-two. However, according to her own account, she was quite shy.

In the summer of 1934, a friend introduced her to the twenty-six-year-old Johnson. He was now in Washington attending law school at night. Lyndon was anything but shy, and he now had his sights set on a political career. All he was lacking was money, which a wealthy wife would bring him. He knew immediately that he wanted to marry Lady Bird and reportedly proposed on their first date. She was more cautious, as the following letters show, but Lyndon persisted, sending her letters almost daily from Washington, asking her to agree to marry.

He insisted that in return she send him a continuous flow of letters. His persistent requests for her to say she loved him show the obsessiveness and arm-twisting that became part of his public persona and his political success.

[Stationery: House of Representatives/Washington, D.C./R.M. Kleberg, 14th Dist., Texas/ Lyndon B. Johnson, secretary]

[Handwritten above letterhead: "This paper made of Texas cotton." The paper is so thin that the handwriting from the other side shows through.]

[9/23/1934]
Sunday 10:30 a.m.

Dear Bird:

. . . The thing I want more every day than anything else is a letter from you. I have asked you to write me daily so often that what pride and self-respect I have been able to retain since meeting you occasionly asserts itself, and consequently, my requests, expectations, and letters to you necessarily have been fewer here of late. It is always such a trial for me to write a personal letter. It has been years since I've written any appreciable number but strangely enough I have a desire to talk to you some-time each day and the only medium I have is via the letter route. Unless you give vent to your desires, if you have such desires, and write more often, I shall naturally try to be equally as self-composed and watch for a letter to answer later in the week.

. . . I could read and reread a letter from you which contained just one central idea, [if] that idea concerned itself only with expressions of your love. I wait to hear you say over and over again that "I love you". You may remember that one time you told me, "Someday I may feel that way and when I do—I shall very likely tell you of my own volition." That should have been enough—ordinarily it would have been too much—but even the strongest of men sometimes don't follow their judgment but submit to a dictate from elsewhere. Tell me soon, dear, just how you know you do feel—if feel you do. . . .

Again I repeat—I love you—only you—Want to always love—only you—It is an important decision—It isn't being made in one night—it probably never will be yours—but your lack of decision hasn't tempered either my affection, devotion or ability to know

*what I want—I don't want to go on this way—Do you? Will you
tell me? Give me lots of letters next week—I'm going to need
them—mix some "I love you" in the lines and not between them—
Adios until tomorrow—Lyndon*

[Kleberg office stationery]
[At the top of the page, above the letterhead, he wrote:]
Question—Attention: Who do you love?

[9/26/1934]

My dearest,

*I feel too good to be a criminal altho when I think of my
complaint about not receiving letters I can conceive of having
been too exacting and expectant. Your letters mean so much that
when I don't get one in the morning mail my stock immediately
starts going down. Yesterday I wrote complaining—only to have
the mail bring me a letter an hour after mine had been posted.
He said it wasn't mailed at the right time to be delivered with the
other letter mail. When I started to school last night I stopped
at the Dodge [Hotel] and to my most pleasant surprise, I had
another letter from you which had been written Friday night. It
was the last letter you have written. It made me so happy to have
you tell me you wanted me. It gave me new life—a real inspiration
and a determination to make you the most happy and contented
little woman in all the world. If I were only sure—if you could
only know how you feel [whether she loved him]—what a different
slant it would put on the whole matter. . . . Hurry and tell me
when you will be here to visit (or to stay??) We must have our
biggest and best celebration when you and Gene are here. Very
likely we will have the dance at the Shoreham [Hotel]. . . . Your
Friday letter gave me new hope, new interest, new plans and to
sum it all up just thrilled me to death.*

*Hurry and send me the Kodak pictures. Don't postpone finding
the large picture you looked for but couldn't locate the night I was*

at your home. Then on top of all of that (and that isn't much for one who loves you and adores to look at you often) I want you to have those new pictures made and really rushed to me. Then I'll have something to thrill me in addition to waiting for the postman.

I have all of your letters—one by one in my room. When I can't "take it" anymore I reread them and last night I noticed that you had only erred 4 days in not writing. For a while I thought you had waited a week to write—then I realized you had only left me less than a week ago—

Honey I can't write very well. I don't know how to spell, punctuate and compose. It is much easier to dictate when you have been doing that for two years.

You wanted a long letter—Here it is—Now I will brief cases for the next 3 hours—Haven't had a date since I enrolled [in law school] and try to work from 8 until 12. Could work later with you looking on—or reading with me. Won't you come and help me to climb? . . .

Tell me what I hope you want to tell me each time after you have sealed your letter. Remember?

I'm ready now—Are you?

All my love—Lyndon Baines

Johnson succeeded in his obsessive pursuit. He and Lady Bird were married on November 17, 1934, at St. Mark's Episcopal Church in San Antonio, only ten weeks after they had first met.

After their honeymoon, their relationship changed. According to the Johnson biographer Robert Caro, Lyndon told his new bride that he wanted her to serve him coffee in bed, along with a newspaper. She also had to lay out his clothes, fill his fountain pen and cigarette lighter, put them along with his handkerchief and money into the proper pockets of his suit, and finally shine his shoes. Caro says she followed his instructions, even though "he made sure that everyone knew that she was performing these chores, loudly reminding her about her duties in front of other people." Even on their honeymoon, while visiting friends,

Lyndon and Lady Bird Johnson were married in San Antonio on November 17, 1934, and honeymooned in Mexico, where they were photographed on a boat in the Floating Gardens in Xochimilco.

he noticed a run in her stocking and told her to go change. When she hesitated, he ordered her to leave the room immediately. Nevertheless, she stuck with him and by all accounts was a key factor in promoting his political career. When we asked Mr. Caro why she endured this treatment, he replied, "I guess she loved him."

Equally puzzling is the fact that Johnson was a notorious womanizer, often bragging about his exploits in bed. After his death, a television producer asked Lady Bird why she put up with his behavior. She replied, "You have to understand, my husband loved people. All people. And half the people in the world were women. You don't think I could have kept my husband away from half the people?" She paused and said, "He loved me. I know he only loved me."

Richard Nixon to
Thelma Catherine "Pat" Ryan

Richard Nixon, the thirty-seventh president of the United States, is the only president to resign, forced from office in his second term in 1975 because of various scandals known as Watergate. The lyrical young man revealed in the following letters is a side of Nixon few others ever saw. Yet the woman who received them stayed loyal throughout his checkered political career.

Twenty-six-year-old Pat Ryan was teaching at a local high school in Whittier, California, in 1938, when she met Richard Nixon in a local theater group. They both had roles in a play called *The Dark Tower*. Nixon was a twenty-five-year-old lawyer, a junior member of a local law firm. He described his meeting with Pat as "love at first sight," and on their first date asked her to marry him. Though Pat later described him as "so much fun," it took him two years to persuade her to accept his proposal.

[no date: Possibly March 16, 1938]

Patricia:

Somehow on Tuesday there was something electric in the usually almost stifling air in Whittier.

And now I know. An Irish gypsy who radiates all that is happy and beautiful was there.

She left behind her a note addressed to a struggling barrister who looks from a window and dreams.

And in that note he found sunshine and flowers, and a great spirit which only great ladies can inspire.

He knew then why he felt so many fine things for this girl he had learned to know.

And though he is a prosaic person, his heart was filled with that grand poetic music, which makes us wish for those we love the realization of great dreams, the fulfillment of all they desire.

And though he knew he should not bore her with these thoughts, he sent them to her, because, you see, they were good thoughts—wished for her, that she might be forever happy.
    Dick

Someday let me see you again? In September? Maybe?

                                                    [no date]
Dearest Heart—
    No one shall see my writing on this stationery but you—because you see I have so much to write to you and so many times I have to send you notes!
    During the past few days with the rain falling—I have thought of you many times—good thoughts too.
    Every day and every night I want to see you and be with you. Yet I have no feeling of selfish ownership or jealousy. In fact I should always want you to live just as you wanted—because if you didn't then you would change and wouldn't be you.
    Let's go for a long ride Sundays; let's go to the mountains weekends; let's read books in front of fires; most of all let's really grow together and find the happiness we know is ours.
    My love to Thee Dearheart
    R

                                                    [no date]
                                         Wednesday afternoon
Dearest Heart
    As I look out the window at the clouds with the sun trying to break through, I am thinking of how much you have meant to me the past two years.
    Do you remember that funny guy who asked you to go to a 20–30 ladies night just about two years ago? Well—you know that though he still may be funny—he's changed since then. But you may not know—dear one—that he still gets the same thrill when you say you'll go someplace with him—that he did

*when you said one time that he could take you for a ride in his
car!*

*And did you know that he still looks out the window wherever
you are and sends you the best he has in love, admiration, respect,
and "best of luck"?*

*And when the wind blows and the rains fall and the sun shines
through the clouds (as it is now) he still resolves, as he did then,
that nothing so fine ever happened to him or anyone else as falling
in love with Thee—my dearest heart—*

Love, Dick

Dick eventually won Pat over and they were married on June 21, 1940,
at the Mission Inn in Riverside, California. Pat later said that she had
been attracted to the young Nixon because he "was going places, he was
vital and ambitious . . . he was always doing things."

Jimmy Carter to Rosalynn Smith

Jimmy Carter first met his future wife, Rosalynn Smith, on a "chance"
meeting that was actually set up by his younger sister Ruth. It was 1945
and Jimmy, age twenty, was enrolled in the Naval Academy. He fell in
love immediately, and though she was just seventeen, she felt an attraction to him as well. On his return to the academy, they continued their
courtship by exchanging what Carter later told an interviewer were "intimate love letters." (Unfortunately, he never shared those letters with
the interviewer or with us.)

At Christmas that year, Jimmy invited Rosalynn to his family's celebration and gave her a silver compact engraved with initials that were
a coded message: ILYTG, or "I Love You the Goodest." He proposed to
her at that time, but because she had promised her father on his deathbed that she would attend college, she turned him down.

A few months later, however, she changed her mind, and when she
visited the Naval Academy with Jimmy's parents, she agreed to marry
him. Accordingly, Jimmy sent her a copy of *The Navy Wife,* a kind of

Jimmy and Rosalynn Carter formed a partnership of equals, sharing the joys of dancing at a Washington ball, as seen here. The couple have had the longest marriage in White House history.

manual written by two real-life navy wives. In the margin of the following passage, he wrote, "You, darling."

"To begin with she is easy on the eyes. Her pretty soft brown hair has a semblance of a natural wave, her features are good, she has pretty teeth and a ready smile. She is slim and has a willowy figure. She dresses well, and knows how to wear her clothes. She is adaptable, is understanding, and can make the best of regulations and conditions as she finds them. She is a good cheery companion, an excellent dancer, never catty, has good manners."

Jimmy and Rosalynn were married on July 7, 1946, in the Plains (Georgia) Methodist Church and remained together until her death in November 2023. Their marriage lasted for seventy-seven years, the longest of any presidential couple.

In her autobiography, *First Lady from Plains*, Rosalynn Carter wrote that Jimmy sent her many letters while he was serving in the US Navy.

Although they were not available at the time of publication, President Carter later published a poem that reveals his love for her. We reprint the first lines of the poem here. His publisher would not permit us to reproduce all of it.

Rosalynn

She'd smile, and birds would feel that they no longer
had to sing, or it may be I failed
to hear their song.

As far as we know, Carter was the only president who published poetry.

George H. W. Bush to
Barbara Pierce Bush

George H. W. Bush met his future wife, Barbara Pierce, at a country club dance when they were still teenagers. She was a distant relative of Franklin Pierce, the fourteenth president of the United States. George was the son of a wealthy banker who later became a US senator. He and Barbara became engaged when George enlisted in the navy after the United States entered World War II in 1941.

The published collection of George H. W. Bush's letters is more than seven hundred pages long but includes only three letters to his wife, Barbara, including this brief but poignant birthday note:

[June 8, 1979]

Happy happy 54th
love you—I love you very much. Nothing—campaign
separations—people, nothing will ever change that—
I can't ever really tell you how much I love you.
Your 55 yr. old husband
Pop

George's two middle names, Herbert Walker, were the names of his maternal grandfather, known to the family as "Pop." Young George thus acquired the nickname "Poppy," or "Pop." He became the forty-first president of the United States in 1989.

Barack Obama to
Michelle LaVaughn Robinson Obama

In 1989, when Barack Obama was about to depart Chicago for his second year in law school, he had to leave behind the woman he had been dating all that summer: Michelle Robinson, a young associate at a law firm. In her autobiography, Michelle relates that Barack told her he preferred keeping in touch via letter writing. "'I'm not much of a phone guy,' was how he put it," she recalled.

"As if that settled it.

"But it settled nothing. We'd just spent the whole summer talking. I wasn't going to relegate our love to the creeping pace of the postal service. . . .

"I informed Barack that if our relationship was going to work, he'd better get comfortable with the phone. 'If I'm not talking to you,' I announced, 'I might have to find another guy who'll listen.' I was joking, but only a little.

"And so it was that Barack became a phone guy."

And so it also was that posterity was deprived of words that passed between them that might give an insight into two of the most interesting people of our time.

The only handwritten message that we could find from the forty-fourth president to his wife was a letter that he sent her on January 17, 2017, her fifty-third birthday, and eleven days after they moved out of the White House:

You're not only my wife and the mother of my children, you're my best friend. I love your strength, your grace, and your determination. And I love you more each day. Happy Birthday.

The inauguration of Barack Obama attracted the largest attendance of any event ever held in the capital. The theme of the inauguration was "A New Birth of Freedom," a phrase from Lincoln's "Gettysburg Address."

Two years went by, and Barack Obama had discovered Twitter, now known as X—the first president to do so. On his wife's fifty-fifth birthday, he posted online a picture of himself and Michelle when they were young. He tweeted this message:

I knew it way back then and I'm absolutely convinced of it today—you're one of a kind, @MichelleObama. Happy Birthday!

PART 2

Separation

Introduction

Each of these letters was penned because the writer and his beloved were separated. Some letters were meant to ease that separation. Whenever William McKinley went on a business trip, he always wrote to his wife, Ida, every day. When someone asked Ida what her husband could find to write about so often, she replied simply, "He can say he loves me."

Many of the letters in this section are from men who were separated from their fiancées or wives because they were at war. The letters had two purposes. One was to convey the horrors of war. The second was to relay what each woman most wanted to hear: that the letter writer was alive. Often those who were about to go into battle wrote of quotidian matters, such as Washington telling Martha that he had made preparations for his will, and in a postscript describing some cloth he had purchased for a new suit.

Ulysses S. Grant, one man who had improved his writing skills (but not his spelling) gave a vivid description of a battle to his beloved Julia:

> *We found the Mexican Army . . . drawn up in line of battle waiting our approach. . . . When we got in range of their Artillery they let us have it right and left . . .*
>
> *Although the balls were whizing thick and fast about me I did not feel a sensation of fear until nearly the close of the firing a ball struck close by me killing one man instantly . . . It was a terrible sight to go over the ground the next day and see the amont of life that had been destroyed. The ground was literally strewed with the bodies of dead men and horses.*

Ulysses and Julia were engaged but not yet married. She feared that his absence would lessen his love for her, and he concluded his letter:

Julia is as dear to me to-day as she was the day we visited St. Louis together, more than two years ago, when I first told her of my love. From that day to this I have loved you constantly and the same and with the hope too that long before this time I would have been able to call you Wife.

Chester A. Arthur and his law partner traveled from New York City to Kansas in 1857. It was a dangerous trip in those days, because Kansas was about to gain statehood, and it would enter the Union as either a slave state or a free state. Angry mobs on both sides roamed the territory, fighting those whose views were different. Arthur and his partner were antislavery and planned to open a law office to give legal advice to people whose views matched theirs.

We get a reminder from Chester Arthur of how important handwritten letters were in the days before cell phones made it possible for anyone to be able to communicate with loved ones at a moment's notice. When a letter from his wife didn't arrive before he left Omaha, Arthur wrote:

It was hard to go away knowing that in a day or two more, the long-wished for letter would come. It was a great trial to be so long without a word to tell me that my darling, dearer to me than all the world beside, is safe and well.

And some years later, Theodore Roosevelt, trying his hand at ranching in the Dakota territory, received a longed-for stack of letters from his wife. His reaction:

How eagerly I seized those dear little 'square letters'! I almost cried over them, I loved them so. They were so like your own blessed self, and I just read them over again and again.

Benjamin Harrison, the grandson of a president, who was destined to become president himself, fought in the Civil War. He described to his wife one of the bloodiest battles of that war:

*. . . We had quite a hard fight at Golgatha Church about two
miles from here on the 15th and lost killed & wounded fifty
men. . . . My Regt [regiment] was advanced without any support
to within three hundred yards of a strong rebel breastwork. . . .
We stood there fighting an unseen foe for an hour and a half
without flinching while the enemy's shells and grapes fell like
hail in our ranks tearing down large trees and filling the air with
splinters. Two or three of my men had their heads torn off close
down to the shoulders & others had fearful wounds.*

But amid such horrors, the men who wrote letters to their wives
never forgot to express their love, as Benjamin Harrison did:

*I cant tell when I can get to go home. I would not like to leave
my Regt [regiment] in the command of another in a fight. I have
got to love them for their bravery & for dangers we have shared
together. . . .*

*When I can leave them. . . . you will be sure I shall come
with swift feet to the wife & home of my heart. Your devoted
Husband. Benj. Harrison.*

George Washington to
Martha Dandridge Custis Washington

The following letter that George Washington sent to his wife, Martha,
was written at an auspicious time—just after the Continental Congress had appointed Washington to head the Continental Army that
would defend the independence of the new nation. Washington had
not sought, or even desired, this honor, for it thrust him into the
forefront of the struggle and if he failed, it would mean the loss of
his freedom, perhaps his life, and the plantation at Mount Vernon
where he would have much preferred to spend his later years, rather

than leading troops into battle. In the following letter, he shared with his wife (whom he calls Patcy) the reasons for his acceptance of the commission.

Philadelphia, June 18, 1775

My Dearest

I am now set down to write you on a subject which fills me with inexpressible concern, and this concern is greatly aggravated and increased, when I reflect upon the uneasiness I know it will give you—It has been determined in Congress that the whole Army raised for the defence of the American Cause shall be put under my care, and that it is necessary for me to proceed imme-diately to Boston to take upon me the command of it. You may believe me my dear Patcy, when I assure you, in the most solemn manner, that so far from seeking this appointment I have used every endeavor in my power to avoid it, not only from my unwill-ingness to part with you and the Family, but from a consciousness of its being a trust too great for my Capacity and that I should enjoy more real happiness and felicity in one month with you, at home, than I have the most distant prospect of reaping abroad, if my stay were to be Seven times Seven years. But, as it has been a kind of destiny that has thrown me upon this Service, I shall hope that my undertaking of it, is designed to answer some good purpose—You might, and I suppose did perceive from the Tenor of my letters, that I was apprehensive I could not avoid this appointment, as I did not even pretend [t]o intimate when I should return—that was the case—it was utterly out of my power to refuse this appointment without exposing my Character to such censures as would have reflected dishonor upon myself, and given pain to my friends—this I am sure could not, and ought not be pleasing to you and must have lessened me considerably in my own esteem. I shall rely therefore, confidently, on that Provi-dence which has heretofore preserved and been bountiful to me, not doubting but that I shall return safe to you in the fall—I shall feel no pain from the Toil, or the danger of the Campaign. My unhappiness will flow, from the uneasiness I know you will feel at being left alone—I beg of you to summon your whole fortitude & Resolution, and pass your time as agreeably as possible—nothing will give me so much sincere satisfaction as to hear this, and to hear it from your own pen. . . .

As life is always uncertain, and common prudence dictates to every Man the necessity of settling his temporal Concerns whilst it is in our power—and while the Mind is calm and undisturbed, I have since I came to this place . . . got Colo Pendleton to Draft a Will for me by the directions which I gave him which will I now Inclose—The Provision made for you in cas[e] of my death will, I hope, be agreeable . . .

I shall add nothing more at present as I have several Letters to write, but to desire you will remember me to Milly and all Frends, and to assure you that I am with the most unfeigned regard,
My dear
Patcy Yr Affecte
Go: Washington

P.S. Since writing the above I have received your letter of the 15th and have got two suits of what I was told wa[s] the prettiest Muslin, I wish it may please you—it cost 50/ a suit that is 20/ a yard.

John Adams to Abigail Smith

Less than a month before their marriage, John Adams wrote to his fiancée, Abigail Smith, about his efforts to find suitable servants to help her manage their new home—a cottage John had inherited from his father. Calling her "Diana," a classical reference that he knew she would understand, Adams confessed to yearning for the time when they could be together—not knowing how often revolution and politics would separate them. He wrote the following after interviewing women to help Abigail keep house—which was an enormous task in an age when al-

*This portrait of John Adams is by the Salem artist
Benjamin Blyth, made around 1766 during the
newlywed couple's visit with Abigail's older sister.
John and Abigail exchanged more than 1,100 letters during their lifetimes.*

most everything, including clothes, soap, and various foods, had to be
made at home.

Sept. 30, 1764

My dear Diana,
   I have this evening been to see the Girl. [He mimics her reaction.] *What Girl? What right have you to go after Girls? Why, my
Dear the Girl I mentioned to you Miss Alice Brackett. But Miss
has hitherto acted in the Character of an House-Keeper, and her
noble aspiring Spirit had rather rise to be a Wife than descend
to be a Maid.* [He explains that Alice is needed to keep house for
her uncle. He continues his letter, naming some other potential
housekeepers.]

Benjamin Blyth painted this portrait of Abigail during the same visit. Their correspondence shows the loving and intellectual friendship they shared. For the time, John showed a real sense of equality with his wife, asking her advice about political as well as personal matters.

. . . *Hannah Crane (pray dont you want to have her, my Dear) has sent several Messages to my Mother, that she will live with you as cheap, as any Girl in the Country. She is stout and able and for what I know willing, but I fear not honest, for which Reason I presume you will think of her no further.*

. . . *Oh my dear Girl, I thank Heaven that another Fortnight will restore you to me—after so long a separation. My soul and Body have both been thrown into Disorder, by your Absence, and a Month or two more would make me the most insufferable Cynick, in the World. I see nothing but Faults, Follies, Frailties and Defects in any Body, lately. People have lost all their good Properties or I my Justice, or Discernment.*

But You who have always softened and warmed my Heart,

shall restore my Benevolence as well as my Health and Tran-
quility of mind. . . .
 Believe me, now and ever yr faithful
 Lysander

During their lifetimes, John and Abigail Adams wrote each other more than eleven hundred letters—and saved most of them. The reason was that during those volatile times, they were frequently separated. One of the longest separations began at the end of 1779, when Congress sent John to Europe to promote American interests with European nations. He took two of his sons—John Quincy and Charles, ages nine and twelve—along with him, to further their education. John and Abigail would not see each other again for more than four years. Among the many letters they exchanged is the following, which he wrote while he was living in Amsterdam. John had sent his son Charles back to America because he was homesick. (Charles proved to be the most unruly of the Adamses' sons. He was nearly expelled from Harvard for running, drunk and naked, through Harvard Yard with a group of friends. Streaking is not just a modern fad.)

        Amsterdam Decr. 2 1781
My dearest Friend
 Your favours [letters] of September 29 and Oct. 21 are before
me. I avoided saying any Thing about Charles, to save you the
Anxiety, which I fear you will now feel in its greatest severity a
long time. I thought he would go directly home, in a short Passage,
in the best Opportunity which would probably ever present. But
I am disappointed. Charles is at Bilbao with Major Jackson and
Coll. Trumbull who take the best care of his Education as well as
his Health and Behaviour. They are to go home with Captain Hill
in a good Vessel of 20 Guns. Charles health was so much affected
by this tainted Atmosphere, and he had set his heart so much
on going home . . . that it would have broken it, to have refused
him—I desire I may never again have the Weakness to bring a
Child to Europe. They are infinitely better at home. [However,

John had already sent his fourteen-year-old son, John Quincy, to St. Petersburg, the capital of Russia, to serve as secretary to Francis Dana, the American diplomatic representative to the Imperial Court.]

I beg you would not flatter yourself with hopes of Peace. There will be no such Thing for several years. . . . [Actually, a peace treaty was signed on September 3, 1783. John Adams was one of the signatories.]

General Washington has done me great Honour, and much public service by sending me, authentic Accounts of his own and Gen. [Nathanael] *Greene's last great Actions. They are in the Way to negotiate Peace, it lies wholly with them. No other Ministers but they and their Colleagues in the Army can accomplish the great Event.*

I am keeping House, but I want [need] *an Housekeeper. What a fine Affair it would be if We could flit across the Atlantic as they say the Angels do from Planet to Planet. I would dart to Pens hill and bring you over on my Wings. But alass We must keep house separately for some time.*

But one thing I am determined on. If God should please to restore me once more to your fireside, I will never again leave it without your Ladyships Company. No not even to go to Congress at Philadelphia, and there I am determined to go if I can . . . get chosen, whenever I return. [Actually, as their exchange of letters in Part 3 shows, he did go to Philadelphia without her.]

I would give a Million sterling that you were here—and could Afford it as well as G. Britain can the thirty Millions she must spend the ensuing Year to compleat her own Ruin.

Farewell. Farewell.

After more than four years without her husband, Abigail finally decided to make the long sea voyage to Europe. There was less danger from English warships now that the war was over. She brought along her daughter Nabby, who was at the time engaged to be married to a man her parents disliked. The resulting separation ended the engagement.

Informed of Abigail's intentions, John sent his son John Quincy (now returned from Russia) to London to meet his mother and sister and bring them to the Hague, where John was US minister to the Netherlands, and had purchased a house that was the first American embassy on foreign soil. He wrote her the following letter for John Quincy to deliver.

The Hague July 26 1784

My dearest Friend

Your letter of the 23rd has made me the happiest Man upon Earth. I am twenty Years younger than I was Yesterday. It is a cruel Mortification to me that I cannot go to meet you in London, but there are a Variety of Reasons decisive against it, which I will communicate to you here. Meantime, I sent you a son who is the greatest Traveller of his age, and without Partiality, I think as promising and manly a youth as is in the World.

He will purchase a Coach, in which we four must travel to Paris. . . . I wish you to see the Hague before you go to France. . . .

Every Hour to me will be a Day, but don't you hurry, or fatigue or disquiet yourself upon the Journey. Be carefull of your Health. . . .

It is the first time in Europe that I looked forward to a Journey with Pleasure. Now, I promise myself a great deal. I think it lucky that I am to go to Paris where you will have an Opportunity to see that City, to acquire its Language &c. It will be more agreable to you to be there, than here perhaps for some time.

For my own Part I think myself made for this World. . . .

Yours with more Ardor than ever,

John Adams

The details of John and Abigail's reunion in London were not recorded. Abigail gave a hint of what it was like to be alone with her husband after more than four years when she wrote to her sister Mary Cranch: *"You will chide me* [for not describing the event], *but you know, my dear Sister, that poets and painters wisely draw a veil over those Scenes which surpass the pen of the one and the pencil of the other; we were indeed a very very happy family once more . . . together after a Separation of 4 years."*

Thomas Jefferson to
Martha Wayles Jefferson

Although Jefferson fulfilled his wife's dying wish that he destroy all the letters they had written to each other, he showed his feelings by inscribing on her tombstone *To the memory of Martha Jefferson, daughter of John Wayles, born October 19th 1748 intermarried with Thomas Jefferson January 1st, 1772, torn from him by death September 6, 1782. This monument of his love is inscribed, "If in the House of Hades men forget their dead, yet will I even there remember you, dear companion."* (This last sentence is a quote from *The Iliad* and is written in Greek on the stone.)

James Madison to
Dolley Payne Madison

In 1799, Madison was elected to the Virginia legislature. While Dolley and her son Payne remained at Montpelier, the Madison family plantation, James Madison went to the state capital for the meeting of the legislature. He had planned that she would join him, but as this letter explains, he got lost on the way to Richmond and it was difficult to find suitable lodging.

Richmond, Monday night December 2d, 1799
My dearest,
    Neither the chart [map] *of your uncle or the memory of your brother* [who thought he knew the way to Richmond] *could save me from two errors on our way down, we made out, notwithstanding to reach Town before sunset. I found at Mr. Watson's a room*

prepared for me, and an empty one immediately over it, but they are both in a style much inferior to what I had hoped. You must consequently lower your expectations on this subject as much as possible before you join me, which I shall look for about the time you suggested. . . . Present me affectionately to all around you— always and truly yours
   J. Madison Jr.

James Monroe to
Elizabeth Kortright Monroe

James Monroe, the fifth president, was perpetually in debt, even though he owned a plantation with enslaved persons providing the labor. He had expensive tastes. Despite his financial issues he married twenty-year-old Elizabeth Kortright in February 1786. This was a particularly reckless move on Monroe's part, because her father was a wealthy New York City ship owner, and Elizabeth was used to wearing fashionable dresses and other luxuries. The twenty-seven-year-old Monroe must have felt that he could earn enough to enable both himself and Elizabeth to continue their expensive lifestyles. The pressure on him increased when she became pregnant before the end of the year.

The only profession Monroe was prepared for was the law. Though he had studied under Thomas Jefferson, he had never really practiced law. He decided to leave his wife and infant daughter in New York with friends and go to Richmond to launch his career as a lawyer. From there, he wrote Elizabeth this letter in April 1787. Notice that he doesn't let poverty stop him from ordering a custom-built carriage, although he also warns his wife that when she joins him, their living quarters may be "painful or afflicting." He is apologetic and hopes that "we shall be able to surmount these difficulties" so that they will not again be forced to separate for such a long time. He refers to their daughter as "the little monkey."

[no salutation]

I arriv'd here this evening after you left me and I have since been in health. I lodge and dine with Mr. Jones [his uncle]. *I hope to hear from you by the post this morning. I have the utmost anxiety to know that your self and our little Eliza* [their daughter] *are well, and that you are well rec'd and kindly treated by Mrs. Lewis* [with whom she was staying]. *Of this I have no doubt but shall be happy to hear it from yourself. Has* [Eliza] *. . . grown any, and is there any perceptible alteration in her. . . . I was sorry that you had not with you the article you mentioned as necessary for the little monkey. I hope she suffers no inconvenience from it. . . . I hope you use much exercise. I am satisfied the pain you complain of in your breast arises from this source. Let me instruct you not to neglect it—it will also contribute much to secure you from the disease of this country* [Virginia], *the ague and fever. Quarrier* [Thomas Quarrier, a Revolutionary War veteran who opened a carriage-making business; Thomas Jefferson was one of his customers] *has engag'd to begin a carriage for us—he objects to making it perfectly flat or straight before—he says it will sink and be apt to leak, that they might also be out of fashion—be so kind as to inform me in what style you wish it and the color you prefer.*

I find it impossible to make arrangements here during the term of the c[our]*t* [the time when courts met, and Monroe would be most likely to find work].

Mr. Randolph has not mention'd it and I have no money. I have partly arranged with Mr. Carrington that we shall get a house together this fall and bring yourself and his lady down for the court . . . His lady will be content to live on very little during the court . . . and I have assured him you will be as easily satisfied. Such difficulties as are insurmountable shod [should] *Be submitted to with fortitude and patience however painful or afflicting they may be. In future I trust we shall have little occasion to exercise this kind of fortitude for I hope we shall be able to surmount those difficulties which the severities of fortune had*

impos'd on us in our commencement as to avoid separation for
such length of time.

Believe me my dear Eliza, most affectionately yours. Jas.
Monroe

[P.S.] *Kiss the little babe for me and take care of yourself and her.*

Monroe would be elected president of the United States in 1816, the fifth person to hold that office, and the last of the founders to do so. This is the only letter from him to his wife that is known to exist. Eliza was not a popular First Lady because, in contrast to Dolley Madison, she was aloof and cold, probably due to the fact that she suffered from chronic convulsions that left her unconscious. During one of these attacks, she fell into a burning fireplace. The inaugural ball was held in their private home in Washington, and Eliza seldom appeared at other social functions.

However, she was responsible for a notable act when her husband was the US ambassador to France. The French Revolution was raging, and the guillotine was working overtime to claim the lives of supposed enemies of the revolution. One of those tossed in jail and awaiting judgment was the wife of the Marquis de Lafayette, who was beloved in America because of the aid he had given the new nation during the American Revolution.

Monroe sent Elizabeth, riding in his carriage, which was marked with the seal of the American government, to visit Madame de Lafayette. French officials, informed of the important American visitor, freed their noble prisoner.

Later, when Monroe was president, the Marquis showed his gratitude with an official visit to the United States.

Andrew Jackson to
Rachel Donelson Jackson

After his wife Rachel's death, people noticed that Jackson always carried a miniature picture of her in a locket and placed it on the table next to his bed at night. Below is the letter—sent fifteen years before his election as president—in which he thanked her for sending that locket, accompanied by her note: "Do not, my beloved husband, let the love of country, fame, and honor, make you forget you have [a wife.]" At the time, Jackson was commanding the West Tennessee militia. Britain had declared war on the United States in 1812 and Jackson was fighting the Creek Native Americans, who were Britain's allies, along the Tennessee River. Despite Jackson's hopes—expressed in this letter—that he would soon return home, he would not be able to see his wife again until 1815, when he defeated the last of the British forces in New Orleans.

January 8, 1813

My love,

I have this evening since dark received, your affectionate letter by Dunwoodie. . . . he has carefully handed me your miniature—I shall wear it near my bossom, but this was useless [unnecessary], *for without your miniature, my recollection never fails me of your likeness . . .*

I thank you for your prayers—I thank you for your determined resolution, to bear our separation with fortitude, we part but for a few days, for a few fleeting weeks, when the protecting hand of providence if it is his will, will restore us to each others arms, In storms, in battles, amidst the raging billows recollect, his protecting hand can save, in the peaceful shade, in cabins, in pallaces, his avenging hand can destroy—Then let us not repine, his will be done, our country calls . . .

It [is] *now one oclock in the morning the candle nearly out, and*

*I must go to bed. May the angelic hosts that rewards & protects
virtue and innocence, and preserves the good, be with you until I
return—is the sincere supplications of your affectionate Husband.*
  Andrew Jackson

While Jackson was commanding Tennessee volunteer troops in the War
of 1812, he sent his wife a letter describing in detail a fierce battle in
which Rachel's nephew, Alexander Donelson, had been killed. She responded on February 10, 1814, expressing her fear that Jackson himself
would be killed. She wrote:

*I received your Letter . . . Never shall I forgit it I have not slept
one night sinc[e]. What a dreadfull scene it was how did I feel
I never Can disscribe it I Cryed aloud and praised my god
for your safety how thankfull I was . . . you have served your
Country Long Enough you have gained maney Laurels . . . you
have been gone a Long time six months in all that time what has
been your trials daingers and Diffyculties hardeships oh Lorde
of heaven how Can I beare it . . . my prayers my tears is for
your safety Daye and night . . . health and happy Dayes until we
meet—Let it not be Long from your Dearest friend and faitfull
wife until Death*
  Rachel Jackson

Andrew Jackson's reply:

Head quarters Fort Strother
February 21st 1814

My love,
  *I have this moment recd. Your letter of the 10th . . . and am
grieved to think the pain my absence occasions, but when you
reflect, that I am in the field, and cannot retire when I please,
without disgrace I am in hopes that your good sense, will yield
to it yet a little while with resolution and firmness, and my love
as it respects my safety, when you reflect, that I am protected by*

*that same overruling providence when in the heart of the [C]reek
nation, as I am at home. His protecting hand can Shield me as
well from danger, here as there, and the only differrence is that
his protecting hand is more conspicuous in the field of Battle than
in our own peacefull dwellings when we are surrounded, by our
boosom friends.*

*The brave must die, in a state of war the brave must face the
enemy, or the rights of our country could never be maintained.
It was the fate of our brave Nephew Alexander Donelson to fall,
but he fell like a hero . . . and he has only gone in the prime of
life, when we had a right to expect, we would be gratified with his
society [company] for a few years, but still we know we have to
die, still the pleasing heavenly thought that we are to meet on high
never to part again where we will enjoy happiness unmingled, by
the interruption of human depravity & corruption—yes my love
our young friend has gone, but he died like a hero he fell roman
like—and we must resign him—it is a pleasing recollection, when
we reflect, that he . . . has left no stain behind [so] that his friends
can with pleasure review his conduct, and speak of his virtues
and his valour with pleasure . . . I have therefore to request that
you will retain your usual firmness—and should it be the will of
divine providence, to smile upon my honest exertions, I have a
pleasing hope of seeing you before long . . . I will soon put an end
to the Creek war . . . and I can honourably, retire, I shall, return to
you[r] arms on the wings of love & affection, to spend with you
the remainder of my days in peaceful domestick retirement . . . I
shall be with you the moment I can with honor and safety to my
country—untill then my dearest heart—summons up your resolution and bear my absence with fortitude . . .*

    Andrew Jackson

Jackson was elected the seventh US president in 1828. Rachel had a special dress made for the inauguration, but she died in December before
the ceremony took place. She was buried in the dress.

William Henry Harrison to
Anna Symmes Harrison

William Henry Harrison, the ninth president, was born in Virginia. His father, the owner of a plantation, had been a delegate to the First Continental Congress and a signer of the Declaration of Independence. William enrolled in medical school but left because he didn't have the money to continue. He enlisted in the army and was assigned to the Northwest Territory, where settlers were encroaching on land traditionally the home of Native Americans.

Harrison soon met and fell in love with Anna Symmes, the daughter of Judge John Cleves Symmes, who had purchased from the government the title to approximately three hundred thousand acres of land.

When Harrison asked the judge for his daughter's hand, Symmes asked how he proposed to support a family. His reply: "With my strong right arm and my sword." The judge didn't find this a satisfactory answer, but when he left the area on business, William and Anna eloped. The judge reluctantly accepted Harrison as his son-in-law and gave him a parcel of land, hoping he would become a farmer.

Harrison continued his military career as well, and continually battled the Native Americans who lived in the territory. Some accepted payments to move westward, but others resisted. The struggle culminated with the Battle of Tippecanoe, where Harrison led his forces to victory, later signing treaties that effectively opened the territory to nonnative settlement.

There is a legend that one of the Native American chiefs placed a curse on Harrison, which resulted in the deaths in office of every American president thereafter who was elected in a year ending in a zero. In any case, Harrison won the presidential election of 1840, becoming the oldest man (sixty-eight) elected president up to that time. To demonstrate his vigor, he wore no overcoat on the cold March day of his inauguration and gave a two-hour inaugural speech, the longest in history. A month later, he died of pneumonia.

(The "curse" lasted every twenty years until 1980, when Ronald

Reagan was elected president and a year later survived an assassination attempt.)

The following may not be the most effusive love letter, but it is one of the few penned by Harrison and has never been published before. Since Anne Symmes Harrison defied her father to marry Harrison and later gave birth to ten children, there is every reason to believe the couple loved each other. Anna, a former schoolmate of Martha Washington's granddaughter, was very well-read and subscribed to all the newspapers she could get, even though she lived in what was then a frontier community. When her husband ran for office, she said, "I wish that my husband's friends had left him where he is, happy and contented in retirement." After he was elected president, she decided not to attend the inauguration, planning to visit Washington in May, when traveling was easier. He died before she arrived.

University, April 15th 1820
[In 1801, Harrison founded the first institute
of higher learning in the Northwest Territories.
It became known as Vincennes University.]

My Dear Anna,

By Mr. Smith I heard yesterday you were all well—I am glad you have paid Cincinnati a visit—Were you to ride about more than you do I have no doubt it would contribute greatly to your health—You mention nothing about visiting this place. You might do it with little trouble. Anna [their daughter, born 1813] *is large enough to stay at home—Your friends enquire of me almost every day when you are coming over—*[Your friend] *would I am confident be glad were you to consent to make a journey to this place—the roads and weather are fine—You would be in no danger of my going too often to the theater or of embracing it . . . I would as soon think of deserting my country's standard in the moment of greatest danger or of abandoning the religion in which I have been educated. Mrs. Taylor and Miss Bambridge arrived in town last evening—They gave me all the news of our city. . . . Give my love to Sister Betsey* [his elder sister]—*tell her I*

*am expecting a letter from her. . . . Did Paula receive a letter from
me? . . . Kiss Anna for me—Scott* [John Scott Harrison, their son,
who would become the father of Benjamin Harrison, the twenty-
third president]—*Benjamin—Emma—Mary—and Harri* [some
of their other children]. *Mr. Bullock Hampton's mother stopped
in a carriage—the other day—at the college gate—and enquired
for me—I was not in college at that time—she was I expect on her
way to Frankfort* [Kentucky] . . . *I shall go to Frankfort in a week
or two—Adieu dear Anna*
   Wm. Harrison, Sr.

James K. Polk to Sarah Childress Polk

James K. Polk, the eleventh president, and his wife, Sarah, had no children, the only presidential couple never to have any—biologically, by
adoption, or from a previous marriage. Their lack is thought to have
been the result of a painful operation James had as a young man to
remove gallstones. However, this freed his wife, who was well educated
for a woman of the time, to take a greater role in his political affairs.
She was meant to be a politician's wife; indeed, she guaranteed it. When
she met her husband, he was the chief clerk of the Tennessee House of
Representatives. After he proposed, she agreed only on condition that
he run for a seat in the House before they got married.

She showed herself to be a useful asset by serving as his secretary,
clipping political news articles from newspapers, briefing him on books
he had no time to read. He knew she was an asset, as his letters show,
and while he was campaigning, he kept her up-to-date on his effective-
ness and chances of victory. Andrew Jackson is said to have advised Polk
to marry her if he wanted to enter politics. "Stop this philandering,"
Jackson told him. "They tell me you are a gay Lothario; you must settle
down as a sober married man."

"What lady should I choose?" Polk asked.

"The one who will give you no trouble," replied Jackson. "Her wealth, family, education, health, and appearance are all superior. You know her well."

"You mean Sarah Childress?" Polk said. Then, after a moment's thought, he said, "I shall go at once and ask her."

They were married January 1, 1824, at the plantation house of her parents. Polk was twenty-eight; Sarah was twenty. That same year, he won another election—this time, to the US House of Representatives. Fifteen years later he was elected governor of Tennessee but lost his reelection bid two years later. The following letter was sent to his wife during a third try at the governorship.

Kingston, June 9th 1843

My Dear Wife,

I received your two letters, the one from Columbus and the other from Murfreesboro, by the mail of this evening. I wrote you from Cleveland and Athens, but you had not received them before you left home. It pains me that you write so despondingly. You must cheer up. It is now but 7 weeks until the election. The worst of the canvass is over. I am blessed with fine health, and am in good spirits. That I have gained considerably in the 8 counties in East Tennessee through which I have passed there cannot be a doubt. My estimate is, that the gain in these 8 counties is from 600 to 800 votes. It may be much greater, by the failure of the dissatisfied Whigs [the opposing party] to attend the polls, and by the fuller vote of the Democratic party [his own]. Our friends every-where are active & confident of success. The Whig leaders are using desperate efforts to rouse their party, but as far as I can judge, without success. My friends in middle Tennessee, I hope will be vigilant and active.

James K. Polk

Polk's optimism was misplaced, and his wife's fears had been perceptive. He lost the election. Therefore, it was a surprise when, the following year, he received the Democratic Party's nomination for president. The term "dark horse," meaning an unexpected political victor, was

This daguerreotype shows the determination and strong bond that James and Sarah Polk shared. After his death Sarah lived on for forty-two years, dedicating herself to honoring his memory—the longest widowhood of any First Lady.

first applied to him. He owed part of his triumph to the fact that when he served in Congress, his wife cultivated a network of Democratic political leaders and their wives. During the presidential campaign, Sarah played an important part, writing newspaper pieces and helping with her husband's speeches. He said that no one knew his affairs as closely as his wife. As First Lady, she was a noted hostess, even though her religious beliefs caused her to ban dancing, card games, and liquor in the White House. (Wine was permitted, however.)

Though Polk served only one term as president, it was eventful, seeing the United States fight and win a war with Mexico, leading to the annexation of Texas and nearly the entire Southwest as well as California. He also settled a dispute with Britain over the boundary of the Oregon

Territory. Despite his popularity he chose not to run for reelection and died three months after his term ended.

Polk's last words were "I love you, Sarah. For all eternity, I love you."

Franklin Pierce to Jane Appleton Pierce

Almost no one thought Franklin Pierce and Jane Appleton were suited for each other. He was gregarious, liked to party, and drank heavily. She abstained from alcohol and was withdrawn, often depressed, and deeply religious. Nobody agrees on how they met, either. Only the fact that Franklin went to law school at Bowdoin College in Brunswick, Maine, where she lived, is certain. One story has it that he saw her standing under a tree during a thunderstorm and went to tell her that it was dangerous. In any case, he courted her for the next seven years; it took that long for her to say yes because her family opposed their marriage.

They finally wed on November 19, 1834. By that time Franklin had been elected to the US House of Representatives, and Jane discovered she disliked politics, in part because of the heavy drinking and boisterous parties that were typical of Washington, DC.

When Jane became pregnant, she moved to her grandmother's house in Concord, Massachusetts, where she gave birth to their first child, a boy named Franklin Jr. Unfortunately, he lived for only three days.

A second son, Frank Robert, was born three years later. By now, Franklin was a US senator, but Jane still avoided Washington, arguing that New Hampshire was a better place to raise a child than the capital. When Franklin's party lost the midterm elections, putting it in the minority in Congress, he resigned from the Senate to go home to his wife and son. Tragically, Frank Robert died at the age of four from typhus.

Pierce and a partner opened a law firm, and he and Jane had a third son, Benjamin, in 1841. Five years later, the United States declared war on Mexico on the grounds that Mexican troops had attacked Americans north of the Rio Grande—known to us as Texas. Pierce used his political connections to gain an officer's commission in the volunteer force raised in New Hampshire. Eventually he became a brigadier general. He wrote his wife (he called her Jeanie) a letter from the ship headed for Mexico:

> *Barque Kepler*
> *At Sea, May 22, 1847*
>
> *Dearest Jeanie,*
>   *We are still 400 or 500 miles on our passage—preposterous voyage thus far for I have not been sick a moment altho' there has been scarcely another exception. I was never better—my horses are getting along nicely. . . . Yesterday my first sabbath at sea—a great and solemn day—service morning and evening—excellent sacred music by the trips all most solemn and impressive. . . . I seize the moment to send back a line to those who are ever in my thought and who are enshrined in my heart of hearts. . . . Kiss dear Benny. I am in good health and spirits with a heart for the service before me. . . . The effect of the voyage upon me is almost magical. My appetite, strength and robustness is a subject of general remark upon the officers. God grant that my dear ones may be preserved from sickness and all harm and that I may again meet them the honored husband and father.*
>   *Yr own affectionate Frank.*

After landing in Mexico Pierce wrote his wife the following letter, previously unpublished, of which only a fragment remains in the Library of Congress. In it he describes falling or being thrown from his horse twice, events that political opponents would use later to taunt him.

> *Headquarters 1st Brigade*
> *3rd Division*
> *August 26, 1847*
>
> *My Dearest Jeanie—*
>   *I wrote you three days since with* [the thought] *that it might go to Vera Cruz with official dispatches . . . I earnestly hope that we may have peace but as yet nothing is settled. I say nothing about the late*

battles because the official reports will probably reach you as soon if not sooner than this letter. It was a bloody battle and resulted in a most brilliant victory to our arms . . . When my horse was at full speed, [I was] leading my brigade through a perfect storm of [bullets and shells]. [Then] he fell with me among the rocks of lava—at first I was not conscious of any serious injury but before I had proceeded 300 yards became faint. I hardly know what would have become of me but for Thicke [an aide?] who was following the colour [brigade banner] closely and came to my relief. In 30 minutes, I was able to walk with difficulty. . . . I found the horse of poor gallant Wm Johnson, who had just received a mortal wound of which he expired in an hour or two. I was permitted to take him (my own having been totally disabled) was helped into the saddle and continued in it until 11 o'clock that night—the night darker, the rain fell in torrents, I was of course separated from my servants without tent or covering. Add to all this that during the afternoon of the 19th we had gained no advantages over the enemy, who remained firmly entrenched with 7000 men opposed to about 6000 of our men . . . the morning of the 20th was as brilliant as the night before was dark & gloomy. Soon after daylight their works were carried with the bayonet, and of their 7000 men . . . probably 4000 cannot be found today. . . . About 1 o'clock . . . I was ordered by Genl [Winfield] Scott to attack with my brigade the enemy in the west, to cut off his retreat. We marched about 2 miles when we reached the position sought and although the line of the enemy was perfectly formed & extended as far as the eye could reach in either direction they were attacked vigorously and successfully—Reaching a ditch which it was impossible for my horse . . . to leap, I sprang from my saddle without thinking of my injury moved on foot at the head of the brigade for 300 yards when turning suddenly when my knee the cartilage of which had been seriously injured I fainted and fell where the bank in the ditch [was] in range of heavy fire of the enemy. That I escaped seems to me now almost like a miracle. . . .

The last page of the surviving letter ends without a closing or signature.

Abraham Lincoln to Mary Todd Lincoln

In 1846, as a member of the Whig Party, Lincoln was elected to the United States House of Representatives, where he served two years. Originally, his wife, Mary, had lived with him and their two sons in Washington, DC, but she returned to Illinois with the children. Now she evidently wished to rejoin him. This is one of the few personal letters from Lincoln to his wife that survive.

This Currier and Ives print shows Abraham and Mary Todd Lincoln with their youngest son, Tad, in 1865. Mary had a tempestuous relationship with Lincoln, who was a better father than a husband.

Washington
June 12, 1848

My dear wife:

On my return from Philadelphia, yesterday, where, in my anxiety I had been led to attend the whig convention I found your last letter. I was so tired and sleepy, having ridden all night, that I could not answer it till to-day; and now I have to do so in the H.R. [House of Representatives] *The leading matter in your letter, is your wish to return to this side of the Mountains. Will you be a good girl in all things, if I consent? Then come along, and that as soon as possible. Having got the idea in my head, I shall be impatient till I see you. You will not have enough money to bring you; but I presume your uncle will supply you, and I will refund him here. By the way you do not mention whether you have received the fifty dollars I sent you. I do not much fear but that you got it; because the want of it would have induced you* [to] *say something in relation to it. If your uncle is already at Lexington, you might induce him to start on earlier than the first of July; he could stay in Kentucky longer on his return, and so make up for lost time. Since I began this letter, the H.R. has passed a resolution for adjourning on the 17th July, which probably will pass the Senate. I hope this letter will not be disagreeable to you; which, together with the circumstances under which I write, I hope will excuse me for not writing a longer one. Come on just as soon as you can. I want to see you, and our dear—dear boys very much. Every body here wants to see our dear Bobby.*

Affectionately
A. Lincoln

Mary Lincoln replied, "How much I wish we were together this evening."

Andrew Johnson to Elizabeth McCardle Johnson

Andrew Johnson, the seventeenth president, was born in Raleigh, North Carolina, in 1808. His father died when Andrew was three, and his mother supported her children by taking in laundry. Neither of Andrew's parents could read or write, and he did not attend school. His mother apprenticed Andrew and his older brother to a tailor, to learn a skill that would permit them to earn a living. Sometimes people came to the tailor shop and read books aloud to the workers. This is thought to have contributed to Johnson's ability as a public speaker, which helped him in his later political career.

Andrew, his mother, brother, and stepfather moved to Greeneville, Tennessee, where he met Elizabeth McCardle, who was attending Rhea Academy. Within a year, they were married. Andrew was eighteen, and Elizabeth (whom he called Eliza) was only sixteen, the youngest person to marry a future president. It is said that Elizabeth taught her husband how to read, write, and do mathematics.

Andrew opened a tailoring business, and with the profits began to invest in real estate. His growing prosperity led him to enter politics. This list of offices he held shows his steady rise: town alderman, mayor, member of the state legislature, congressional representative, governor of Tennessee, senator. When the Civil War broke out in 1861, Johnson spoke out against secession, but by popular vote, his home state of Tennessee chose to join the Confederacy. Johnson opted to remain in the US Senate, the only senator from a Confederate state to do so.

When Union forces captured control of parts of western and central Tennessee, President Lincoln appointed Johnson military governor of the state. In an attempt to increase Johnson's popularity, Lincoln exempted Tennessee from the Emancipation Proclamation. The following letter was written shortly afterward, when Johnson was in Washington and his wife in Nashville. One thing the letter indicates is that although Johnson had learned to write, spelling was not one of his strengths. It may be embarrassment over this lack of skill that made his descendants destroy all the letters he wrote to Elizabeth except this one.

Washington City March 27th 1863.

My dear Eliza,

It is so difficult for me to write I am almost deterred from now trying after having commenced

I Desire to know how your health is. [She suffered from tuberculosis.] *I am kept in suspence all the time in reference to Some one of the family—Col Stover telegraphed that your health is about the same and that Mary* [their daughter] *is not well—I have heard nothing from Robert & Charles* [their sons] *since I left Nashville. I hope all is right with them. Martha* [another daughter] *and* [her] *children I fear I shall never see them again* [because they were living in Confederate-controlled territory]. *I feel sometimes like givg all up in dispare! But this will not do we must hold out to the end. This rebellion is wrong and must be put down let cost what it may in the life and treasure. I intend to appropriate the remainder of my life to the redemption of my adopted home East Tenessee and you & Mary must not be weary. It is our fate and we Should be willing to bear it cheerfully. Impatience and dissatisfaction will not better it or shorten the time of our Suffering. I expected to have been back some time ago, but have been detained her by the Govmt. . . . Things do not look in Tennessee at this time as* [we] *would like to see them, but must take them as they are. I would like to see the confederate Army* [driven] *back before you and Mary goes to Nashville, but by the time I reach there we will see more about it. You have no doubt seen that there are more* [Union] *troops being sent into Ky and the intention is to send them from there into Tennessee unless they are beaten back by the Rebels which I do not think will be the case. However we must wait and See the result. Washington is about as usual as far as I have seen, nothing more than common. The weather since I left you has been uninterruptedly bad. I have scarcely had a well*

*day since reaching the north; aboniable cold, with horseness,
sore throat and a bad cough. I have been speaking and exposed
to some extent which has kept it up. I hope you are gai[n]ing
strength and some flesh. I trust there is nothing serious the matter
with Mary and that she will soon be well again. Tell Mary she
must devote much of her time and attention to the instruction and
trai[n]ing of her children and say to them that the're grand father
thinks of them every day and prays for their future happiness. You
must tell Andrew that his father's hopes rest upon him now and
that he must make a man of himself he [can] learn to do it if he
will and I expect it of him. If he will only educate him Self he has a
destiny of no ordinary Character. When I get to Louisville I Shall
expect to find that he has made considerable progress in writing
as well as in his books. If he will be a good boy and learn as he
can there is nothing that he wants that I can procure for him but
what he shall have. . . .*

*Give my love to all and accept for yourself the best wishes of a
devoted husband's heart.*

Andrew Johnson

At Lincoln's behest, the new Republican Party nominated Johnson in
1864 for the vice presidency in Lincoln's second term. Lincoln planned
to restore the Union by pursuing a lenient policy toward the defeated
Confederate states. However, he was shot by an assassin on April 14,
1865, and died the following day, making Johnson the president. His
wife, Elizabeth, still battling tuberculosis, spent much of her time as
First Lady in her bedroom. Their daughter Martha assumed the social
duties usually performed by the president's wife.

The Radical Republicans who were now in control of Congress
tried to pursue a more punitive postwar policy, which Johnson opposed. He was not by nature a compromiser and clashed repeatedly
with congressional leaders. On March 2, 1868, the House of Representatives passed an impeachment bill against Johnson—the first ever
against a sitting president. The bill went to the Senate, where it had to

be passed by a two-thirds majority. By a single vote, the impeachment failed.

After his term as president ended, Johnson returned to Tennessee, where he was again elected to the US Senate, the only ex-president to serve there. However, he died of a stroke after less than a year in office. His wife joined him in death within a year.

Ulysses S. Grant to Julia Dent

After becoming engaged to Julia Dent, Grant was assigned to a military unit under General Zachary Taylor (later to become the twelfth president) to protect newly independent Texas against Mexico, a move that eventually resulted in war. In this letter, Grant refers to the fact that before he left, he and Julia exchanged rings with each other's initials inside.

Corpus Christi Texas
March 3d 1846

My Dear Julia

. . . This morning before I got awake I dreamed that I was some place away from Corpus Christi walking with you leaning upon my arm, your hand was in mine and I felt very happy. How disappointed when I awoke and found that it was but a dream. However I shall continue to hope that it will not be a great while befor such enjoyment will be real and no dream. . . . My Dear Julia as long as I must be separated from your dear self evry moove that takes place I hail with joy. I am always rejoised when an order comes for any change of position hoping that soon a change will take place that will bring the 4th Inf.y [the Fourth Infantry, his unit] to a post where there are comfortable quarters, and where my Dear Julia will be willing to accompany me. . . . You must write to me often Julia and . . . I will write to

*you very often and look forward with a great deal of anxiety—
to the time when I may see you again and claim a kiss for my
long absence.—Do you wear the ring with the letters U.S.G. in
it Julia. I often take yours off to look at the name engraved in
it . . .*

> *Your Most Devoted*
> *Ulysses*

Grant had his first experience with combat in the Mexican War. He
wrote vividly about what it was like.

> *Head Quarters Mexican Army*
> *May 11th 1846*

My Dear Julia

*After two hard fought battles against a force far superior to our
own in numbers, Gen. [Zachary] Taylor has got possession of the
Enemy's camp and now I am writing on the head of one of the
captured drums. . . . About two days after I wrote* [his last letter]
*we left Point Isabel with about 300 waggons loaded with Army
supplies. For the first 18 miles our course was uninterrupted but
at the end of that distance we found the Mexican Army . . . drawn
up in line of battle waiting our approach . . . Our waggons were
immediately parked and Gen. Taylor marched us up towards
them. When we got in range of their Artillery they let us have it
right and left . . .*

*Although the balls were whizing thick and fast about me I
did not feel a sensation of fear until nearly the close of the firing
a ball struck close by me killing one man instantly, it nocked
Capt. Page's under Jaw entirely off and broke in the roof of his
mouth . . . Capt. Page is still alive. When it became to dark to see
the enemy we encamped upon the field of battle and expected to
conclude the fight the next morning. Morning come and we found
that the enemy had retreated under cover of the night. . . . It was
a terrible sight to go over the ground the next day and see the
amont of life that had been destroyed. The ground was literally*

strewed with the bodies of dead men and horses. The loss of the enemy is variously estimated from about 300 to 500. Our loss was comparatively small. . . .

On the 9th of May about noon we left the field of battle and started on our way to Matamoras. When we advanced about six miles we found that the enemy had taken up a new position in the midst of a dense wood, and as we have since learned they had received a reinforcement equal to our whole numbers. Grape shot and musket balls were let fly from both sides making dreadful havoc. Our men continued to advance and did advance in spite of their shots, to the very mouths of the cannon and killed and took prisoner the Mexicans with them, and drove off with their own teams, taking cannon ammunition and all, to our side. In this way nine of their big guns were taken and their own ammunition turned against them. . . . I understand that General Lavega, who is a prisoner in our camp has said that he has fought against several different nations but ours are the first that he ever saw who would charge up to the very mouths of cannon. . . .

Now that the war has commenced with such vengence I am in hopes my Dear Julia that we will soon be able to end it. In the thickest of it I thought of Julia. How much I should love to see you now to tell you all that happened . . . When we have another engagement [battle], *if we do have another atall, I will write again, that is if I am not one of the victims. . . . Dont forget to write soon to your most Devoted*
ULYSSES

At the Battle of Monterrey, Grant distinguished himself when assigned to carry a dispatch past Mexican snipers. He accomplished his task by hanging off the side of his horse, concealing himself from the snipers. After the battle, he wrote to Julia, still his fiancée. In the last letter he had received from her, she was evidently wondering whether his love for her had waned. He doesn't mention his military exploits.

Camp Near Monteray Mex.
Oct. 3d 1846

My Dearest Julia

I wrote to you while we were still storming the city of Monteray and told you then that the town was not yet taken but that I thought the worst part was then over. I was right for the next day the Mexicans capitulated and we have been ever since the uninterrupted holders of the beautiful city of Monteray . . . If it was an American city I have no doubt it would be considered the handsomest one in the Union . . . I have written two pages and have not told you that I got a letter a few days ago from my Dear Dear Julia. It has been a long long time since I got one before but I do not say that you have not written often for I can very well conceive of letters loosing their way following us up. What made you ask me the question Dearest Julia "if I thought absence could conquer love"? You ought to be just as good a judge as me! I can only answer for myself alone, that Julia is as dear to me to-day as she was the day we visited St. Louis together, more than two years ago, when I first told her of my love. From that day to this I have loved you constantly and the same and with the hope too that long before this time I would have been able to call you Wife. Dearest Julia if you have been just as constant in your love it shall not [be] long until I will be entitled to call you by the affectionate title. You have not told me for a long time Julia that you still loved me, but I never thought to doubt it. Write soon to me and continue to write often. . . . Give my love to all at White Haven.

Ulysses

Grant and Julia were married after the Mexican War was over in 1848, and by this time Ulysses had decided to make the army a career. Within five years, they had two children, Frederick and Ulysses Jr. Their arrivals evidently led to further separations, because Julia returned to her parents' home to give birth, and the children were often left with their grandparents. In the meantime, Grant was transferred to posts on the

West Coast. Here is part of a letter he wrote from what was then the Washington Territory:

> *Columbia Barracks, W.T.*
> *July 13th 1853*
>
> My Dearest Julia,
>   It is about 12 o'clock at night, but as the Mail is to leave here early in the morning, I must write tonight—I got your long sweet letter, giving an account of our dear little boys at the pic nic where Fred. started [riding a horse] behind his Grand ma, but wanted her to ride behind him before he got through. You know before he could talk he would always persist in having his hands in front of mine when driving [a horse-drawn wagon]. The loose end of the lines never satisfied him. . . .
>   [In her previous letter, Julia had sent him some leaves that she had kissed.] My dear Julia I have said nothing about the pink leaves upon each of which you say you presed a sweet kiss. I cannot, in this, return the favor on flowers but you may rest assured that I will imprint them when we first meet upon your lips and those of our dear babes. . . .
>   Adieu dear Julia, the Steamer is in sight that is to take this.
>   Your affectionate husband
>   Ulys.

Rutherford B. Hayes
to Lucy Webb Hayes

Lucy Webb Hayes was a fervent abolitionist, and she convinced her husband that slavery was evil. After getting his law degree, he became a volunteer lawyer for the Underground Railroad, helping escaped enslaved persons gain their freedom. So, it was only natural that when the Civil War began, he was one of the first to volunteer for the Union army. The first recruits from southern Ohio were sent to Camp Dennison, north-east of Cincinnati. It was near enough to the city that people came to watch the soldiers drill.

Lucy was unhappy when her husband was soon transferred to a more distant camp, because she could not visit him there. But he had a different opinion.

> *Columbus* [Ohio]
> *Monday, 10 p.m.*
> *June 10, 1861*
>
> *Dearest Lu:*
>
> *I thought I'd write a few words to my dear wife before sleeping. We have been at the camp all the afternoon. Our quarters are not yet built; all things are new and disorganized; the location is not nearly so fine as Camp Dennison, but with all these disadvantages, we . . . came away feeling very happy. We visited our men; they behaved finely; they are ambitious and zealous, and met us in such a good spirit. . . . We are glad we are away from the crowds of visitors who interfere so with the drills at Camp Dennison . . .*
>
> *But I must stop this. You know how I love you; how I love the family all; but Lucy, I am much happier in this business than I could be fretting away in the old office near the courthouse. It is living. My only regret is that you don't like our location. We shall probably spend the summer here, or a good part of it, unless we go into Virginia. No more tonight. Much love.*
>
> *Sincerely,*
> *R. B. Hayes*

Hayes was offered the position of judge advocate general, probably because he was the only lawyer in the battalion. He was disappointed in this assignment, since he wanted to fight. He got his wish when his regiment went to western Virginia, where it encountered Confederate forces and drove them off. Later, he wrote Lucy:

Cross Lanes, near Gauley River, below
Summersville, Virginia, September 19,
Thursday a.m. [1861]

. . . You have no fear of my behaviour in fight. I don't know what
effect new dangers might have on my nerves, but the other day I
was several minutes under a sharp guerrilla fire—aimed particu-
larly at Captain Drake and myself (being on horseback), so I know
somewhat of my capacity. It is all right. In the noisy battle, for it
was largely noise, none of our regiment was under fire except the
extreme right wing of my little command; two were wounded and
I could hear the balls whistle away up in the air fifty feet over my
head; but it amounted to nothing. A portion of Colonel Lytle's
men caught nearly all the danger, and they were under a very
severe fire.

. . . The paymaster is expected soon. I shall be able to send you
lots of money if he does [come] *as I now spend next to nothing.*
Kisses for all. Dearest, I love you so much.

Affectionately,
Rutherford

By November 1861, Hayes's war was still a series of skirmishes, as he
describes in this letter:

Camp Ewing [at Bowyer's Ferry on the
New River, in West Virginia]
November 5, 1861
Tuesday morning

Dearest Lucy:
. . . We are having stirring times again. The enemy on the other
side of the New River are trying to shell such of our camps as
lie near the river bank. We are just out of reach of their shot.
McCook, in sight of us below, is camped in easy range, and they
are peppering at him. I hear their guns every two or three minutes
as I write. He doesn't like to move, and probably will not until

they do him some serious harm. They fired all day yesterday without doing any other mischief than breaking one tent pole. A ball or shell would hardly light before his men would run with picks to dig it up as a trophy. It is probable that we shall cross the river to attempt to drive them off in a day or two. . . .

I thought of you all yesterday, and wished I could look in on you at Birch's birthday dinner. You were thinking of the absent father and uncles. [Birch was Birchard, one of their three sons; Lucy had sent Hayes a letter describing the birthday party and wishing that Rutherford and Lucy's two brothers had been there. All three were in the army.]

. . . We love each other so much that on all sad or joyous occasions we shall always have each other in mind. . . . Good-bye. Love to all.

Lovingly,
Rutherford

Though he had been wounded several times, and was known to his men as a fearless commander who often led the way into battle, Hayes seemed to increasingly enjoy the fighting, as the following letter shows:

Camp near Berryville [Virginia],
September 4 [1864]
Sunday evening

Dearest—

We had one of the fiercest fights yesterday I was ever in. It was between the [Confederate] *South Carolina and Mississippi divisions under General* [Joseph B.] *Kershaw and six regiments of the Kanawha Division* [of the Union army]. *My brigade had the severest fighting, but . . . none of us suffered as might have been expected. We were under cover except when we charged and then darkness helped. We whipped them, taking about one hundred prisoners and killing and wounding a large number. Captain Gillis was killed, shot near the heart, Captain Austin dangerously wounded through the right shoulder, George*

*Brigdon, my color-bearer, bearing the brigade flag, mortally
wounded. . . .*

   *It was a pleasant battle to get through, all except the loss of
Gillis and Brigdon and Austin. I suppose I was never in so much
danger before, but I enjoyed the excitement more than ever before.
My men behaved so well. One regiment of another division nearly
lost all by running away. The Rebels were sure of victory and
ran at us with the wildest yells, but our men turned the tide in
an instant. [The Rebels were t]he crack division of [Confederate
General James] Longstreet. They say they never ran before.*

   *Darling, I think of you always. My apprehension and feeling is
a thousand times more for you than for myself. . . .*

   Love to all. The dear boys, God bless them.

   Affectionately ever, your

   R.

Lucy was having health problems and Hayes, by now a general, tried
to reassure her. A bit of news in this letter was that he had gone to see
Lincoln's second inauguration on March 4 and felt that his new vice
president, Andrew Johnson, "spoiled it."

Camp Hastings,
March 12, 1865

My Darling,

   *I am very glad to have heard from or of you several times
during the last week. While your rheumatism stays with you I
naturally feel anxious to hear often. If you should be so unlucky
as to become a cripple, it will certainly be bad, but you may be
sure I shall be still a loving husband, and we shall make the best
of it together. There are a great many worse things than to lose the
ability of easy locomotion. Of course, you will have to use philosophy or something higher to keep up your spirits . . .*

   *It is lucky you didn't come to the inauguration. The bad
weather and Andy Johnson's disgraceful drunkenness spoiled it.*

   I have bought a "Gulliver's Travels" which I will give to Webb [the second of their sons] *if he can read it. I remember he was fond of my telling it, and with his sweet voice often coaxed me to tell him about "the little people." . . .*

Affectionately ever,

R.

President Lincoln was assassinated on April 14, 1865, just five days after Robert E. Lee surrendered his army to Ulysses S. Grant, effectively ending the war. Hayes went to Lincoln's funeral five days later and described his conflicting feelings to Lucy:

> *New Creek, West Virginia,*
> *April 19, 1865*

My Darling,

I have just returned from Cumberland to meet Dr. Joe [Lucy's brother] from Winchester and to see the funeral ceremonies, etc. at department headquarters.

Had a good time. I feel the national loss, but even that is nothing compared to the joy I feel that this awful war is ended in our favor. Joe and I moralized over it, and agreed that no one man, not even so great a one as Lincoln, was anything by the side of the grand events of the month. We are to leave the [military] service hereafter when things take shape a little, if possible at the same time.

I asked you in a late letter to be ready to come to me on short notice. I, or somebody will meet you at Parkersburg or somewhere. Come without much baggage ready to travel. We will perhaps take a journey of three weeks or so when I quit. Joe will go along and possibly two of my staff. Can we take Birch [their eldest son] without Webb? Can you leave George [their youngest son]?

I am so anxious to be with you . . . I am so happy in the prospect of being with you for good soon.—Reply at once.

Affectionately, ever,

R.

Chester A. Arthur to Ellen Herndon

In 1857, when this letter was written, Chester A. Arthur and his law partner, Henry D. Gardiner, were traveling from New York City to Kansas,
where they hoped to set up a law office. Back in New York, Arthur had
been a leading opponent of slavery. He once successfully represented
a woman who sued the transit company for denying her a seat on a
streetcar because she was Black. (Shades of Rosa Parks a century later.)

At the time, Kansas was still a territory, although its citizens were
petitioning Congress to grant it statehood. The burning question of the
day was whether it should have the status of free state or slave state. Organized mobs from both sides, pro- and antislavery, fought each other
and terrorized citizens who held views contrary to theirs. The conflict
led to the name "Bleeding Kansas." Arthur and Gardiner idealistically
felt they would be able to give legal advice and assistance to those who,
like them, were abolitionists.

It was a sacrifice for Arthur to make this journey, because he had recently become engaged to Ellen Herndon (whom he called "Nell"). As
this letter, which was written on her birthday, indicates, he had brought
along a picture of her to keep his memory of her fresh.

Sunday, 30 August, 1857

My dearest Nell,

We are at St. Joseph [Missouri] *. . . on our way down the*
[Missouri] *river. . . . I did not receive any letter from you, Nell, up
to the time I left Omaha . . . We took the first boat that came after
we were ready to go, for we might have been obliged to wait many
days for another.*

*It was hard to go away knowing that in a day or two more, the
long-wished for letter would come.*

*It was a great trial to be so long without a word to tell me that
my darling, dearer to me than all the world beside, is safe and
well.*

I hope you get my letters regularly, and that you have lost none of them. I think that if you send a letter to me at St. Louis immediately on your receiving this, I shall get it before I leave there on my way home. I trust you are well, darling, though at times I feel anxious and fearful for you.

This is your birthday my own precious darling—my own Nell. The remembrance came with my first awaking in the early morning, as the thought of you always does—and as I kissed your image, darling, my heart was full to overflowing with love and prayer for you! And when I looked out and saw it was a glad, bright morning and everything looked fresh and beautiful, I thought it was a happy omen! How full of joy & happiness the world seemed to me, for I felt that you are my own Nell—that you love me!

I said "I am content." I was happy and thanked God that he had blessed me!

The day has fulfilled its morning promise, it has been most bright and beautiful even to the last rays of its gorgeous sunset, still lingering on the sky.

Who is there, dear, darling Nell, who can today anxiously & lovingly, wish you all earthly happiness—richer blessings with each returning year and God's blessing and protecting care, here and here after—as your own loving Chester? May these blessings all be yours and, oh, if any part of that earthly happiness be in my keeping, my darling, my precious one, it is a precious, sacred trust dearer than life itself!

I have never been with you on your birthday . . . two years ago—I can not realize it now—neither of us had heard the other's name—a year ago, I was away from you, although my heart was with you then, and now I am a long, long way from you, yet nearer than ever before, darling.

I would that the next [birthday] may find me with you, and that I may tell you all I would wish, all that my heart is now too full for me to write. My heart is full indeed for my thoughts have been of you all the day.

I sat down to write this hours ago, but I could not.

*The sun went down, and I sat in the coming on of the still soft
Sabbath evening dreaming of the soft moonlight nights of June,
a year ago, in our old place in the window-seat of the happy,
happy days at Saratoga* [a summer resort town in upstate New York,
where Arthur had proposed to her], *the golden, fleeting hours at
Lake George and all the precious days I have been with you, since
a year ago today, I wrote you wishes for your happiness. It has
been a happy year to me, the happiest of my life. It has given me
the precious blessing of your love, and it has been a happy year
to you, dearest love, for I believe you when you tell me that it is
happiness to you, to know that I love you fondly, truly devotedly,
always—that you are my own darling Nell.*

*I know you are thinking of me now. I feel the pulses of your
love answering to mine. If I were with you now, you would go and
sing for me "Robin Adair." Then you would come & sit by me—
you would put your arms around my neck and press your soft
sweet lips over my eyes. I can feel them now.*

*Yes darling, my heart is indeed full to night—full of love for
you, of happiness and gratitude for your love. Swelling with all
these recollections & with the thought, that with God's blessing,
I shall soon hold you in my arms again! The hours grow longer
every day.*

Good night. May God bless & keep you always my darling.

Your own

Chester

Chester Arthur and Ellen Herndon were married in 1859. They had
three children, one of whom died young. Though Arthur didn't run
for elective office until 1880, he was active in Republican politics in New
York City. He occupied a position that enabled him to dispense jobs and
favors to those who had helped the Republican Party. This was known
as the spoils system.

In January 1880, Ellen contracted pneumonia and died after a short
illness. Her devoted husband was shattered, but that year he was nom-

inated for the vice presidency in a political deal to balance the ticket. His running mate, James Garfield, won the presidency, and Arthur was expected to fade into the background. However, Garfield was shot by an assassin and, after lingering for months, died.

Arthur was now the twenty-first president of the United States, a job few people felt he was qualified for. He was expected to be a caretaker president, but he signed a bill establishing the civil service system, where government workers were given jobs on merit, instead of service to the political party in power. This was a remarkable change from the way government and politics in his native New York operated.

While president, Arthur had a portrait of his beloved "Nell" hung in the White House and had a fresh rose placed in front of it every day. He donated a stained glass window to a church near the White House and had a light placed behind it so that he could see it at night from his private rooms. In their New York residence her room was kept exactly as she left it, with a bookmark in the last page she had read.

Benjamin Harrison to Caroline Lavinia Scott Harrison

Benjamin Harrison, the twenty-third president, was the one who was the grandson of another president, William Henry Harrison. Benjamin married Caroline Scott, a music teacher and the daughter of a minister, when he was twenty and she was a few months older. By the time the Civil War broke out in 1861, the Harrisons already had two children. Benjamin was one of the early supporters of the antislavery Republican Party and wished to join the Union cause, but he worried that he could not support his family on the small salary he would receive from army service, as the following letter shows. At the urging of the governor of Indiana, where Harrison lived, he began to recruit other men and decided he could not ask them to make a sacrifice he himself was unwilling to make. So, he signed up and was made a colonel, in charge of a regiment. To his disappointment, in the first year of the war, he was not given a chance to take part in the fighting. He wrote his wife a letter on Christmas Eve 1862, expressing his feelings:

December 24, 1862

. . . And this is Christmas eve, and the dear little ones are about this time nestling their little heads upon the pillow, filled with the high expressions of what Santa Claus will bring them, and Papa is not there. How sad and trying it is for me to be away at such a time as this, and yet I cannot allow my complaining spirit to possess me. There are tens of thousands of fathers separated like me from the dear ones at home, battling with us for the preservation of our noble government which, under God, has given us all that peace and prosperity which makes our houses abodes of comfort and security. I am enduring very heavy trials in the army, but I believe that I was led to enter it by a high sense of Christian patriotism and God has thus far strengthened me to bear all cheerfully . . . I know you must be very lonesome and oppressed with many anxieties, but God will give you strength to bear them all and will, nay I believe already has, drawn you closer to Himself as the source of all comfort and consolation. It is a blessed promise that "all things shall work together for good to those who love God." Let us have faith to receive the promise in all its royal fulness."

Your devoted Husband. Benj. Harrison.

Six days later, Harrison and his men could hear the sounds of artillery fire, part of what became known as the Battle of Stones River. He learned that Caroline's brother John Scott had been severely wounded in the fighting. Harrison wrote to his wife:

I almost envy John his honorable wound, and hope we may soon exchange the ease and quiet of our present camp for the hardship and dangers of the field . . . not that I am ambitious of military fame, but because I want to feel that I am accomplishing something for the cause, which I sacrificed to espouse.

Eventually, Harrison got his wish to see combat. He took part in one of the bloodiest battles of the war, describing it in detail to his wife.

Camp 70 Ind. Vol. Infty
Near Kenesaw Mountain
June 18th 1864

My dear Wife
*   . . . We had quite a hard fight at Golgatha Church about two miles from here on the 15th and lost killed & wounded fifty men. . . . My Regt [regiment] was advanced without any support to within three hundred yards of a strong rebel breast-work where they had eight pieces [of artillery] in position & nicely covered and we being entirely exposed. We stood there fighting an unseen foe for an hour and a half without flinching while the enemy's shells and grapes fell like hail in our ranks tearing down large trees and filling the air with splinters. Two or three of my men had their heads torn off close down to the shoulders & others had fearful wounds. . . . Our Surgeons had got separated from us & putting our wounded in a deserted house I stripped my arms to dress their wounds myself. Poor fellows. I was but an awkward surgeon, but I hope I gave them some relief. There were some ghastly wounds. . . . I pulled out of one poor fellows arm a splinter five or six inches long & as thick as my three fingers. . . . We are in reserve today for the first time and right glad of it. God does indeed most mercifully preserve my unworthy life. May it continue to be His Care not mine to Keep it. . . .*

*   I got a letter from you yesterday. Do write me more often & longer letters, telling me everything that is going on. . . .*

*   But must close. I cant tell when I can get to go home. I would not like to leave my Regt in the command of another in a fight. I have got to love them for their bravery & for dangers we have shared together. I have heard many similar expressions from the men toward me.*

When I can leave them & the Service you will be sure I shall come with swift feet to the wife & home of my heart. Your devoted Husband. Benj. Harrison.

While still serving in the war, Harrison received word that his wife was seriously ill, causing him to consider asking for a leave of absence, but on his thirty-first birthday he received two letters from her, telling him she had recovered. The news caused him to write the following:

August 20, 1864

My dear Wife

I feel as if I ought to write today not only to acknowledge the receipt of these letters . . . but because it is my birthday and suggests many memories of the past, among the happiest of which your sweet form is closely interwoven . . . I am thirty-one years old today, and nearly eleven years of this, we have been man and wife. For how many more years God has decreed my life to be lengthened out, He only knows, and whether they shall be as full of blessings as those that are gone. But whether they be many or few, I hope they will bear witness of a faithful discharge of duty both to those I love on earth and my Father in heaven. . . . I hope to be a better husband and father, a better citizen and a better Christian in the future than I have been in the past.

You may think it strange that I promise nothing to my present occupation as a soldier. The reason is that I hope my mission as a soldier will end before another birthday. . . .

Write to me often and tell me everything. I am in excellent health, and since I have heard of your recovery, in fine and hopeful spirits. May God abundantly bless you and the dear children and bring me to your arms again when my duty is done. Love to all friends. Benj. Harrison.

Even amid the reminders of battle, Harrison found something to help him declare his love. In war-torn South Carolina, wandering through the remnants of a house that had been part of a plantation, he came upon a garden and found rosebuds blooming. He picked two and sent them to his wife with this message:

Imagine my whispering in your ear with this simple gift all that could be delicate and affectionate in a lover in his first declaration.

Harrison narrowly won the presidential election of 1888, and his wife found a project for herself in redecorating the White House, which had not been renovated in years. Her other favorite activity was growing flowers in the greenhouse that stood on the grounds. A reporter estimated there were five thousand decorative plants in the East Room alone, and throughout the rest of the house, "5,000 azalea blossoms, 800 carnations, 300 roses, 300 tulips, 900 hyacinths, 400 lilies of the valley," and countless small green plants. Caroline was also a talented artist, and painted an entire set of dishes that can be seen in the White House today.

Tragically, Caroline contracted tuberculosis and died in October 1892, during her husband's campaign for a second term. He lost and resumed his law practice. Nearly four years later, Harrison married his wife's niece, Mary Scott Lord, a young widow almost twenty-five years younger than Harrison, who had lived with the Harrisons in the White House. Harrison's grown children disapproved and refused to attend the wedding.

William McKinley to
Ida Saxton McKinley

Ida Saxton was one of the most attractive young women in Canton, Ohio. She was beautiful, well educated, and lively. Added to this was the fact that her father was one of the richest men in town. Many of Canton's young men courted her, but she chose William McKinley, who had become a lawyer after returning from service in the Civil War. (He would become the last president to serve in that war.) His career as a politician seemed bright, for he was elected county prosecutor when only twenty-six years old. The following year, Ida accepted his proposal of marriage, and less than a year later, she gave birth to a daughter they called Katie.

Two years later, Ida gave birth again, but this time the experience was long, difficult, and painful. Four months later, the infant died, and Ida was never the same—physically or emotionally. She developed what people of the time called "the falling sickness" and which today is thought to have been epilepsy. Her husband remained solicitous of her well-being, even as his political career thrived.

After his election as the twenty-fifth president, he had Ida sit next to him at formal dinners, rather than at the opposite end of the table, as was customary. He could sense when she had a seizure coming on and would place a napkin over her face to hide her distorted features. After the seizure passed, he would remove the napkin as if nothing had happened.

Before he became president, McKinley was frequently out of town on business, but each day he always found time to write to his wife. Here is an undated letter that he wrote to her while on a business trip. Someone asked Ida what he could possibly find to write about in all those letters, and she said simply, "He can say he loves me."

The following letter has never been published before and shows a side of McKinley that few modern readers would expect, judging him only by the photographs that show him as a stern, taciturn individual.

I received your precious letter a moment or two ago and it fell on me like sunlight in a dark day. It is a beautiful rainbow in my sky, giving me courage, hope, love and promise. I am sorry you are staying up so late and I don't want you to do so for the purpose of writing me. Your health is dearer to me than your letter written at the hazard of the former. . . . I feel like flying for home in the morning but then I would only get there before I must return. Accept much love for yourself and Katie—
   Your devoted Husband
   Wm McKinley Jr.

Following is another letter, written when McKinley served in Congress. It, too, has been unpublished until now.

> *My Precious Wife:*
> *I received your dear good letter this morning and it has given me new inspiration. I suppose from the tone of your letter you are rather unwell or expecting to be. I hope you are safe though. If not take three doses of Bromide, during that period. I am very well . . . It is awful lonesome without you. I am anxious for the next two weeks to roll around when I will join you, bring you here with me. Your friends all send much love.*
> *Yours faithfully,*
> *Wm McKinley, Jr.*

In September 1901, after being elected to a second term as president, McKinley and his wife visited the Pan-American Exposition in Buffalo, New York. Ida was too tired to stand in a receiving line, but the president enjoyed meeting the public, and he was shaking hands with a long line of people when an anarchist named Leon Czolgosz, concealing a pistol in a handkerchief, shot McKinley twice in the abdomen as the president held out his hand.

Doctors could not locate the second bullet, and McKinley lingered for eight days as gangrene set in. His wife at his bedside, he told the doctors that further efforts were useless, and he and Ida sang "Nearer, my God, to Thee" as he passed away.

After her husband's death, Ida McKinley ceased to suffer from seizures.

Theodore Roosevelt to
Alice Lee Roosevelt

Although Theodore Roosevelt's beloved wife was pregnant with their first child, he embarked on a trip to the Dakota Territory. He was examining the possibility of starting his own ranch, to make money to pursue either a political or a literary career. Sickly as a child, he always valued the benefits of an outdoor life and was clearly ambitious. But not even he could foresee that one day his face would be hewn into the side of a mountain in the Dakotas, alongside the images of Washington, Jefferson, and Lincoln.

Ferris Ranche
Little Missouri
Dakotah
Sept. 23rd, 1883

Darling Wifie,
Today a friend of mine, a cattle man, coming up the river, brought my mail: "There's the greatest pile of little square letters I ever see" he remarked as he handed them to me. Eagerly I seized those dear little "square letters"! I almost cried over them, I loved them so. They were so like your own blessed self, and I just read them over again and again, in the order in which they were written. My own tender true love, I never cease to think fondly of you; and oh how doubly tender I feel towards you now! You have been the truest and tenderest of wives, and you will be the sweetest and happiest of all little mothers.
In a couple of days now I start for home, so this will be the last news, in all probability, that you will hear from me, unless I write you from St. Paul, where I expect to be forced to stop a day or two. This has been by all odds the pleasantest and most successful trip I have ever made. I have three splendid trophies, and the heads of the buffalo and stag will look grandly in our hall, and I am feeling in such health as I have certainly

not been in for the past four years. . . . We have all we can eat of buffalo meat, venison, duck, and grouse; the temperature is below freezing each night, but we generally sleep in a hunters "shack" or shanty, and are always warm in our blankets; and all day long I spend, rifle in hand, tramping over the rugged hills, or, much more often, galloping or lopeing for hour after hour among the winding valleys or through the river bottoms. Of course I am dirty—in fact I have not taken off my clothes for two weeks, not even at night, except for one bath in the river— but I sleep, eat and work as I never could do in ten years time in the city.

During these ten days I have also been making up my mind to go into something more important than hunting. I have taken a great fancy to the three men, Merrifield and two brothers named Ferris, at whose ranche I have been staying several days, and one of whom has been with me all the time. I have also carefully examined the country, with reference to its capacity for stock raising; and the more I have looked into the matter—weighing and balancing everything, pro and con, as carefully as I know how—the more convinced I became that there was a chance to make a great deal of money, very safely, in the cattle business. Accordingly I have decided to go into it; very cautiously at first, and, if I come out well the first year, much more heavily as time comes on. Of course it may turn out to be a failure; but even if it does I have made my arrangements so that I do not believe I will lose the money I put in; while, if it comes out a success, as I am inclined to think that on the whole it will, it will go a long way towards solving the problem that has puzzled us both a good deal at times—how I am to make more money as our needs increase, and yet try to keep in a position from which I may be able at some future time to again go into public life, or literary life. But, my own darling, everything will be made secondary to your happiness, you may be sure. . . . I have carefully looked over the chances; I know I run a certain risk, but I do not consider it a very large one, and I believe that the chances are very good for making more of a success than I could in any other way. Goodbye, sweet-heart; best love to all; I shall probably be with you on Tuesday or Wednesday week . . .

Ever your loving Thee

In 1884, Alice died two days after giving birth to their only child, a daughter. On the same day, Roosevelt's mother died. In his diary, he just drew an X.

He left the daughter in care of a relative and went west again, to live as a cowboy.

Theodore Roosevelt to Edith Kermit Carow Roosevelt

But time healed even this wound, and Theodore married his child-hood friend Edith Carow in 1886, less than two years after his first wife's death. He continued a political career that would take him to the pres-idency but never lost his lust for hunting, writing to Edith while he was on an African safari in 1909, after his presidency.

In camp on 'Ngor river,
near Mt. Elgon, B.E.A. [British East Africa]
Nov. 12th 1909

Oh, sweetest of all sweet girls, last night I dreamed that I was with you, and that our separation was but a dream; and when I waked up it was almost too hard to bear. Well, one must pay for everything; you have made the real happiness of my life, and so it is natural and right that I should constantly [be] more and more lonely without you. The other day here I sat down under a tree and found my clothes covered with "pitch-forks" [insects]; and I laughed so hard as I thought of the Sweet Cicily [a plant that attracts insects] at home. Do you remember all about the Sweet

Cicily, you darling? Do you remember when you were such a pretty engaged girl and said to your lover "no, Theodore, that I can not allow"? Darling, I love you so. In a very little over four months I shall see you. Now, when you get this [letter] *three fourths of the time will have gone. How very happy we have been for these twenty-three years! Five days hence, on the 17th, is the anniversary of our engagement. . . .*

We are now camped on one of the streams that make up the headwaters of the Nile; a rapid, muddy river, with hippos and crocodiles in it. The banks are fringed with strange trees, and the country is covered with grass so high as to make it well nigh hopeless to look for lions. But we have killed many antelopes of kinds new to us; their names would mean nothing to you—bohor, sing sing, oribi, lelivel, kob. This seems to be a healthy country for men; but half our horses have died, and we may have to go in to the railroad on foot.

I have no idea how my articles in Scribners [a magazine] *have done, or whether they have been failures; at any rate I hope you have liked them. I have worked faithfully at them; and it has been a very real resource to have them to do.* [Apparently he could afford the trip because he earned money from the articles.] *Of course I never in the world would have taken this as a mere pleasure trip, a mere hunting trip. Kermit solemnly reads over the articles with a strong proprietary feeling. He and I are really attached to our personal attendants—poor, funny grasshopper-like black people!*

Kiss Ethel and the two little boys for me—they really are hardly "little boys" any longer. Give my dearest love to Aunt Lizzie; and Laura

Your own lover.

Woodrow Wilson to
Ellen Axson Wilson

When Woodrow Wilson married his first wife, Ellen Axson, in June 1885, they pledged never to part from each other. Fortunately for posterity, they failed to keep that pledge, often separating for various reasons and being forced to keep in touch by writing letters, which give us a closer look at the dynamics of what was obviously a love match. While Woodrow was teaching at Bryn Mawr, Ellen went south to her aunt's home in Gainesville, Georgia, to deliver each of their three children. Her stated reason was that, as a southerner, she didn't want to bear a child north of the Mason-Dixon Line. (It had been twenty years since the Civil War, but feelings still ran high.) They even formed the habit of taking separate vacations, and Wilson also traveled to give speeches.

Wilson wrote the following letter when his wife was visiting Chicago for the World's Fair. He stayed home to take care of their three daughters, aged three, six, and seven.

Princeton, September 10, 1893

. . . . *You seem to me to contain in your sweet person and your sweet nature, everything that is worth living for in the world,—besides duty. Duty is worth living for, no man could think otherwise; but there is often no joy in living for it. Everything connected to living for you is full of joy, if only it can be combined with you. Nellie* [the eldest daughter] *told the whole secret to-day. I said, "Nen, why do you want mama to come back?" and she said in that sweet, quick way of hers, "To love her!" That's the whole matter. To live for you is to love you.*

You serve me as a sort of perpetual source of youth. The sort of love I have for you has no age; it is as much a young man's love as a mature man's. It is at once the pledge of youth and of manhood. You are the companion of all my growth, whether of mind or of heart, and I associate you with all my ages. I loved you long

*before I ever met you, for you are my ideal. You have been with
me, in my desires, ever since I was a boy; you know and keep me
close company as a man; you are all that I would be, brought into
my life and kept constantly at hand, to excite my enthusiasm, to
kindle my heart into a constant blaze of joy. . . .*
  Woodrow

Wilson wrote the letter below when he was in Baltimore to teach at Johns
Hopkins, while Ellen remained in Princeton, New Jersey, with their
three children. If the letter seems excessively passionate—certainly by
the standards of the nineteenth century—recall, too, that the Wilsons
had been married almost ten years at the time of the writing and their
passions had certainly not gone stale.

Baltimore, 6 February, 1894
My own darling,
  *. . . When you get me back you'll smother me, will you, my
sweet little lover? And what will I be doing all the while—simply
submitting to be smothered? Do you think you can stand the innumerable kisses and the passionate embraces you will receive? Are
you prepared for the storm of love making with which you will be
assailed? [Do] you not know by experience to what lengths and
extravagancies of . . . demonstrativeness on your part hurries your
intemperate lover—and are you prepared to take the risks?*
  *Oh, sweetheart, sweetheart, my precious, precious darling!—
what a terrible longing it brings into my heart—how it makes all
my pulses start, while my heart itself seems to stand still, when
I think of having you in my arms again, of being in your arms
again—touching your lips,—hearing you say you love me—seeing
the burning light in your eyes as we are strained close to each
others' embraces! If I were to allow myself to think of it much, I
simply could not stay here!*
  Your own
  Woodrow

Warren G. Harding to Florence Kling Harding

Warren G. Harding was Florence Kling's second husband, and he was five years younger than she. Florence had a son by her first husband, but after her divorce, she allowed her father, with whom she often clashed, to adopt the boy. When she met Warren, she was earning a living by giving piano lessons. At the time, Warren was owner of the local newspaper, the *Marion* [Ohio] *Star*. When they became engaged,

Five years older than her husband, Florence was the first First Lady to vote in a presidential election and opened the White House to celebrities such as Albert Einstein, tennis star Bill Tilden, and entertainer Al Jolson. Unfortunately, she could not keep Warren's libido in check.

her father opposed the marriage, spreading a rumor that the Harding family was part black—a charge his political opponents later repeated. Warren and Florence married on July 8, 1891.

Warren had to be hospitalized for depression in January 1894, and Florence took over the newspaper, organizing a circulation department for the first time and hiring newsboys—including Norman Thomas, who later ran six times for president on the Socialist Party ticket. The paper thrived under her leadership. When Warren was released from the hospital, Florence continued to take an active role. About this time, he gave her the nickname "Duchess."

In 1899, she encouraged her husband to run for the Ohio state senate and sometimes wrote his speeches. When he won, she drummed up support for him from other newspapers. Four years later he ran and won for lieutenant governor. While living in Columbus, the state capital, Florence began to consult fortune-tellers.

With Florence's encouragement Warren ran for the US Senate in 1914 and won his first national office. The Hardings moved to Washington, where Florence made influential friends, including Evalyn Walsh McLean, wife of the owner of the *Washington Post* and the *Cincinnati Enquirer*. Florence became interested in the causes of women's suffrage and animal rights.

As the following letter shows, Warren's genial personality helped him to move to the inner circles of the Republican Party. Members of an informal group known as the Little Mothers met at the Hotel Bon-Air, in Augusta, Georgia, for golf, drinking, card games, and discussions of politics. This never-before-printed letter was written in 1919, when it was clear that 1920 would probably be a good year for a Republican candidate for president.

[Stationery: Hotel BonAir, Augusta, Georgia]
Sunday, 23 March [1919]

My Dear Duchess:
I sent you a night wire [night telegram] *yesterday, instead of writing, for two reasons. First, it would be a word on Sunday morning, when no mail is delivered. Second, I couldn't write*

before the departure of the mail. We went out to the military
camp—Camp Hancock, to be abandoned next week after costing
millions—to see the machine gun school. George Edwards and a
bunch of officers and mechanics came for us a little before five
and we never got back till nearly eight. Had to curtail dressing for
dinner and an after dinner letter is too late to mail . . .

After dinner we played auction [bridge]—*a funny, or rather*
a strange incident arose. Sandberg and I were partnered against
Gillette and Frelinghuysen. Sandberg . . . was playing the hand.
Spades were led and he trumped them. As dummy I asked if
he had no spades. He said no, and trumped them three times.
Later on he found that he had the ace of spades in with his clubs.
Gillette then promptly claimed 300 points . . . I insisted only one
hundred points could be claimed . . . because Sandberg's play of
the ace would have won us game and rubber. But they took the
300. Never heard a case like it. I don't like excessively rigid rules
among friends for a small stake. . . . I mean to omit the auction
tonight and read after I get home. . . .

Mean to have golf with Taft tomorrow. [President William
Howard Taft, like Harding, was from Ohio and they were both
avid golfers. Harding had given the nominating speech for Taft
at the Republican National Convention of 1912.] *Hale arranged*
all the matches. He and Frelinghuysen nearly quarreled on
Friday, and have since kissed and made up. Hale is often very
disagreeable. . . .

It has been very attractive here. The weather has been absolutely
grand, save for a light shower one afternoon. It is an attractive
place, too, just across the Savannah river from South Carolina.
I think Pine House is about 100 miles away. Everyone here talks
golf—the greatest bunch of golf nuts you ever saw anywhere. . . .
Sitting about at night you generally hear about "dubbing an
approach" or a "dandy drive" or a "sliced iron shot . . ."

Taft speaks tonight on the League [of Nations, which President
Wilson had proposed as part of the settlement that ended World
War I; it was hotly debated whether the United States should join it,

and the Senate finally voted it down] *at the Methodist church. We are rather expected to go, but nothing doing. The group at the hotel is not strong for the League. I wonder if you read the Lodge-Lowell debate.* [Senator Henry Cabot Lodge was the chief opponent of the United States joining the League. He was debated by Harvard president A. Lawrence Lowell, who supported it.] *I did not think Lodge covered himself with glory. It read like a rather trivial affair, I thought.*

Guess this is all today. I will close with an expression of my love.

Affectionately,

W.G.

In 1920, Warren received the Republican nomination for president. Florence consulted an astrologer named Madame Marcia to determine what the future held. Madame Marcia said that Warren would become president but would die in office. Florence set to work getting him elected.

Warren won with a "front-porch campaign," where he and Florence mostly stayed at home and answered reporters' questions. His campaign slogan was "normalcy," which grammarians laughed at because the proper word was "normality." Today, everybody uses "normalcy," which Americans in 1920 took to mean Harding would take the country back to the "good old days" when it didn't get involved in European wars and had low taxes. (Not so well-known is the fact that Harding is also credited with coining the phrase "Founding Fathers." He first used it in the keynote address of the Republican National Convention of 1916.) The election of 1920 was the first in which women were allowed to vote in national elections, and Florence became the first First Lady to vote for her husband as president.

On November 2, Harding won the election as the twenty-ninth president of the United States—and the only one elected on his birthday. As the couple entered the White House, Florence was quoted as saying, "Well, Warren, I got you here. Now what are you going to do?" In the third year of his presidency, he and Florence took a cross-country trip to Alaska. On the way back, Harding fell ill, and they stopped at a hotel in San Francisco, where he died of what was said to be a heart attack.

On the way back, Harding's body was displayed through the glass side of a railroad car, and hundreds of thousands of people turned out to view it, because he had been a highly popular president. Few people other than Florence knew that some of his closest cronies had used their positions to enrich themselves. That would soon come out, but to save Warren's name, she began to burn his papers. It took her several days to finish the job. For this reason, very few of his letters to her are available today. She may have saved the ones, like the one above, that he sent her when he was happiest—enjoying the company of other powerful men who accepted him as one of them.

Franklin Delano Roosevelt to Eleanor Roosevelt

Though they were distant cousins, Franklin and Eleanor did not spend much time with each other growing up. But after they met by chance on a train, they felt an immediate attraction. Eleanor's parents had died when she was young, and she considered herself a kind of "ugly duckling." For Franklin, her appeal may have been that she was the niece of Theodore Roosevelt, the twenty-sixth president of the United States. Franklin was ambitious and told people he could be president himself someday. (Someone once replied, "Does anyone else think so?" No one could have guessed that he would in fact be the only person elected president four times.)

Their wedding was held in New York City on St. Patrick's Day, March 17, 1905, and Theodore gave the bride away. Meanwhile, the sounds of thousands of Irish celebrating in the streets almost drowned out the ceremony inside. Afterward, "Teddy" led the guests to the church library, where refreshments were being served. He regaled the crowd with political anecdotes, while Franklin and Eleanor stood by, almost unnoticed. It illustrated the truth of what his daughter said about him:

"Father always wanted to be the bride at every wedding and the corpse at every funeral."

Franklin and Eleanor had been married for three years at the time this letter was written, but it is the earliest surviving correspondence between them. Eleanor stayed home taking care of their two children, aged two and six months. James, the younger child, was suffering from pneumonia. Franklin and his uncle Warren Delano were on a business trip to Kentucky and Tennessee, where the family had interests in some coal mines. It was the first time Franklin had ventured south of Washington, DC, and he wrote to Eleanor (whom he always addressed as "Babs" in his letters) to describe the scenery.

Hotel Johnson
Pennington Gap, VA.
June 12, 1908
Friday

My own dear Babs—

. . . The trip today has been so wonderful to me that I can't begin to tell you about it now. We woke up near Hagerstown, Maryland, and ever since have been coming through Virginia, the valley of Virginia or rather a succession of wonderful valleys and hills. In some places we were over 2,000 feet up, and the train ran thro gorges that for sheer beauty beat anything that we saw in the Black Forest.

Loads of love, my own dearest. I do hope you are taking very good care of yourself and that the lambs are well. I am so anxious to hear how Anna likes Seabright [a house on the New Jersey shore they had rented for the summer].

It is now 11 o'clock and I have had a bath and am almost asleep. Ever your own devoted,

F.

In his first venture into politics, in 1910, Roosevelt won a seat in the New York State Senate by a narrow margin. Thus, in summertime, Franklin had to stay behind to attend sessions of the legislature while

Eleanor and the children, now numbering three, went to Campobello Island in Canada, where they had been spending summers since 1909. In the following letter, Franklin responds to the news that his family had arrived safely.

> *Hyde Park, N.Y.*
> *July 1, 1911*
> *Saturday*
>
> *Dearest—*
> *Your telegram came about an hour ago and I was thankful to get it. I was getting very worried. I had expected one from Portland, but am glad you got there all right. . . . I now hope to get away on Tuesday, reaching Campo Wednesday. I can't tell you how I miss you. . . . I do hope you have found things in a semblance of order, and that the chicks are all right. I am sure they are delighted at being there again. The Campo is all I need now and I will surely be up.*
> *Loads of love and kisses.*
> *Ever your devoted*
> *F.*

In the presidential election of 1912, Franklin supported the candidate of the Democratic Party, Woodrow Wilson, even though Franklin's distant cousin Theodore Roosevelt was running against Wilson that year on the third-party Progressive ticket. A grateful Wilson appointed Franklin to the post of assistant secretary of the navy, which Franklin, an avid sailor, felt particularly qualified for. He felt fortunate that it was also the job Theodore Roosevelt had held on his way to the presidency.

In August 1914, World War I broke out in Europe. President Wilson was successful in keeping the United States out of the war, but at the Navy Department, Roosevelt followed the conflict with growing interest. The German plan of attack called for it to send its troops through neutral Belgium, which resisted longer than anyone had expected. In this letter, Franklin shows his sympathy for England and France, enemies of Germany in the war, though President Wilson called on Americans to remain neutral. As usual, Eleanor was spending the summer at Campobello.

> *Washington*
> *August 10, 1914*
> *Monday*

Dearest Babs—

The heat has come again, and today is the third scorcher but one doesn't have much time to think about it. There is little real news from Europe. . . . The Belgian defense has been as magnificent as unexpected. I hear on good authority that the French War College

When Franklin Roosevelt contracted polio in 1921, he feared his political career might be over. It was Eleanor who helped keep his name before the public and often acted as his legs. Notice that the brace on FDR's leg is showing around the bottom of his trousers.

figured on only three days of delay to the German advance by the Belgian forces. Thank God England has gone in in earnest. Now she has landed 20,000 with 80,000 more in this first movement. . . .

I've been disappointed that England has been unable to force a naval action—of course it is the obvious course for Germany to hold its main fleet back and try to wear out the blockading enemy with torpedo and submarine attacks in foggy and night conditions. [It was German attacks on American shipping that ultimately brought the United States into the war.]

. . . Please on receipt of this wire me whether Miss S. [apparently a midwife; Eleanor's fourth child was due soon] *thinks I had better come at once or can stay till the 17th. I still hope to come on the 15th, and can of course come any day but I may be able to accomplish more by staying two days longer. . . .*

Tell Sister [their daughter Anna] *and James that I have loved their letters but that there is hardly time enough to eat!. . . .*

Loads of love. I long to be with you dearest these days and you are constantly in my thoughts.

Your devoted,

F.

The baby, named Franklin Delano Jr., was born on August 17. Franklin Sr. had arrived in time for the birth. (A previous baby had received the same name but died soon after its birth.)

Harry S. Truman to
Elizabeth Virginia "Bess" Wallace

Truman felt that he had to become more successful before he could marry Bess, and tried various ventures such as oil drilling and zinc mining in hopes that he could make enough money to renew his proposal. Those efforts had not succeeded by 1917, when the United States entered World War I. Truman now enlisted in the US Army and was given the rank of first lieutenant, which he had formerly held in the Missouri National Guard.

Bess apparently suggested that they marry before Truman went overseas with the troops, but he declined because he feared that he might be maimed in the war, as he makes clear in the following letter.

Kansas City, Mo.
July 14, 1917

Dear Bess,

. . . Bess I'm dead crazy to ask you to marry me before I leave but I'm not going to because I don't think it would be right for me to ask you to tie yourself to a prospective cripple—or a sentiment. You, I know, would love me just as much, perhaps more, with one hand as with two, but I don't think I should cause you to do it. Besides, if the war ends happily and I can steal the Russian or German crown jewels, just think what a grand military wedding you can have, get a major general maybe.

If you don't marry me before I go, you may be sure that I'll be just as loyal to you as if you were my wife. I'll not try to exact any promises from you either if you want to go with any other guy, well all right, but I'll be as jealous as the mischief although not begrudging you the good time.

Bess, this is a crazy letter but I'm crazy about you and I can't say all these nutty things to you without making you weep. When you weep, I want to. If you'd looked right closely the other night, you might have discovered it, and a weeping man is an abomination unto the Lord. All I ask is love me always, and if I have to be shot I'll try and not have it in the back or before a stone wall, because I'm afraid not to do you honor.

Sincerely,
Harry

An epidemic of influenza, called "Spanish flu," spread through the world during 1918 and 1919. It is said to have killed more people than

World War I. Though the war ended in November 1918, Truman and many other American servicemen were still in France while the disease was raging. He was alarmed to hear that Bess had caught the deadly illness. However, in January he learned that she was recovering. He wrote her the following:

Camp La Beheholle, near Verdun
January 12, 1919

Dear Bess,

Last evening was a glorious one even if it was raining. A mail brought me three letters from you dated December 13, 16, 18 . . . I am so glad you are out of danger from that awful flu. You've no idea how uneasy I've been since hearing you and Mary [his sister] had it. We over here can realize somewhat how you must have felt when we were under fire a little. Every day nearly someone of my outfit will hear that his mother, sister, or sweetheart is dead. It is heartbreaking almost to think that we are so safe and so well over here and that the ones we'd like to protect more than all the world have been more exposed to death than we. I am hoping that the worst is past and that from now on we'll never hear of it again. It seems that war and pestilence go hand in hand. If it isn't the Black Death it is something equally as fatal. We hear that the poor Russians are dying by the hundreds and the damnable Hun [German] is murdering himself for pleasure. I suppose it will be some time before we have a golden age of health, peace, and prosperity such as the ten years before 1914 were. . . .

I do hope you are well and all right by this time. Be sure and write when you feel like it. I love you.

Always,
Harry

After the war, Truman felt he had proved himself and wanted to do something as quickly as possible after he arrived home, as he told Bess from France:

[Rosières, near Bar-le-Duc]
February 18, 1919

Dear Bess:

. . . Please get ready to march down the aisle with me just as soon as you decently can when I get back. I haven't any place to go but home and I'm busted financially but I love you as madly as a man can and I'll find all the other things. We'll be married anywhere you say at any time you mention and if you want only one person or the whole town I don't care as long as you make it quickly after my arrival. I have some army friends I'd like to ask and my own family and that's all I care about, and the army

Harry and Bess Truman on their wedding day, June 28, 1919. After the ceremony, the newlyweds left for a honeymoon in Chicago and Detroit. They then returned to Missouri and moved into Bess's mother's house, which would be their home for the rest of their lives.

*friends can go hang if you don't want 'em. I have enough money
to buy a Ford and we can set sail in that and arrive in Happyland
at once and quickly.*

Don't fail to write just 'cause I'm starting home.
Yours always,
Harry

Harry and Bess were married on June 28, 1919. He opened a haber-
dashery with Eddie Jacobson, a friend he had met in the army, but it
was unsuccessful. In February 1924, Bess gave birth to a daughter they
named Margaret.

Harry found his true calling in politics. During his army service,
he had befriended Tom Pendergast, whose uncle, Jim, headed the
local Democratic machine back in Missouri. With Jim's backing Harry
was elected county judge, an administrative rather than a judicial position. Truman proved to be popular with the voters, and in 1934, he
was elected to the United States Senate. Thus, he was present at the
1936 Democratic National Convention in Philadelphia, which was to
nominate President Franklin D. Roosevelt for a second term. Harry described the activity in a letter to Bess on June 28, which also happened
to be the couple's seventeenth wedding anniversary.

Washington, D.C.
Sunday, June 28, [1936]

Dear Bess,

*I was so lonesome last night I just had to spend four dollars to
call you up. If I'd stayed in Philly, it would have cost me five for a
hotel and I* [would have] *gotten wet besides* [because Franklin D.
Roosevelt gave his acceptance speech outside, in Franklin Field, and
it rained.] *The New York Times said this morning that everyone
got soaked but they stayed anyway, 105,000 of them, to hear
and see the President and Cactus Jack* [John Nance Garner, vice
president during Roosevelt's first two terms]. *That's a real tribute.
His* [Roosevelt's] *speech was a masterpiece, I think. The convention* [indoors] *was like all such gatherings, just one grand yell*

from start to finish, and in order to find out what went on it was necessary to read the papers or go down to a hotel and listen to the radio. . . . You couldn't tell what was happening by being on the floor [of the convention hall, Municipal Auditorium] . . .

I hope you are enjoying the day. It's just about as hot here as it was in Independence [Missouri] *June 28, 1919* [their wedding day]. . . . *There is no special prize for seventeen years of married life that I could discover, so you'll have to make out without any. I'd like to be there to take you out to dinner though. Lots of water has gone under the bridge since then . . . I think my sweetheart is better looking today than ever, if that is possible, and you know it is not fashionable now to think that of the same one* [the same woman, that is]. *Please kiss Margie* [their daughter, Margaret] *and I hope I get that letter tomorrow. It wasn't in the mail this morning.*

Love to you and I hope for at least seventeen more.

Harry

Much of the time, Bess stayed at home, caring for her mother and thinking that Independence, Missouri, was a better place to raise Margaret. This provided Harry with an opportunity to write letters.

Truman was becoming a national figure. After the entry of the United States into World War II in 1941, he became head of a special Senate investigative committee—which became known as the Truman Committee—charged with uncovering wasteful defense spending. He described the committee's work as protecting the "little man" from the greedy predations of big labor and big business. Soon he was called on to give speeches around the country.

At the Democratic National Convention of 1944, Truman received the party's nomination as vice president, with Franklin D. Roosevelt running for his fourth presidential term. Those close to Roosevelt suspected he would not survive to complete the four years, so it was likely that Truman would become president. He wrote Bess about one of the only times he met Roosevelt:

Washington, D.C.
August 18, 1944

Dear Bess.

. . . . I went in [to see the president] *at about five to one and you'd have thought I was the long lost brother or the returned Prodigal. I told him how I appreciated his putting the finger on me for Vice President and we talked about the campaign . . .*

Then lunch was announced and we went out into the back yard of the White House under an oak tree planted by old Andy Jackson, and the movie men and then the flashlight boys went to work. He finally got hungry and ran 'em out. Then his daughter, Mrs. [Anna] *Boettiger, acted as hostess and expressed a lot of regret that you were not there. I told the President that you were in Missouri attending to my business there, and he said that was O.K. He gave me a lot of hooey about what I could do to help the campaign and said he thought I ought to go home for an official notification and then go to Detroit for a labor speech and make no more engagements until we had had another conference. So that's what I'm going to do. . . .*

The President told me that Mrs. R. was a very timid woman and wouldn't go to political meetings or make any speeches when he first ran for governor of N.Y. Then he said, "Now she talks all the time." What am I to think?

Kiss Margie, lots and lots of love to you,
Harry

Roosevelt died of a cerebral hemorrhage on the afternoon of April 12, 1945. When Truman was informed, he recalled that he felt "like the moon, the stars, and all the planets had fallen on me." When he phoned his wife to tell her, she burst into tears. Her mother and daughter asked what was wrong. The reason she was crying was that she knew her cherished privacy was no more.

Roosevelt had failed to brief his vice president on many important matters, including the Manhattan Project to build an atomic bomb. Truman, as ever, sat down to work: His wife was not at first sympathetic to the demands of the presidency. She insisted on spending that first Christmas at her family house in Independence. Harry had to fly on the presidential plane, through a sleet storm, to join her. Bess even chided him for doing so, telling him he should have stayed in Washington. Irritated, Truman wrote her the following letter after he returned:

December 28, 1945

Well I'm here in the White House, the great white sepulcher of ambitions and reputations. I feel like a last year's bird's nest which is on its second year. Not very often I admit I am not in shape. I think maybe that exasperates you, too, as a lot of other things I do and pretend to do exasperate you. But it isn't intended for that purpose. . . . You can never appreciate what it means to come home as I did the other evening after doing at least one hundred things I didn't want to do and have the only person in the world whose approval and good opinion I value look at me like I'm something the cat dragged in and tell me I've come in at last because I couldn't find any reason to stay away. I wonder who we are made so that what we really think and feel we cover up?

This head of mine should have been bigger and better proportioned. There ought to have been more brain and a larger bump of ego or something to give me an idea that there can be a No. 1 man in the world. I didn't want to be. But, in spite of opinions to the contrary, Life and Time say I am.

If that is the case, you, Margie, and everyone else who may have any influence on my actions must give me help and assurance, because no one ever needed help and assurance as I do now. If I can get the use of the best brains in the country and a little bit of help I have on a pedestal at home, the job will be done. If I can't, no harm will be done because the country will know that Shoop, the Post-Dispatch, Hearst, Cissy, and Patterson [newspaper critics of Truman] were right.

Kiss my baby and I love you in season and out.
Harry

The letter was probably never sent, and the Trumans' daughter, Margaret, found it in his desk after his death twenty-seven years later. Somehow, her father had made his feelings known in a more tactful manner and Bess returned to Washington, resigned to the role she and her husband now had to play.

Dwight D. Eisenhower to Mary "Mamie" Geneva Doud Eisenhower

Dwight David Eisenhower was born in Texas in 1890 and his family moved to Abilene, Kansas, when he was two. His parents had seven sons and could not afford higher education for them. Growing up, Eisenhower read through his mother's collection of history books and when he took the test for US Military Academy students, he passed. He entered West Point and graduated in 1915, even though his mother was a pacifist—a deeply religious Mennonite.

While in basic training in Fort Sam Houston in San Antonio, Texas, that year, Eisenhower met Mary Geneva "Mamie" Doud, who was the daughter of a wealthy family who were visiting friends. He offered to give Mamie a tour of the grounds. She recalled, "He was the handsomest man I ever laid eyes on." He began to visit her family and proposed to her on Valentine's Day in 1916. She said yes.

Mamie knew from the beginning that marrying Eisenhower would make her the wife of a career military officer—and all the hardships that would mean. After the United States entered the Second World War in 1941, they moved to Washington, DC, where her husband was appointed to the army general staff. Later, Ike was sent to Europe, where he supervised the invasions of North Africa and Sicily and was later responsible for the planning of the D-Day invasion of France. Mamie could not join him during this assignment, but he wrote to her regularly. His letters show the deep affection he held for her—such as the following one, which was marked "Not to be opened until November 14," her birthday.

London
[sent around October 30, 1942]

By the time you read this your newspapers will probably have told you where I am and you will understand why your birthday letter had to be written some time in advance. [He had been named commander of the Allied Expeditionary Force assigned to invading North Africa and had secretly moved to the AEF's headquarters on the island of Gibraltar.] *You will also realize that I have been busy—very busy—and any lapses in the arrival of letters will be explained to you . . .*

I hope you won't be disturbed or worried. War inevitably carries its risks in life and limb—but the chances, in my case, are all in my favor—a fact which you must always remember. Moreover—even if the worst should ever happen to me, please don't be too upset. . . .

Anyway—on the day you open this letter you'll be 46. I'd like to be there to help you celebrate, and to kiss you 46 times (multiplied by any number you care to pick) . . . In any event I will be with you in thought, and entirely aside from the usual congratulations and felicitations I will be thinking with the deepest gratitude of the many happy hours and years you've given me. I am quite aware of the fact that I'm not always easy to live with—that frequently I'm irascible and even mean—and my gratitude is all the greater when I realize how often you've put up with me in spite of such traits.

The crowning thing you've given me is our son—he has been so wonderful, unquestionably because he's so much you—that I find I live in him so very often. Your love and our son have been my greatest gifts from life, and on your birthday I wish that my powers of expression were such as to make you understand that thoroughly—clearly and for always. I've never wanted any other wife—you're mine, and for that reason I've been luckier than any other man. . . .

[The editor of Eisenhower's letters, his son John S. D. Eisenhower, did not include signatures.]

In November 1942, American troops landed in North Africa, preparing to engage German and Italian forces that held much of the area to the east. Even though the landing was a success, Eisenhower had a ticklish problem in dealing with French forces in the area. Since the Nazis had overrun much of France, these troops initially resisted Eisenhower's attempts to occupy what were French colonies in Africa. However, he soon convinced their leader that the Americans had no intention of taking control away from the French. But it put a strain on him that he confided to his wife in this letter, in which he includes interesting observations on leadership.

ALGIERS, December 30, 1942

Sometimes I get to missing you so that I simply don't know what to do. As pressure mounts and strain increases everyone begins to show the weaknesses in his makeup. It is up to the Commander to conceal his; above all to conceal doubt, fear and distrust, especially in any subordinate, and to try to overcome the defects he finds around him. When the strain is long continued the commander gets to feeling more and more alone and lonesome, and his mind instinctively turns to something or someone that could help. This, of course, is not well explained—but I mean only to tell you that constantly I think of you as someone who could provide a counter balance for me—and send me back to work fitter to do a good job. No one else in this world could ever fill your place with me—and that is the reason I need you. Maybe a simpler explanation is merely that I LOVE you!! Which I do, always. Never forget that, because, except for my duty, which I try to perform creditably, it is the only thing to which I can cling with confidence.

Not that I'm abused—it's just that situations such as this bring on many daily and hourly problems to solve, and many

"Ike's" infectious grin and his military success in World War II made him a popular candidate for the presidency. The Eisenhowers are shown here at the Republican Convention in 1960.

disappointments in persons that in normal times seem so robust and able, so that finally a man gets somewhat cynical, and has to fight against becoming morose. All this creates a feeling of isolation and aloneness—and this is made more acute by the fact that eventually you find yourself sneaking off alone so as to get away from talking and arguing the same things—It would be lots more fun to sneak off to see you. . . .

John F. Kennedy to Jacqueline Bouvier Kennedy

Because John F. Kennedy wrote almost nothing to his fiancée, Jacqueline Bouvier, before they were married, and very little afterward, there are few letters like this one. As president, Kennedy found that his wife's glamour and charm made her quite popular when she traveled abroad, so he sometimes sent her on goodwill missions. He arranged for a state visit to India and Pakistan in the spring of 1962. Crowds gathered to see her everywhere she went. In India, she was referred to as "Amerika Maharani" (America's Queen).

Jacqueline sent her husband progress reports on her trip, and he responded, telling her:

> *The stories and pictures of your trip have been wonderful. The reports and pictures seem to confirm that you are well and happy. Galbraith* [the US ambassador to India, who accompanied Jacqueline] *is looking a little tired. Caroline and John* [the Kennedy children] *came home yesterday and are very well and brown. We all miss you very much.*
> *All love.*
> *Jack.*

George H. W. Bush to Barbara Pierce

George was sent to pilot school and flew more than fifty missions in the Pacific during World War II. In the introduction to his collection of letters, he explains that his wife, Barbara, lost all the letters, except this one that he wrote her during the war. It describes his feelings on seeing the announcement of their engagement, and he tells Barbara about naming his plane *[Bar #2]* after her.

December 12, 1943

My darling Bar,
This should be a very easy letter to write—words should come easily and in short it should be simple for me to tell you how desperately happy I was to open the paper and see the announcement of our engagement, but somehow I can't possibly say all in a letter I should like to.
I love you, precious, with all my heart and to know that you

love me means my life. How often I have thought about the immeasurable joy that will be ours some day. How lucky our children will be to have a mother like you—

As the days go by the time of our departure draws nearer. For a long time I had anxiously looked forward to the day when we would go aboard and set to sea. It seemed that obtaining that goal would be all I could desire for some time, but, Bar, you have changed all that. I cannot say that I do not want to go—for that would be a lie. We have been working for a long time with a single purpose in mind, to be so equipped that we could meet and defeat our enemy. I do want to go because it is my part, but now leaving presents itself not as an adventure but as a job which I hope will be over before long. Even now, with a good while between us and the sea, I am thinking of getting back. This may sound melodramatic, but if it does it is only my inadequacy to say what I mean. Bar, you have made my life full of everything I could ever dream of—my complete happiness should be a token of my love for you.

Wednesday is definitely the commissioning and I do hope you'll be there. I'll call Mum tomorrow about my plan. A lot of fellows put down their parents or wives and they aren't going so you could pass as a Mrs.—Just say you lost the invite and give your name. They'll check the list and you'll be in. How proud I'll be if you can come.

I'll tell you all about the latest flying developments later. We have so much to do and so little time to do it in. It is frightening at times. The seriousness of this thing is beginning to strike home. I have been made asst. gunnery officer and when Lt. Houle leaves I will be gunnery officer. I'm afraid I know very little about it but I am excited at having such a job. I'll tell you all about this later too.

The wind of late has been blowing like mad and our flying has been cut to a minimum. My plane, #2 now, is up at Quonset, having a camera installed. It is Bar #2 but purely in spirit since the Atlantic fleet won't let us have names on our planes.

George and Barbara Bush wave to the crowd at the Republican National Convention in 1992. Less than ten years later, they would see the nomination and election of their son, George W., to the highest office in the land.

Good nite, my beautiful. Everytime I say beautiful you about kill me but you'll have to accept it—

I hope I get Thursday off—there's still a chance. All my love darling—

Poppy
public fiancé as of 12/12/43

After George returned from the war, he and Barbara were married on January 6, 1945. George was elected president in 1988, and their son George W. Bush became the forty-third president in 2001, which made Barbara only the second woman to be both the wife and the mother of a president (after Abigail Adams).

PART 3

Adversity

Introduction

Maybe the true test of a loving relationship is whether it is strong enough to survive adversity. The kinds of adversity couples can face are endless: foreign invasion, debilitating illness, rumored infidelity, political disagreements, the death of a child, and, in the case of Louisa Adams, abandonment by her husband. One marriage was even disrupted by a voodoo doll! Finally, there is the death of one of the partners. Ulysses S. Grant knew death was near, and the letter he wrote to his wife may still bring tears.

Dolley Madison, wife of President James Madison, was famous for her parties in the first years of his term. She liked to invite people who were ordinarily political enemies, and soon the wives of foreign diplomats urged their husbands to get invitations to Dolley's parties as well.

But during the War of 1812 Dolley showed she could do more than throw parties. Her husband left the White House to oversee the troops who were gathered where British forces were expected to land. He wrote her that he hoped to return home "later in the evening."

However, the British landed elsewhere and headed for Washington. When Dolley heard the sound of artillery guns approaching, she and her servants loaded a wagon with valuables from the White House, including the original copy of the Declaration of Independence, which she stuffed into a suitcase. But Dolley insisted on delaying their departure until she could bring the painting of George Washington by Gilbert Stuart. It was almost eight feet high and needed to be unscrewed from the wall. Finally, she ordered the frame to be broken and the canvas removed. Only then would she leave—just in time, for the British soon arrived and burned the White House. And so Dolley also became famous for her courage.

———

Nellie Taft's lifelong dream of becoming First Lady came true when her husband, William Howard Taft, became president in 1909. Tragically, a few months later she suffered a debilitating stroke and had to leave the unhealthy climate of Washington to recuperate. Her husband wrote to her almost every day to inform her of what was going on in the capital. Here is part of one typical letter:

> . . .
>
> *I am longing to see you. The White House is not the same without you. Flowers are wanting and that essence or atmosphere that you alone can supply. . . .*
> *With devoted love My dear—Yours, Will*

When Dwight D. Eisenhower was commanding the US military forces in Africa, *Life* magazine spread a rumor that he was having an affair with his driver, a British woman named Kay Summersby. The rumor continued after the war and his wife, Mamie, was asked about it. She replied, "Why would it bother me? I wouldn't have stayed with him five minutes if I hadn't had the greatest respect for him."

There is just one letter from President Gerald R. Ford in this book. It is the only one Ford's children have made public. It is a handwritten note from Ford to his wife, Betty, who had just been diagnosed with breast cancer. Instead of seeking to hide her disease, she had made it public, urging women everywhere to get regular breast exams. This saved many lives. Ford tells her, "We know how great you are and we, the children and Dad, will try to be as strong as you."

Betty Ford's cancer treatment was successful, and she lived for another thirty-seven years.

Perhaps the most moving letter in this book was written by Ulysses S. Grant a month before his death. He concealed it in his coat pocket, where he knew his wife would find it. The man who once expressed his love with a series of dashes spoke eloquently here, and if you read only one letter, read that one.

John Adams to Abigail Smith Adams

John and Abigail Adams were married for fifty-four years, and although they didn't always agree, they argued with wit and civility. The following exchange began when Abigail wrote what is one of the most famous letters in American history. Her husband was attending the Second Continental Congress in Philadelphia while she remained in Boston. The most pressing issue before the Congress was whether to issue a Declaration of Independence, which would be a drastic step, because it meant a clean break with Britain. Before he left home, John had been talking about establishing a new code of laws, though that would come later. Abigail had very definite ideas about what the Congress should do:

Braintree
March 31 1776

. . . I long to hear that you have declared an independency—and by the way in the New Code of Laws which I suppose it will be necessary for you to make I desire you would remember the Ladies, and be more generous and favourable to them than your ancestors. Do not put such unlimited power into the hands of the Husbands. Remember all Men would be tyrants if they could. If perticuliar care and attention is not paid to the Laidies we are determined to foment a Rebelion, and will not hold ourselves bound by any Laws in which we have no voice, or Representation.

That your Sex are Naturally Tyrannical is a Truth so thoroughly established as to admit of no dispute, but such of you as wish to be happy willingly give up the harsh title of Master for the more tender and endearing one of Friend. Why then, not put it out of the power of the vicious and Lawless to use us with cruelty and indignity with impunity. Men of sense in all Ages abhor those customs which treat us only as the vassals of your Sex. Regard us then as Beings placed by providence under your protection and in immitation of the Supreme Being make use of that power only for our happiness.

John Adams's reply is somewhat lesser known.

April 14, 1776

. . . As to Declarations of Independency, be patient . . .
As to your extraordinary Code of Laws, I cannot but laugh.
We have been told that our Struggle has loosened the bands of Government every Where. That Children and Apprentices were disobedient—that schools and Colledges were grown turbulent— that Indians Slighted their Guardians and Negroes grew insolent to their Masters. But your Letter was the first Intimation that another Tribe more numerous and powerfull than all the rest were grown discontented. This is rather too coarse a Compliment, but you are so saucy, I wont blot it out.

Depend upon it, We know better than to repeal our Masculine systems. Altho they are in full Force, you know they are little more than Theory. We dare not exert our Power in its full Latitude. We are obliged to go fair, and softly, and in Practice you know We are the subjects. We have only the Name of Masters, and rather than give up this, which would compleatly subject us to the Despotism of the Peticoat, I hope General Washington, and all our brave Heroes would fight. I am sure every good Politician would plot, as long as he would against Despotism, Empire, Monarchy, Aristocracy, Oligarchy, or Ochlocracy. A fine Story indeed. . . . After Stirring up Tories, Landjobbers, Trimmers, Bigots, Canadians Indians, Negroes, Hanoverians, Hessians, Russians, Irish Roman Catholicks, Scotch Renegadoes, at last they have stimulated the [he leaves a long space here: women?] *to demand new Priviledges and threaten to rebell.*

In July 1777, Abigail Adams was expecting the couple's sixth child. One of them had already died in infancy, and now she was worried about her current pregnancy. As she wrote John, "I have been very unwell for this week past, with some complaints that have been new to me, tho I hope not dangerous.

"I was last night taken with a shaking fit, and am very apprehensive that a life was lost . . . I would not Have you too much allarmed. I keep up some Spirits yet, tho I would have you prepaired for any Event that may happen."

John replied the following day:

Philadelphia July 10, 1777. Thursday

My Mind is again Anxious, and my Heart in Pain for my dearest Friend.

Three times have I felt, the most distressing Sympathy with my Partner, without being able to afford any Kind of Solace, or Assistance.

When, the Family was sick of the Dissentery, and so many of our Friends died of it.

When you all had the small Pox.

And now I think I feel as anxious as ever. Oh that I could, be near, to say a few kind Words or shew a few Kind Looks, or do a few kind Actions. Oh that I could take from my dearest, a share of her Distress, or relieve her of the whole.

Before this shall reach you I hope you will be happy in the Embraces of a Daughter, as fair, and good, and wise, and virtuous as the Mother, or if it is a son I hope it will still resemble the Mother in Person Mind and Heart.

On July 16, Abigail wrote John that "a life I know you value, has been spaired and carried thro Distress and danger although the dear Infant is numberd with its ancestors."

James Madison to
Dolley Payne Madison

When Thomas Jefferson became the third president in 1801, he named James Madison as his secretary of state, widely regarded as the second most powerful post in government. Madison was easily elected to be the fourth president in 1808.

Becoming First Lady was not a new position for Dolley. Since Jefferson was a widower, he had asked her to be his official hostess at White House functions.

Dolley came from a Quaker family that moved to Philadelphia when she was fifteen. Her father chose as her husband a prosperous lawyer named John Todd, with whom she had two sons. After her father's death, an epidemic of yellow fever struck the city, taking the lives of Dolley's husband and one of her sons. She moved to a boardinghouse that her mother had established, and it was there that James Madison met her. He was not a particularly imposing figure. He would become the shortest president, standing only five feet, four inches tall. Also, he was forty-three, and she only twenty-six. In addition, he was not a Quaker, so when she accepted his proposal of marriage, she was expelled from her Quaker faith.

That was just as well, because she had grand plans for redecorating the White House, but then she developed an ulcerated knee, which required medical treatment. For most of the latter part of 1805, she was confined to a hospital bed in Philadelphia. She worried that she might never walk again. Unfortunately, Madison had to be in Washington most of the time and was separated from his wife. But he kept in touch with letters such as this one. When he refers to "Miss P," it is an inside joke about Dolley's friend Betsy Pemberton, who Dolley pretended was in love with James.

Washington
Oct. 31 [1805]

Your second letter my dearest . . . is this moment read and flatters
my anxious wishes & hopes for your perfect recovery, and your
safe return to Washington. I am glad to find you so determined to
your adherence to the Drs. Prescriptions. Be assured that he will
give none that are not indispensable, & that you will not rejoice
in having strictly observed [them]. . . .

I repeat my kisses to Miss P. I wish I could give her more
substantial ones than can be put on paper. She shall know the
difference between them the moment she presents her sweet lips
in Washington—after I have set the example on those of another
person whose name I flatter myself you will not find it difficult to
guess. I shall comply with all the commands in your letter. With
unalterable love I remain Yrs.

James Madison

A later letter revealed that her knee had healed. James replied:

Washington Monday Novr: [no date; 1805]

. . . I am rejoiced to hear that your knee remains perfectly healed.
Take care of it I beseech you, till it can defy ordinary exercise,
and that you may the sooner undertake your journey home. Being
obliged to write in a hurry, I can only add my best love to you,
with a little smack for your fair friend [Miss P.], *who has a sweet*
lip, tho' I fear a sour face for me.

J.M.

It was a good thing that Dolley's knee healed, because great things
were in store for her. In 1808, James Madison was elected the fourth
president of the United States. His strongest opponent was Charles
Cotesworth Pinckney of South Carolina, who said after his defeat that

This print is a copy of a portrait of Dolley Madison painted by Gilbert Stuart. Dolley virtually invented the model for a First Lady. She presided over the first Inaugural Ball and was both a perfect hostess and a political asset for her husband James, who was shy in large groups.

he had lost to "Mr. and Mrs. Madison. I might have had a better chance if I faced Mr. Madison alone."

Dolley made the most of her new status and set a standard for First Ladies that has seldom, if ever, been surpassed. Under her leadership, Washington society became fashionable. On Wednesday nights, she presided over receptions in what were then called drawing rooms in the White House. Invited guests came to meet the presidential couple, enjoy platters of food that were brought around by servants, and listen to music. The tasty food offerings included Dolley's favorite dessert: ice cream in warm pastry shells.

Among the guests were diplomats from foreign countries, whose wives were eager to attend. The evenings became so popular that they had to be extended to several rooms, which buzzed with topics of the day: political, intellectual, social, and current events. Dolley set a fashion tone, too, by wearing a turban adorned with plumes. The term "First Lady" was not then used for the president's wife, but Dolley was often referred to as "Lady Presidentress."

Since Madison's political opponents were included among the guests at these affairs, the evenings helped to encourage an atmosphere of cooperation among the two opposing parties. Furthermore, they demonstrated to foreigners that the United States, which was then an experiment in republican government, could create a social event as civilized as any in Europe. President Madison's innate shyness would have prevented him from organizing this kind of affair. Dolley's role in it made her the first female Washington power broker.

Then her weekly soirees literally went up in flames. For years, Great Britain had been at war with Napoleonic France. Britain's chief strength was its navy, and it declared that other nations could no longer carry on trade with France, cutting off a lucrative business for the United States. In addition, the British navy had a policy known as impressment, in which it seized from other nations' ships sailors who it claimed were British citizens. Both policies affected the United States, and on June 1, 1812, President Madison sent a message to Congress outlining American grievances against Britain. Congress responded by declaring war—although the vote was by no means unanimous.

The war was fought on many fronts in North America, but the most important event for the Madisons was the landing of British troops only five miles from the White House, on August 17, 1814. Four days later, President Madison left Washington to review the troops who were supposed to defend the capital. From there, he wrote Dolley this letter:

> *Mr. William's about 6 or 7 miles from Washington*
> *Tuesday, August 23*
>
> *My dearest,*
> *We reached our quarters last evening at the Camp between 8 &*
> *9 o'c. and made out very well. I have passed the forenoon among*
> *the troops, who are in high spirits & make a good appearance.*
> *The reports as to the enemy have varied every hour. The last &*

*probably truest information is that they are not very strong, and
are without cavilry and artillery and of course that they are not
in a condition to strike at Washington. It is believed also that
they are not about to move from Marlbro unless it be from an
apprehension of our gathering force and a retreat to their ships. It
is possible, however they may have a greater force or expect one,
than has been represented . . . We expect every hour to have something further from the camp concerning the Enemy. If it should be
a matter to make it advisable to return to the Camp; you will not
see me this morning, otherwise I hope I shall be with you in the
course of . . . perhaps later in the evening.*

   Your devoted husband
   J.M.

Unfortunately, James Madison's optimism about the strength of the
British forces was unwarranted. Dolley herself, writing to her sister the
same day, described the situation at the White House as the redcoats
approached:

Tuesday, Augt. 23d. 1814.

Dear Sister

   *My husband left me yesterday morng. to join Gen. Winder. He
enquired anxiously whether I had courage or firmness to remain
in the President's house until his return . . . and on my assurance
that I had no fear but for him and the success of our army, he
left me, beseeching me to take care of myself, and of the cabinet
papers . . .*

   *Wednesday morng., twelve o'clock. Since sunrise I have been
turning my spy glass in every direction and watching with unwea-
ried anxiety, hoping to discern the approach of my dear husband
and his friends, but, alas, I can descry only groups of military
wandering in all directions, as if there was a lack of arms, or of
spirit to fight for their own firesides!*

   Three O'clock. Will you believe it, my Sister! We have had a

battle or skirmish near Bladensburg, and I am still here within
sound of the cannon! Mr. Madison comes not: may God protect
him! Two messengers covered with dust, come to bid me fly; but
I wait for him . . . At this late hour a wagon has been procured. I
have had it filled with the plate and most valuable portable arti-
cles belonging to the house . . .

Our kind friend, Mr. [Charles] Carroll, has come to hasten my
departure, and is in a very bad humor with me because I insist
on waiting until the large picture of Gen. Washington [painted
by Gilbert Stuart, it was almost eight feet high] *is secured, and it*
requires to be unscrewed from the wall. The process was found
too tedious for these perilous moments. I have ordered the frame
to be broken, and the canvass taken out . . . And now, dear sister,
I must leave this house, or the retreating army will make me a
prisoner in it. . . . When I shall again write you, or where I shall be
tomorrow, I cannot tell!

The British army did enter the capital and set fire to both the White
House and the Capitol building. However, it was only a temporary victory for them, as Madison's next letter to Dolley makes clear:

Brookville Aug. 27, 10 OC.
My dearest,
Finding that our army had left Montgomery Court House
we pushed on to this place, with a view to join it [the army], *or*
proceed to the City [Washington] *as further information might*
prescribe, I have just recd. a line from Col. Monroe, saying that
the Enemy were out of Washington, & on the retreat to their Ships
& advising our immediate return to Washington. We shall accord-
ingly set out thither immediately. You will all of course take the
same resolution. I know not where we are in the first instance to
hide our heads [sleep]; *but shall look for a place on my arrival. . . .*
Truly yours,
J. Madison

The War of 1812 ended more or less in a draw. The British agreed to maintain the prewar boundaries in North America. And Dolley? Now that she had a blank slate to work with, she began to redecorate the White House so that she could continue her Wednesday night soirees.

John Quincy Adams to Louisa Catherine Adams

Although Louisa Catherine Adams titled her autobiography *Adventures of a Nobody*, she showed strength of character that few others had. In 1815, when her husband was the American minister to the Imperial Court of Russia, he was assigned to negotiate a treaty elsewhere in Europe. He left her with their seven-year-old son in St. Petersburg. After a year's absence he notified her that she should join him in Paris.

It was not until many years later that she was able to describe her harrowing forty-day journey across war-torn Europe, where outlaws and renegade soldiers threatened her and her son. They often had to spend the night in run-down inns that served food that was unfamiliar. The wheels of the carriage sometimes bogged down in roads that had been made hazardous by rain and melting snow. She feared that her guide was going to steal her possessions and desert her.

Louisa's husband had supposedly left letters for her at what he thought would be places she would pass through, but she received only one of them. In it, he said he wished merely "to let you know where I am and with what impatience I am waiting to receive you." In fact, he recalled later, the months he had spent waiting for her were "in many respects the most agreeable interlude of my life."

Twenty-one years later, after her husband had spent one unsuccessful term as president, Louisa decided to write an account of her journey. Her purpose, she wrote, was to "show that many undertakings which appear very difficult and arduous to my Sex, are by no means as trying as imagination forever depicts them."

Andrew Jackson to
Rachel Donelson Jackson

By 1814, Jackson was a major general commanding volunteers from Tennessee in the War of 1812. He led his troops against the Creek tribe, who were allies of the British. Because he was known for his toughness, his men began to call him "Hickory," a wood known for its strength. Eventually, this became "Old Hickory." He showed how apt the nickname was in two letters to his wife. In the first, dated August 23, 1814, from his headquarters in Mobile, Alabama, he wrote:

> *My Love . . .*
> *My arm has broke, and has been running for some days, and has become painfull. I entertain some fears, that it will rise and break in the underside, I hope this will not take place before I can reach you, for which I will set out in two weeks from this date unless prevented by the appearance of an enemy, or bad health, neither of which I hope will intervene . . . wishing you good health, and a calm mind untill I have the pleasure of meeting you, I remain affectionately yours, &c &c*
> *Andrew Jackson*

A month later, Jackson was still in Mobile. In the meantime, he had received a letter from James Monroe, then serving as secretary of war (and who would be elected president in 1816), ordering Jackson to take his men to New Orleans to ward off a British invasion. Jackson doesn't mention this to his wife, but instead reports:

> *September 22nd 1814*
> *My Love—*
> *I have the pleasure to inform you, that since the bone came out of my arm which I sent you, it is healing and strengthening very fast, I hope all the loose pieces of bone is out, and I will not be longer pained with it—*

I hope you will reconcile yourself to our separation as well as possible—the very moment that the situation of this lower country, would make it prudent, I shall direct you to Join me. . . .
I am verry affectionately yr Husband
Andrew Jackson

PS say to my sweet little andrew [their adopted son], *that his papa wants to see him & his suit verry much—that he must ride the cosee* [a horse] *to see me—*

The fact that Jackson does not mention his orders to go to New Orleans reflects his fear that the letter might be intercepted and give away a military secret. He did in fact defeat the British at New Orleans, preventing them from capturing a crucial port at the mouth of the Mississippi. That made him a national hero, even though the battle had been fought after a peace treaty had been signed in Europe. History does not record Rachel Jackson's reaction to receiving a bone from her husband's arm *["which I sent you"]* as a kind of memento.

When her husband was elected president in 1828, his wife, Rachel, was immensely proud. She chose a white gown to wear at the inauguration. Tragically, she died of a heart attack on Christmas Eve, weeks before the inaugural ceremony. Jackson was crushed. "I try to summon up my usual fortitude, but it is in vain. The time, the sudden and afflicted shock, was as severe as *[it was]* unexpected."

John Tyler to Letitia Christian Tyler

John Tyler made steady and swift progress in his political career, and by the time he was thirty-seven, he had served in both the US House of Representatives and the Senate. The political scene at the time was fluid, with the fledgling Whig Party united only on one issue: its opposition to the longer established Democratic-Republicans. Tyler held strong states' rights views and gravitated toward the Whigs because the

Democratic-Republicans generally favored a more powerful central government.

Letitia usually did not join her husband in Washington; she much preferred plantation life. Tyler kept her abreast of goings-on in the capital, and when he was a senator, he wrote the following letter telling her that he had just witnessed an attempt on President Andrew Jackson's life—possibly the first near-assassination in American history:

Washington, February 1, 1835.

My Dear Wife. We had a most extraordinary scene at the capitol on Friday last.

Warren R. Davis, of South Carolina, had died two nights before, and his funeral ceremonies were performed in the House of Representatives. The body was then moved in procession to the east porch of the capitol, from whence it was to be taken to the burial ground. The members of the House went first, the Senate second, and the President and executive officers third. I was one of the last of the senators . . . and being unwell resolved not to go to the grave, and therefore stepped out of the line of procession . . . The President followed on, some six or eight paces behind me.

While I stood contemplating the scene . . . I heard a sharp noise like that proceeding from the explosion of a [fire]cracker. I turned around to see from whence the noise proceeded, when I saw, but a few steps off, and somewhat in front of the President . . . a man presenting a pocket pistol at the President. . . . The President immediately raised his cane and put at him, but the crowd seized the man in an instant, threw him down, disarmed him, and handed him over to the marshal. He is now in jail to await his trial.

The fact was that he had two pistols with percussion locks. The caps exploded as finely as ever caps did, but for some cause, possibly the dampness of the day, the pistols did not go off. If they had the President must have been killed . . . The pistols, it is said, were afterwards examined and found to be properly loaded. The

*man is ascertained to be a madman—a painter by trade, and an
Englishman by birth. . . . It is said that he made an effort not long
since to kill his sister, and afterwards to kill himself. I stood near
by and saw the whole affair. The old general sprung at him like a
tiger, and manifested as much fearlessness as one could possibly
have done; but he got into a furious rage, and said some things
very unnecessarily. However many allowances should be made
for his situation at the moment. . . .*

*Yesterday I called to see and to congratulate him on his escape.
He was highly pleased at my laughing and saying to him: "Why,
Mr. President, when I looked at you yesterday while springing on
that man with your cane, I could have taken you for a young man
of twenty-five."* [Jackson was sixty-seven] . . .

*Well, this is the first day of February, and four more weeks
will soon run by. Tell Alice* [their daughter] *that she must hem a
handkerchief for me, and to learn her book; that father will soon
be home now. I hope the weather will continue good; but I fear
we shall have a wet month. Since writing thus far, I have received
a letter from Robert* [their son], *in which he speaks of parties
without end. Miss Mary Cook Smith seems now to be his flame.
He tells me of his bidding her farewell on her quitting Williamsburg, and of her inviting him to Doctor Chamberlayne's whenever
he should happen to visit Richmond. He is a curious fellow. . . .*

Yours affectionately, J. Tyler

In the presidential election of 1840, the Whig Party chose William
Henry Harrison of Indiana as its candidate at the head of the ticket.
They nominated Tyler for the vice presidency, because as a Southerner
he would attract votes from that section of the country. A supporter
wrote a song with the line "Tippecanoe and Tyler too." As a military
leader, Harrison had defeated Native Americans in the Battle of Tippecanoe, and even though that had been more than thirty years earlier, it
was still his best-known achievement. "Tyler too" suggested that the vice
presidential candidate was more or less an afterthought. Voters would
be in for a surprise.

Harrison's death, a month after he took office, resulted in another first: John Tyler became the first vice president to become president because of the president's death. Because the Constitution was vague about what powers the new president had in that situation, some thought Tyler should be little more than a caretaker. But he showed his intentions by giving his own inaugural address and pursuing bold policies, like the annexation of Texas, which, because it entered the Union as a slave state, was opposed by abolitionists. The Whig Party formally expelled him, and he was nicknamed "His Accidency." When he vetoed a popular bill, Congress overrode his veto with a two-thirds majority—the first time a president had ever received that rebuke. One of his opponents in the House of Representatives even introduced a bill to impeach him—the first time that was attempted—but it went nowhere.

Her husband's rise to the highest office in the land could not have been good news to his wife Letitia because she had suffered a stroke in 1839 that left her unable to walk. She lived in the White House but remained in her bedroom, appearing in public only for the marriage of one of her daughters. She died in September 1842, the first time a First Lady had died in the White House. Her body was taken back to Virginia, where she was buried on the plantation she had lived on as a child.

While he was still president, her husband married again.

John Tyler to Julia Gardiner Tyler

Julia Gardiner grew up on Gardiner's Island, located off the eastern end of Long Island, New York. The island was and still is owned by her wealthy family, whose original forebear bought it from the local Native Americans in 1639. Julia tended to be a free spirit. Once, after she appeared with an anonymous man in a newspaper advertisement for a clothing store, her family took her to Europe until the scandal died down. Appearing in ads was not something a proper young woman did.

Julia was introduced to President John Tyler at a White House reception in February 1843. Tyler's wife had died only five months earlier, but the president was smitten with Julia. He invited her family, including her parents and sister, to his private quarters, where they chatted for several hours. As they were preparing to leave, Julia's older sister, Margaret, recalled, "What does he do but give me a kiss! *[on the hand, presumably]* He was proceeding to treat Julia in the same manner when she snatched away her hand and then flew down the stairs with the President after her around chairs and tables until at last he caught her. It was truly amusing."

According to family history Tyler first proposed to Julia the following February. She was twenty-two, and he thirty years older. The age difference wasn't all that set them apart: he was formal and (normally) serious; she was beautiful, unconventional, and fun-loving. She later recalled that she had responded to his proposal by shaking her head, brushing his face with a tassel on her cap, and saying "No, no, no."

He persisted, proposing several more times, not deterred by her refusals. Every time there was a White House ball, she received an invitation, and she gradually fell in love. The deciding factor, in any case, came when the president invited her, her sister, and their father, David Gardiner, to a cruise on a US naval ship. A huge gun, named the Peacemaker, exploded when it was being demonstrated, killing several people, including Julia's father.

President Tyler took the role of consoling the bereaved Julia, and they grew closer. Finally, she accepted his proposal at the White House's George Washington Ball. They were married in New York City by the Episcopal bishop of New York. They tried to keep the affair a secret—Tyler told only one of his children beforehand—but the newspapers discovered it and made much of the couple's age difference.

They needn't have worried. Two years later, their first child was born, a boy named David, after Julia's father. Six more children would follow, making Tyler the father of fifteen in all, the most of any president. (One of their children also married at a late age, resulting in the surprising fact that as late as 2023, one of John Tyler's grandchildren was still living.)

Neither political party nominated John Tyler for reelection, and so

John Tyler was the first president to be married while in office. He wed Julia Gardiner, known as "the Rose of Long Island."

Julia's reign as First Lady was short. She made the most of it by throwing a final White House ball for three thousand guests. She permitted her guests to dance the waltz, though her husband had previously thought it immoral. (She was also the person who insisted that a band play "Hail to the Chief" at the president's appearances.)

After Tyler's term, the couple retired to his Virginia plantation, which he had dubbed Sherwood Forest. Life was leisurely, and of course there were all the children to care for. Then, twenty years and one month after the Tylers left the White House, Fort Sumter was attacked, marking the beginning of the Civil War.

There was no doubt about the Tylers' loyalty. To the Confederacy, that is. Julia had even published a book defending slavery, and the Tylers had many enslaved people on their plantation. John Tyler was elected to the Virginia Secession Convention, which was to decide on Virginia's formal departure from the United States. He wrote his wife that war would likely result:

Richmond, April 16, 1861

Well, dearest, your letter received this morning placed me much
at ease relative to the dear children. I hope you will still keep
an eye upon them, and not suffer them to expose themselves to
the weather. Our noble boys are of high spirit, and if God spares
them, I think they will reflect honor on our names.

The prospects now are that we shall have war, and a trying one.
The battle at Charleston [Fort Sumter] has aroused the whole
North. I fear that division no longer exists in their ranks, and that
they will break upon the South with an immense force. Virginia
will deserve much credit for boldness, if in face of all this, in
debt and without disciplined troops, she throws herself into the
melee, taking upon trust the action of the Border slave-States;
but events prove so rapidly on each others heels that we have,
I think, no alternative. Submission or resistance is only left us.
My hope is that the Border States will follow speedily our lead.
If so, all will be safe. The convention is sitting with closed doors.
Another day may decide our course. To-morrow night is fixed for
a great torch-light procession and illumination for the battle at
Charleston. If to this is added an ordinance of secession, there will
be an immense outburst. I wish the boys could be here. . . .

These are dark times, dearest, and I think only of you and our
little ones. But I trust in that same Providence that protected our
fathers. These rascals who hold power leave us no alternative. I
shall vote [for] secession, and prefer to encounter any hazard to
degrading Virginia. If the ordinance passes, it is to be submitted to
the people.

Love and kisses to all. Always your devoted,
J. Tyler

On April 17, 1861, the Virginia Secession Convention voted 88 to 55
in favor of secession. Seeing the way things had gone, some delegates
changed their votes, so the final tally was 103 to 46. The next day, Tyler
optimistically wrote to his wife, predicting victory:

Richmond, April 17, 1861 [He dated the letter the day before, because it was so significant.]

Well, my dearest one, Virginia has severed her connection with the Northern hive of abolitionists, and taken her stand as a sovereign and independent State. By a large vote she decided on yesterday, at about three o'clock, to resume the powers she had granted to the Federal government, and to stand before the world clothed in the full vestments of sovereignty. The die is thus cast, and her future is in the hands of the god of battle. The contest into which we enter is one full of peril, but there is a spirit abroad in Virginia which cannot be crushed until the life of the last man is trampled out. The numbers opposed to us are immense; but twelve thousand Grecians conquered the whole power of Xerxes at Marathon, and our fathers, a mere handful, overcame the enormous power of Great Britain.

The North seems to be thoroughly united against us. . . . Things have gone to that point in Philadelphia that no one is safe in the expression of a Southern sentiment. Poor Robert [his son, in Philadelphia] *is threatened with mob violence. I wish most sincerely he was away from there. I attempted to telegraph him to-day, but no dispatch is permitted northward, so that no one knows there, except by some secret agent, what has transpired here. At Washington a system of martial law must have been established. The report is that persons are not permitted to pass through the city to the South. I learn that Mrs. Garrick and her children, on her way here to join her husband, who is on the convention, has been arrested and detained. . . .*

The city [Richmond] *is full of all sorts of rumors. To-morrow night is now fixed for the great procession; flags are raised all about town.*

If possible I shall visit home on Saturday. . . . I wish much to see you after so long an absence, and the dear children, since they have had the measles. Do, dearest, live as frugally as possible in the household—trying times are before us.

Kisses to all.

Your devoted, J. Tyler

John Tyler, ever the politician, was elected to the House of Representatives of the Confederacy, but died on January 18, 1862, before the Confederate legislature had met. Nevertheless, the president of the Confederacy, Jefferson Davis, organized a grand funeral, celebrating Tyler as a hero of the new nation. His body was draped with the Confederate flag, making him the only US president not to be buried with the American flag.

Julia Tyler lost the plantation during the war and moved to her mother's house on Long Island, New York, with her children. Union troops nearly burned the Long Island house when she flew the Confederate flag from it. Later, she returned to Virginia. In 1880, Congress granted an annuity of five thousand dollars to the widows of former presidents, including Julia.

Millard Fillmore to
Abigail Powers Fillmore

Millard Fillmore, the first president to be born in the nineteenth century, was the son of a tenant farmer who lived in what was then the wilderness of upper New York state. His father didn't want Millard to become a farmer, so he apprenticed him, at age fourteen, to a clothmaker. After finding that his duties consisted almost entirely of chopping wood, young Millard went home. He obtained what little education he could from a village school and paid two dollars for membership in a lending library. He met his future wife Abigail Powers when she became his teacher. Abigail was two years older, but they fell in love.

Millard met a local judge, who agreed to mentor him in the law. After starting to earn money by taking law cases of his own, he and Abigail wed. She continued to teach, making her the first First Lady to hold a job after she was married. (She would also become the last First Lady born in the eighteenth century.)

Millard entered politics, rising through the ranks to national office. On the night he wrote the following letter to his wife, Fillmore was vice

president of the United States. Since at that time there was no official
residence for the vice president, he was staying in the Willard Hotel
and was pining for Abigail, whose frail health had caused her to return
to their home in Buffalo, New York. He attempted to cheer her up by
sharing gossipy news in this previously unpublished letter.

Willard Hotel, Washington
Sunday evening, 10 o'clock, April 1, 1850

My Dear Abigail,

*How lonesome this room is in your absence. I can hardly bear
to sit down and Mr. Stanby and myself have been making calls
on the President and others all the evening. But you have scarcely
been out of my mind since you left. I suppose you are now on the
River and will be at home to-morrow. How I wish I could be with
you! I want to see the children very much. But you will remember
me to them and to sister Mary. . . .*

*Mr. Calhoun's death on Sunday morning has cast a melancholy
gloom over the city.* [John C. Calhoun was one of the Senate's
three most important members, the other two being Henry Clay and
Daniel Webster.] *No business was transacted in the Senate to day.
But some very handsome eulogies were lavished on the deceased,
especially by Messrs. Clay and Webster. You will doubtless see
them in the papers. A singular anecdote is mentioned in connection with his last illness. A black servant, as nurse, accompanied
him from the Hotel to the boarding house where he was confined
during his last illness. This servant was a slave who had saved
enough to purchase his freedom, which he did, and died on the
same day and the same hour as his benefactor. A most singular
coincidence. . . .*

But as there is no one to play backgammon with [something
the couple often did together], *I must close and go to bed. I spent
yesterday in my room investigating the question of how to call
a senator to order for words spoken in debate and came to the
conclusion that . . . it was my duty; and I intend to announce it
in the senate day after tomorrow. . . . The weather has been very*

pleasant here since you left. I hope it has been so where you were. I shall look for a letter from N.Y. tomorrow. I sent you 3 Albany Registers [newspapers] *today that you might have the remainder of Dr. Webster's trial.* [A notorious murder trial in which John White Webster, a Harvard professor of chemistry, was accused of killing a physician to whom he owed a large sum of money. Webster had attempted to destroy the body in his laboratory, but in an early use of forensics, the remains were identified. The judge in the case, a close relative of the victim, instructed the jury that they must bring in a verdict of guilty.] *I perceive that the poor man is convicted. I saw Mr. Latterof this evening, who has just returned from Boston* [where the trial was held], *where he says no man seems to consider him innocent and where he appears to be without sympathy or friends. Is it not horrible?*

I received a note from Frank Taylor on Saturday evening saying that the flags which he wanted could not be found in this city.

Speaking of flags reminds me of [Edwin] *Forrest.* [An American Shakespearean actor whose wife sued for divorce on the grounds of infidelity. At the trial, which was supposed to be closed, Forrest responded by introducing letters from her own lovers. The transcript of the trial was later published on the front page of the *New York Herald*, causing a sensation. Forrest then publicly thrashed the *Herald*'s editor in Washington Square.] *Have you read the letters just published between him and his wife in reference to his divorce case? He must be a very wretched man and she a very wretched woman. She is covered with infamy and he with mortification and shame. Doubtless he would exchange all his wealth and fame if his confidence in the virtue of his wife could be restored. But that can never be. They are ruined forever.*

But I have gossipped enough, and have only room enough left [on the page] *to say what you very well know, that I am your own, devoted*
Millard

Three months after the next letter was written, President Zachary Taylor laid the cornerstone of the Washington Monument. It was the Fourth of July, a hot day, and he refreshed himself by eating cherries and cold milk. This is generally regarded as causing a digestive upset. His doctor concluded that he had contracted cholera, a bacterial infection of the small intestine. Whatever the cause, it resulted in his death four days later—and made Fillmore the president.

Fillmore's term began with the resignations of nearly all the members of Taylor's cabinet—the only time in American history that has happened. However, their departure left him free to appoint friends and cronies from his days practicing law in New York state.

When Abigail Fillmore became First Lady, she was shocked to find that the White House had no library nor music room—two things she regarded as part of every cultured home that could afford it. At her urging, Congress appropriated funds for both, including three pianos.

By all accounts, Millard relied heavily on Abigail's advice. She schooled herself on pending legislation and current affairs. One of their friends noted that Millard often said that he "never took any important step without [Abigail's] counsel and advice." Unfortunately for him, he didn't always follow her advice.

The burning issue of the day was slavery. Fillmore regarded the enslavement of others as immoral but felt that the federal government had no power to end it. Congress passed a bill called the Fugitive Slave Act. Against Abigail's advice, Fillmore signed the act, hoping it would be part of a compromise. As Abigail had warned him, the act angered antislavery advocates with its provisions that required escaped enslaved people to be returned to their masters and set punishments for anyone who had aided them to escape.

The Whig Party, to which Fillmore belonged, refused to nominate him for a second term because he had signed the Fugitive Slave Act. That enabled Franklin Pierce, a Democrat, to win the election. His inauguration took place outdoors on a cold March day, but Abigail Fillmore insisted on standing with her husband throughout the ceremony. She caught pneumonia and died the same month. Fillmore was grief-stricken. He wrote, "For twenty-seven years, my entire married life, I was always greeted with a happy smile."

Franklin Pierce to Jane Appleton Pierce

Franklin Pierce began his inaugural address with the words, *"It is a relief to feel that no heart but my own can know the personal regret and bitter sorrow over which I have been borne to a position so suitable for others rather than desirable for myself."* He also refused to take the oath of office on a Bible and used the words "I affirm" instead of "I do solemnly swear" in the oath itself. This was to signify that he had lost his faith because of a personal tragedy.

His wife, Jane Pierce, was probably the only First Lady who prayed for her husband's defeat at the polls (or maybe just the only one who didn't make a secret of it). From the time they were married, Jane hated politics, even though her husband seemed born for it. His father had been a general in the Revolutionary War and was later elected governor of New Hampshire. Carrying on the family tradition, Franklin was in his second term in the US House of Representatives when he and Jane married, and later was elected to the Senate.

During Franklin's absence in the Mexican war, Jane and her only living son, Benny—the first two had died at early ages—grew ever closer, and she was relieved when Franklin returned without further injury. He was now regarded as a war hero, and his good looks and phenomenal memory for names and faces made him an ideal political candidate. When Pierce's party met to nominate a presidential candidate in 1852, he was at first regarded as too young for the office, but after forty-eight ballots without settling on a leader, the Democrats picked Pierce. Jane fainted when she heard the news, and that was when she began her prayers beseeching God to keep her husband out of the White House. They were unavailing, and worse was yet to come.

After Franklin won the election, he, his wife, and eleven-year-old Benny boarded a train returning from the funeral of Jane's uncle. The

*Jane Pierce never wanted to be First Lady—she
even prayed that her husband, Franklin, would
lose the election. Because of the death of her son
Benjamin, she made almost no appearances as
First Lady.*

train derailed and the car they were in tumbled down a bank. Franklin
kept his wife from falling, but their son was in the seat behind them and
suffered a severe injury to his head, which killed him instantly. Both
parents were distraught, but Jane, who had seen her son's bloody body,
suffered a psychological wound from which she never recovered. After
Franklin's inauguration (becoming, at forty-eight, the youngest man
ever elected president up to that time) Jane spent most of her days in
her bedroom at the White House, writing letters to her dead son Benny.
A previously unpublished sample:

*My precious child—I must write to you, altho' you are never
to see it, or know it—How I long to see you and say something
to you as if you were as you always have been . . . oh! how
precious do those days now seem, my darling boy—And how*

I should have prised [prized] the days passed with you had I suspected they might be so short . . . I know not how to go on without you—you were my comfort dearest far more than you thought . . . and oh! my precious boy how gladly would I recall all that was unreasonable or hasty—or mistaken in my conduct toward you—I see surely, and I did frequently afterward that I had wronged you—and would gladly have acknowledged it only that I feared it might weaken your confidence in me . . . and oh! to look around and see your books and every thing so connected with your own dear self—and now on the Sabbath which you loved so much as you said so often . . . and oh to think of you kneeling by me at our evening prayer to night, dear child—has not the Savior made you His, as we so often asked—But now I must kneel alone—and beg for strength and support under this crushing sorrow, that the Blessed Savior would comfort the heart of your poor stricken Mother—and help me better to bear the burden of your loss which has brought desolation such as I have never (with all my former griefs) known . . . and now this Sabbath evening—you will come in fancy before me—and I sit close by you with your hand in mine perhaps or you will lean against me on the sofa, or as sometimes you did on Sunday evening, sit on my lap a little while and we talk together, and say hymns—and then pray, and then by and by you go to bed, first putting your arms around me, and laying your dear head on my shoulder—and then you get in your bed and we have our Sabbath night kiss—but to think I can never have another—Oh Benny, I have not valued such a sweet blessing as I ought—

Because of his strong enforcement of the Fugitive Slave Act, Pierce was not nominated by his party for a second term, the only time in history that has happened with a president who had been elected to his first term. He purchased a large tract of land in Concord, but his wife would not live there because it reminded her of Benny. When the Civil War broke out, she supported the Union and the abolition of slavery, while her husband backed the legalization of slavery in order to preserve the

Union. Jane died in 1863 and her husband followed her six years later. They lie together in the Old North Cemetery in Concord.

Abraham Lincoln to Mary Todd Lincoln

Pictures of Mary Todd Lincoln make her appear stout by modern standards. In fact, her full figure was quite attractive to most people of her day. Here her husband makes it clear that he liked her that way. She was about twenty-nine at the time this letter was written. Lincoln was serving in the House of Representatives. After moving to Washington, DC, they lived in a cramped boardinghouse with their two children. It was an unsatisfactory life for Mary Lincoln, and Abraham, too, so he had encouraged her in her decision to move back to Illinois with the children. But now Lincoln was feeling lonely.

Washington, April 16, 1848

Dear Mary,

In this troublesome world, we are never quite satisfied. When you were here, I thought you hindered me some in attending to business; but now, having nothing but business—no variety—it has grown exceedingly tasteless to me. I hate to sit down in this old room by myself. You know I told you in last Sunday's letter, I was going to make a little speech during the week; but the week has passed away without my getting a chance to do so; and now my interest in the subject has passed away too. . . .

I went yesterday to hunt the little plaid stockings, as you wished; but found that McKnight has quit business, and Allen had not a single pair of the description you give, and only one plaid pair of any sort that I thought would fit "Eddy's dear little feet." . . .

I wish you to enjoy yourself in every possible way; but is there no danger of wounding the feelings of your good father by being so intimate with the Wickliffe family? [Two of Mary's best friends were daughters of Robert Wickliffe, who had strongly disagreed with Mary's father, a holder of enslaved persons, on the issue of slavery.]

Mrs. Broome [a neighbor in the boardinghouse] *has not removed yet; but she thinks of doing so tomorrow. All the house—or rather, all with whom you were on decided good terms—send their love to you. The rest say nothing. . . .*

And you are entirely free from head-ache? That is good—good considering it is the first spring you have been free from it since we were acquainted. I am afraid you will get so well, and fat, and young, as to be wanting to marry again. Tell Louisa I want her to watch you a little for me. Get weighed and write me how much you weigh.

I did not get rid of the impression of that foolish dream about dear Bobby till I got your letter written the same day. What did he and Eddy think of the little letters father sent them? Don't let the blessed fellows forget father. . . .

Most affectionately
A. Lincoln

Ulysses S. Grant to Julia Dent Grant

Though Grant had been promoted to captain during the Mexican War, his postwar requests for transfers to posts closer to home had been denied, and he missed his wife and children. Furthermore, he had a commanding officer who was a strict disciplinarian. When Grant allegedly began to drink heavily in spite of his commander's warnings, the commander ordered him to resign his commission.

Returning to his family, Grant tried a variety of business ventures, none of which were successful. (The idea of becoming a mathematics professor had been discarded.) Julia's father gave him an enslaved person so that Grant could start a farm, but Grant gave the man his freedom. He was working in his own father's leather goods store in Illinois when the Civil War broke out. Because of Grant's military experience, the governor of Illinois put him in charge of a regiment of volunteers. His many successes over the next three years (and the failures of other Union generals) led President Lincoln to name Grant commander in chief of all the Union armies in March 1864. The following letter indicates that he was still the down-to-earth man Julia had fallen in love with:

June 7th/64

Dear Julia,

I wrote to you last night but having had my hair cut to-day and remembering that you asked me to send you a lock I now write again to send it. I have nothing to add. To-day has been the quietest since leaving Culpepper. There has been no fighting except a little Artillery firing and some skirmishing driving the enemy's pickets south of the Chickahominy . . . War will get to be so common with me if this thing continues much longer that I will not be able to sleep after a while unless there is an occasional gun shot near me during the night.

Love and kisses for you and the children.

Ulys.

At the conclusion of the war, Grant became a national hero. Julia joined him in Washington, where they were asked to attend many celebrations. President Lincoln invited them to join him and his wife at a production of a play in Ford's Theatre on the night of April 15, 1865. However, Mrs. Grant was eager to leave town and visit their children in New Jersey, and they were not present when Lincoln was shot by an assassin.

After Andrew Johnson completed Lincoln's term, Grant was elected president. Less than a month after taking office he became the first sitting president to speak to a Black man as an equal. The man was Oscar Dunn, recently elected lieutenant governor of Louisiana. Grant also named Ebenezer D. Bassett as minister to Haiti, making him the first Black diplomat in American history. Grant further placed hundreds of other African Americans in federal positions throughout his first term. Grant was elected to a second term by a landslide.

President Grant and his wife, Julia, who habitually turned her head to the side in photographs to hide her crossed eyes, with their son Jesse relaxing at a cottage in Long Branch, New Jersey. The Grants were devoted to each other and their four children.

Grant died of throat cancer on July 23, 1885, just days after finishing work on his memoir. Less than a month before, he had written this letter to his wife:

> *Mt. McGregor, Saratoga Cty, N.Y.*
> *June 29th 1885*
>
> *My Dear Wife:*
> *There are some matters about which I would like to talk but about which I cannot. The subject would be painful to you and the children, and, by reflex, painful to me also. When I see you and them depressed I join in the feeling.*
> *I have known for a long time that my end was approaching with certainty. How far away I would not venture to guess.*

I had an idea however that I would live until fall or the early part of winter. I see now, however, that the time is approaching much more rapidly. I am constantly loosing flesh and strength. The difficulty of swallowing is increasing daily. The tendency to spasms is constant. From three or four in the afternoon until relieved by Morphine I find it difficult to get breath enough to sustain me. Under these circumstances the end is not far off.

We are comparative strangers in New York City; that is, we made it our home late in life. We have rarely if ever had serious sickness in the family, therefore have made no preparation for a place of burial. This matter will necessarily come up at my death, and may cause you some embarrassment to decide. I should myself select West Point above all other places but for the fact that in case West Point should be selected you would, when the time comes, I hope far in the future, be excluded from the same grounds. I therefore leave you free to select what you think the most appropriate place for depositing my earthly remains.

My will disposes of my property. I have left with Fred. [their son] a memorandum giving some details of how the proceeds from my book are to be drawn from the publisher, and how disposed of.

Look after our dear children and direct them in the paths of rectitude. It would distress me far more to think that one of them could depart from an honorable, upright and virtuous life than it would to know they were prostrated on a bed of sickness from which they were never to arise alive. They have never given us any cause of alarm on their account. I earnestly pray they never will.

With these few injunctions, and the knowledge I have of your love and affections, and of the dutiful affection of all our children, I bid you a final farewell until we meet in another, and I trust better, world.

U.S. GRANT

P.S. This will be found in my coat after my demise.
U.S.G.

Twenty-four days later, Grant died. Within hours after hearing of his death, the mayor of New York City offered to build a suitable tomb for Grant and his wife. Land was found in Riverside Park, and Julia joined her husband there after her death in 1902.

Rutherford B. Hayes to Lucy Webb Hayes

At the beginning of the Civil War, Lucy was expecting a baby, which was due in December. By this time, Rutherford's unit had moved into Virginia, but he wanted her to imagine he would be nearby when the baby was born.

Fayetteville, Virginia
December 16, 1861

Dearest:

. . . I think of you constantly now. Keep up good courage. Let me know all about you all the time. I will send you a dispatch from here as soon as our [telegraph] operator is at work just to show you that we are not far apart. . . .

I see somebody knits woollen gloves for soldiers. That's sensible. A few stockings, gloves, woolen shirts, and the like are always wanted at this season . . .

Kisses for all the boys and "love you much."
Affectionately,
R.

Camp Union
December 23, 1861

Dearest:

I am so happy to hear today by telegraph that your troubles are over (at least the worst, I hope) and that "mother and son are doing well." Darling, I love you so much and have felt so anxious about you. The little fellow, I hope, is healthy and strong. It is best

it was not a daughter. These are no times for women. . . . What do the boys say? . . . Tell me all about this. . . .
Kiss the boy, yes, "all the boys" for me.
Affectionately
R.

During the war, Hayes was wounded five times, including injuries he received when horses were shot out from under him. The worst wound occurred in the Battle of South Mountain when, as he described in a letter to Lucy's mother, "a musket-ball passed through the centre of the left arm just above the elbow."

He had written to his mother-in-law because Lucy was on her way to him in a prearranged visit. In the war, when there was a shortage of medical personnel, female relatives customarily visited the troops to nurse the wounded. As an officer (by now a colonel), Hayes had private quarters that he shared with his wife. After a later visit, during which she brought their sons, he recalled it with pleasure:

> *Camp Reynolds*
> *May 1, [1864]*
>
> *Dearest,*
> *I am in the old log cabin at a desk where our bed stood. The troops are on the hill overlooking the Falls. . . . I write you merely to finish the good-bye so hastily spoken on the steamboat. Your visit has been the greatest possible happiness to me. I carry with me the pleasantest recollection of you dear ones all. Good-bye.*
> *Affectionately,*
> *R.*

While Hayes was still serving in the army, he was nominated for the House of Representatives and his backers urged him to resign his commission in order to campaign. He responded that an "officer fit for duty who at this crisis would abandon his post to electioneer for a seat in Congress ought to be scalped." He won anyway. This was the beginning of a political career that took him to the governorship of Ohio and, finally, to the presidency. During his term, his wife refused to allow alcoholic beverages in the White House, giving her the nickname "Lemonade Lucy." Hayes, as he had promised, served only one term and he and Lucy retired to their home in Ohio. She died in 1889, and he four years later. His last words were "I know I am going to where Lucy is."

James Garfield to Lucretia ("Crete") Rudolph

James Garfield graduated from Williams College in August 1856. Lucretia Rudolph, the woman to whom he had pledged his love with such passion, attended the ceremony. But so did Rebecca Selleck, another young woman Garfield had met. Noticing the close attention James paid to Rebecca, Lucretia began to have doubts about his oft expressed desire to marry her. Garfield returned to Hiram College, where he was later named president, but Lucretia took a job teaching in Cleveland, partially to test the strength of his affection. Since their mutual friends and colleagues expected them to marry, Garfield felt pressured to do so. Lucretia sensed his lack of enthusiasm, and even after they had set a date, she sent him an invitation to his own wedding as a reminder.

Marriage did not result in Garfield settling down to domestic tranquility. He became involved in politics and was elected state senator, a post that kept him in Columbus, the Ohio capital, for much of the time. Then, when the Civil War broke out in 1861, he organized a regiment of volunteers to fight on the side of the Union. Instead of using his limited free time to come home (where his wife had given birth to a daughter), he visited Rebecca Selleck, and even told his wife he had done so. When she wrote him a letter expressing her discontent, he wrote the following:

Washington, Oct. 25, 1862

My Dearest Crete [his nickname for Lucretia],

. . . I am glad to hear that you are perfecting your arrangements for a home of our own. I only wish I were well through

*this war and could enjoy it with you. I am glad to have you write
me frankly and fully as you do in the last letter of the 20th now
before me. I was however sorry to know that you had been sad
and had passed through a struggle on account of my visit to
Rebecca. I hope you will not harbor any thought that I have practiced any deception toward you in my last communication. I hope
you will see me as I am conscious of being, indeed a true man,
and that I am true to my whole history. I had a very pleasant and
yet sad visit with Rebecca, pleasant because I was glad to revisit
the scenes of six years ago and was enabled to do so without
having my horizon clouded or having the thorns again pierce me,
pleasant because I am more than ever assured that he that is true
to his own nature is happier and better in being so, and I can
say in truth that I love you none the less for having seen Rebecca
again and she is no less dear to me from the fact that the sunshine
has sweetly dawned upon your life and mine—pleasant because I
took pleasure in telling her that I had passed a very happy month
with you and that henceforth my life with you was full of promise
of sweet peace and sunlight. I was sad in this that I found her just
arisen from a bed of pain and suffering, that I feared the insid-
ious approach of consumption* [tuberculosis], *that I found her
surrounded by those who do not contribute much to make her life
agreeable, nor do they seem to be worthy to be companions of so
noble a woman. . . .*

Kiss our darling [daughter] *for me. I regret that I cannot be with
you on the 11th Nov, but I am preparing something for you which
will answer nearly as well.* [He later sent her a photograph.]

*Loving you and hoping to hear from you very often, I am
forever*
Your own James

Despite his protests, Garfield continued his affairs with Rebecca and
other women as well, and if his wife tried to pretend they didn't happen, so-called friends and even Garfield's mother (with whom Lucretia
was living) made her aware of them. She wrote her husband that when

Wallace Ford, a longtime friend of Garfield's, was visiting, "he took occasion to say before *[Garfield's]* Mother and my hired girl, 'James will not be contented with any one thing any more than he will be with one woman.' And when by various and sundry remarks nearly as pleasant, he roused Mother to say, 'If Miss Booth *[Almeda Booth, another of Garfield's lovers]* should tell James the moon was made of green cheese and he had got the first slice, he would believe it.'"

On occasion, Lucretia would give vent to her feelings in letters to James. In the following, he replies to one of these letters and tries to justify himself. Modern readers will note that he attempts to turn the blame on her!

Washington, Dec. 26, 1862

My Dear Crete,

. . . [He begins with reports on military matters, including the fact that he has heard he was going to be promoted to major general. Then he adds, on a separate sheet of paper, the following, headed "Private and Confidential."]

I have taken this new sheet to say a few words in regard to ourselves. I know you want me to be frank in everything, and I want to assure and reassure you that I write what follows with the tenderest regards for our mutual happiness. In your letter which now lies before me there is the following passage: "<u>Jamie, I should not blame my own heart if it lost all faith in you. I hope it may not, indeed I am not going to let it, but I need not be forever telling you I love you when there is evidently no more desire for it on your part than present manifestations indicate.</u>" [underlined in the original] I had to read that sentence over several times before I could become fully convinced that you have written the passage which I have underscored. Waiving the consideration out of which this sentence arose (my letters to you, their relative brevity and infrequency) for I have spoken of that in my last letter which you have received before this . . . I want you to look at your words again and ask yourself whether you ought to have written

*them to me. A husband should not only be a faithful husband
but should also be a noble manly friend and a wife should be a
noble womanly friend. Now Crete, if a mere friend should write
such a sentence to me, I should consider it an imputation upon
my honesty, a direct slight to my manhood which if unexplained
would compel me to drop that correspondence. I am clearly of
the opinion that [it] is very wrong for you to write to me in that
way, and I beg you with all the earnestness of my heart that you
will not do it again. We came so much near[er] to each other and
have been, Oh how much happier than before in consequence
of my last visit home. It is a perpetual source of thanksgiving to
me that we were so blessed. I am all the more rejoiced to know
that that new joy was not an ephemeral existence but a fixed and
permanent part of our lives henceforth, and I believe that nothing,
unless it be such things as that above written, can fling me back
into the old darkness and shadow of death in which my soul dwelt
so long. Understand me: I don't want you to write what you do
not feel, nor indeed do I want you to conceal your real feelings
from me, but it seems to me that you wrote that in a temporary
feeling of dissatisfaction which was not at all an exponent of your
fixed belief. If you really felt what was there suggested, I should
consider it wrong for us to continue any other than a business
correspondence. But I hope and most fully believe we love each
other in a nobler and truer way than that. Be assured that I say all
this (an hour and a half after midnight) from a heart that longs to
clasp your doubts by the warmth of its presence and love. Write
to me and forgive me if I have wronged you. Ever and forever,
Your James*

The birth of a daughter, named after Garfield's mother but always referred to as "Trot" by her parents, brought the couple closer together.
However, Trot died of diphtheria when she was only three. The following letters, written when Garfield had left the army after being elected
to Congress, reveal that her loss brought out Garfield's better qualities.

Washington, Dec. 13, 1863

My Dearest Crete,

Your dear noble letter of the 8th inst. came to me yesterday. It was balm to my heart, and it made me feel more than ever before how noble and true you are. Pray for me, dearest, that my heart may, like yours become more resigned and see the hand of our good Father in this great sorrow. It is a lovely day, after a cold and cheerless morning of storm. I ought to be cheerful and happy as are the sun and the sky, and though your brave words have made me calmer and stronger, I still struggle with my grief and think [of] our precious darling with such a yearning agony of heartbreak that at times it seems as though I could not endure it. I have read twice over this morning the passage you told me of from Thessalonians [1 Thessalonians 4:13]. It is touchingly tender and hopeful. I would that my heart could rest upon it as I when a child rested in my mother's words. I pray that my faith may grow stronger. I try to be helpful but Tennyson speaks for me when he says,

"Yet in these ears till hearing dies,
One set slow bell will ever toll
The passing of the sweetest soul
That ever looked with human eyes."

How her image and little nature has grown upon me since she is gone . . .

With all my heart, I am ever, Your own James.

Washington, Feb. 14, 1864
[Valentine's Day]

Dearest Crete:

Let me be your Valentine, and write you a word at the close of this beautiful day. For almost the first time since I have been here, I have broken away from work and enjoyed a part of [the] Sabbath. I went to the hall of the House to hear Rev. Mr. Furniss of Boston, and he preached a strong earnest sermon which did

*me good and I hope made me better. How I wanted you with me
to enjoy it. I came back to my room . . . and I have had a little
rest. It was needed for I was very tired. How I longed while here
alone to lie upon your breast and tell you how deep and true is
my love for you. The memory of our precious Trot came back
to my heart so fresh today as if she had only just left us. Where
is the dear one now? Can she not send us one word—sign or
token—to tell us she still knows and loves us? How I yearn to
know of her new life and its wonders! The time seems long, that
we must wait to see her, but it may be very short. Blessed little
soul. Were not my hours so full of work and weariness they
would overflow with sorrow that she is gone forever. . . . Ever
and forever your own, James.*

Garfield was elected president in 1880, after serving in the House of
Representatives and being selected for the Senate—a position he declined after being nominated for president. The following year he was
waiting in a train station when he was shot in the back and arm by a
man who had been frustrated in his efforts to gain a job in the federal
government. Garfield lingered for the next eighty days as doctors tried
to find the bullet that had struck him in the back. There were no X-ray
machines in those days and doctors stuck their unsterilized fingers in
the wound, probably leading to the infection that caused his death.
His wife was comforted by her five living children and a trust fund was
raised so that she could live comfortably. She died in 1918.

Theodore Roosevelt to
Edith Kermit Carow Roosevelt

Theodore Roosevelt became president after the assassination of William McKinley. After being reelected in his own right, he kept his promise not to run for a third term, leaving his friend and fellow Republican
William Howard Taft to run for and win the presidency. However, when

Roosevelt later disagreed with Taft on several issues, he decided to form his own political party, the Progressive, and run for president in the election of 1912. While preparing to give a speech in Milwaukee on October 14, 1912, Roosevelt was shot by a would-be assassin (who later claimed that McKinley had appeared to him in a dream and told him to avenge his death by killing Roosevelt). Fortunately, the assassin's bullet was deflected by a copy of Roosevelt's fifty-page speech and a metal glasses case. Roosevelt actually delivered the speech before going to the hospital. Not wanting his wife to learn of the attack in the newspapers, he sent her this telegram:

Am in excellent shape. Made an hour and a half speech. The wound is a trivial one. I think they will find that it merely glanced on a rib and went somewhere into a cavity of the body, it certainly did not reach a lung and isn't a particle more serious than one of the injuries any of the boys used continually to be having. Am at the Emergency Hospital at the moment, but antici-pate going right on with my engagements. My voice seems to be in good shape. Best love to Ethel [his younger daughter].

When reporters later asked Roosevelt how he felt, he replied, "I am fit as a bull moose," and his party was ever after referred to as the Bull Moose Party. In the election he received more popular and electoral votes than Taft, but the Democratic candidate, Woodrow Wilson, won the presidency.

William Howard Taft to Helen "Nellie" Herron

Taft and Nellie became engaged in May 1885. However, the following previously unpublished letter reveals that his mother wrote him a letter that indicated she disapproved of the marriage. Unwisely, Taft showed it to his fiancée, who, unsurprisingly, was not pleased. Here is his letter attempting to patch things up. It is interesting to see how he presents his case much the way a lawyer would.

[probably June 17, 1885]

My darling Nellie,

The color of this ink [blue] *is an indication of my feelings. That an act of mine should have imperilled all my hopes of happiness makes me first angry with myself and then with her who wrote the letter. I am afraid I have been unfilial in my thoughts this morning and yet Nellie I know she will love you and I believe you will love her when you know her. What I most dislike about the letter and what first made me regret giving it to you was the tone of worldliness that crept into some parts of it. To think that I should feel ashamed of my own mother! But I did and do when I come to think over what she has said.*

You say that you are in doubt because you think I have reasoned myself into loving you and have made a mistake. Would it please you better or give better security of your happiness if I had fallen in love with you without reason? My love for you grew out of a friendship, intimate and of long standing. That friendship of course was founded on a respect and admiration for your high character, your sweet womanly qualities and your intellectual superiority over any woman I know and for that quality in you which is called sympathy but I call it selfforgetting companionableness. Thus far I plead guilty to the use of some reason in cultivating as far as what lay in my power the friendship that I felt to be doing me good every day it was my good fortune to enjoy it. But that the transition from that feeling of friendship to the one of love which I have now was the result of any thing but the involuntary action of my heart I deny. You ought to know above all others how unconscious I was of such a feeling until it came on me with overwhelming force. You are all in all to me Nellie. Even the fear that in the closer relations of married life, you with your clear insight into character may discover more of my weaknesses of character than you know now does not deter me because I am

so confident that you will strengthen me where I need it. Much as
I should love where you love me now and say so now, there is a
proud satisfaction that I feel in that such a heart as yours can not
be won in a woman. It only make[s] me certain that when won it
will be a source of joy forever to him, however unworthy he might
[be], who wins it. This last week has been so full of happiness
for me that it is perhaps to be expected that it could not continue
without a break. But Nellie do have pity on me and write me a
note in which you dispel some of the gloom that has settled on me
in spite of this beautiful morning. Four men are waiting for me
and I must stop but not without telling you again my darling that
I love you and sending with this a kiss which I wanted to leave
with you this morning.
    W.H.T.

Taft's mother eventually became resigned to her son's choice of a wife, and they were married on June 19, 1886.

The wish Nellie Herron made when she was seventeen that one day she would be the First Lady was granted in 1908 when her husband, William Howard Taft, was elected president. However, Alice Roosevelt, the malicious twenty-four-year-old daughter of the outgoing president, buried a voodoo doll resembling Nellie in the White House lawn before her father left office. That may (or may not) have had something to do with the fact that barely two months after William Howard Taft moved into the White House, his wife suffered a severe stroke that impaired her ability to speak. She left Washington with its stifling summer to begin her recuperation. To keep her spirits up, her husband wrote her letters almost daily, describing his efforts to get Congress to approve his policies, mixed in with Washington gossip, the oppressive weather, and the progress he was making with his golf game—to which he devoted almost as much time as his presidential duties. The policy parts of the letters, Taft knew, would be interesting to Nellie, because she had frequently advised him on his career. Today they are of great interest to historians, but less so to the general reader. So, we publish here a few excerpts in which he expresses his affection and concern for her.

The White House
May 16, 1911

My darling Nellie:

[After she had suffered a second stroke] *I telephoned the doctor last night after I had unsuccessfully attempted to rouse somebody at Harry's* [his brother]. *This morning I talked to Harry and Helen* [their daughter] *and they say you had a good night and are better. . . . I have notes from Mrs. McClintock, Mabel, Mrs. Townsend, and Mrs. Gerry, anxiously asking after you. The Chief Justice and Mrs. White and many of the ambassadors & ministers called to inquire. Mac Dickinson* [the secretary of war] *sent you six bottles of fine old Rye Whiskey. That ought to rejoice your heart. . . .*

I am longing to have Tuesday come, my darling, so that you may [be] *safely housed in the White House and begin directing matters again and so that I can see you grow better & stronger under my eye.*

With love to all.

Your loving, Will

May 17, 1911

This will reach you, I hope, before you leave Harry's to come to the White House. By telephone from the Doctor and Helen I have followed your progress. . . . It is pretty hot here and you must be prepared to have a rise in temperature on your way down. Last night I went to the Jewish Synagogue to listen to a Baptist minister praise the Jews and to help along the erection of a memorial to a Jewish banker [Haym Salomon] *who was of great assistance to us in the Revolution. . . .*

I am longing to see you. The White House is not the same without you. Flowers are wanting and that essence or atmosphere that you alone can supply.

I hope you will look out your window on the Garden party. May your trip here be easy.

With devoted love My dear—Yours, Will

July 14, 1911

*. . . I have not heard from you for a day or two and I am afraid
you are [not?] keeping up with your promise to write a line
each day . . . I would like to know how you are getting on. We
just had a flying machine land in the grounds. Atwood is the
young aviator. Tell Charley [their son] he used a Burgess Wright
machine—I am off to my afternoon golf. Lovingly yours Will*

July 27, 1912

*. . . I shall be delighted to see you here when you come on
Wednesday. When I am away from you I somehow feel as if the
situation were temporary and ought to end as quickly as possible.
I feel as if I were living a life that was not quite respectable. I am
always missing something, and I feel a bit aimless as well—so
hurry back. . . .*
    Lovingly yours,
    Will

Franklin Delano Roosevelt to
Eleanor Roosevelt

In the summer of 1917, Eleanor seemed reluctant to take the children
to Campobello without Franklin. She may have suspected there was another reason why Franklin was staying in hot, humid Washington besides the pressure of his job. This letter was part of Franklin's effort to
reassure her.

July 16, [1917]

Dearest Babs,
    *I had a vile day after you left, stayed at home, coughed, dozed,
tried to read. . . . I really can't stand that house all alone without*

you and you were a goosy girl to think or even pretend to think
that I don't want you here all summer, because you know I do!
But honestly you ought to have six weeks straight at Campo,
just as I ought to, only you can and I can't! I know what a whole
summer here does to people's nerves and at the end of this
summer I will be like a bear with a sore head until I get a change
or some cold weather. In fact you know I am unreasonable and
touchy now but shall try to improve.
    F.

The following excerpt is of interest because of Franklin's mention of
Lucy Mercer, for it was she who was carrying on an affair with Franklin—
though Eleanor did not yet know that for sure. He wrote this breezy
letter in an attempt to conceal from Eleanor his romantic relationship
with Lucy. Nigel Law, who Franklin implied was her escort on the yacht-
ing trip, was a secretary in the British embassy. Charlie Munn was a classmate of Franklin's at Harvard, and Cary Grayson was President Wilson's
doctor—a man who kept secret the extent of Wilson's disability after his
stroke and would keep Roosevelt's romantic secrets as well.

Washington
[July 25, 1917]
Wednesday

Dearest Babs,
    . . . The trip on the Sylph [a government yacht available for use by
the assistant secretary of the navy] *was a joy and a real test, though I*
got in a most satisfactory visit to the fleet. Such a funny party, but it
worked out wonderfully! The Charlie Munns, the Cary Graysons,
Lucy Mercer and Nigel Law, and they all got on splendidly. We
swam about four times and Sunday afternoon went up the James
to Richmond. . . . We inspected the fleet in a destroyer and lunched
with Admiral Tommy Rodgers on the Arkansas. . . .
    It has been pretty hot and today a tremendous rain—3 inches
and a leak in the sewing room extending to F Jr.'s room and the
dining room ceilings!

I am very well and do my exercises with regularity!
Your devoted
F

When Franklin was returning from a diplomatic mission to Europe shortly after World War I, he caught the influenza that was sweeping the world and had to go to bed immediately upon arriving home. Eleanor began to unpack his luggage and found love letters from Lucy Mercer, who had originally been Eleanor's secretary but was now working for Franklin at the Navy Department.

Eleanor was deeply hurt and told Franklin she wanted a divorce. His domineering mother stepped in, because she knew Franklin's political career would be ruined, and told him if he gave Eleanor a divorce, she would cut him off from her considerable fortune in her will. Franklin patched things up by promising Eleanor he would never again see or communicate with Lucy Mercer, a promise he didn't keep. According to their children, the Roosevelts' marriage was never the same after that and they did not have a physical relationship. Nevertheless, he continued to write Eleanor affectionate letters like the following one:

Washington
[July 22, 1919]
Tuesday

Dearest Babs,

It is surely a rainy time. It has poured every day since I got here on the half and half system. Deluge one hour then sunlight one hour and the papers say continuation! . . .

This a.m. I was awakened at 6 a.m. by a drip, drip, drip and found your bureau afloat, rushed upstairs and found the sun parlor a lake. Worked hard for an hour in my pyjamas with bath towels and tooth mugs and saved the house! . . .

It is fearfully muggy, not so hot but all the doors and windows won't move from the damp.

Do hope you had a fairly good trip though I fear you too were in the rain.

Kiss the chicks and I miss you so much. Wasn't it a nice 9 days at Hyde Park.
Your devoted
F

At his summer retreat on Campobello Island, Canada, in the summer of 1921, Franklin D. Roosevelt was stricken by what was diagnosed as polio, or infantile paralysis. The result was that he was paralyzed from the waist down. For the rest of his life Roosevelt sought a cure that would enable him to walk unassisted. The best treatment he could find was at Warm Springs, Georgia, where swimming in the warm, mineral-laden water seemed to give relief to some patients, including him. He purchased the resort there and formed the National Foundation for Infantile Paralysis, which raised money through what was called the March of Dimes, which invited children throughout the nation to send in ten cents to help find a cure. It eventually contributed to the development of a vaccine that virtually wiped out the disease in the United States. (That's the reason FDR's image appears on the US ten-cent coin today.)

Though Roosevelt never recovered the ability to stand without braces on his legs, he never lost his optimistic spirit, as the following letter shows:

Warm Springs
[October 1924]
Sunday

Dearest E.
It is just a week since you left, but the time has passed without or realizing it, as the life is just the same day after day and there is no variety to give landmarks. The mornings are as you know wholly taken up with the pool and four of the afternoon we have sat out on the lawn or as Roy calls it the "yard," and I have worked at stamps or cheques or accounts or have played rummy with Missy [LeHand, his new secretary].
. . . The legs are really improving a great deal. The walking and general exercising in the water is fine and I have worked out some

special exercises also. This is really a discovery of a place, and there is no doubt that I've got to do it some more. . . .

Much love, and take care of yourself.

Your devoted

FDR

In the following letter, FDR, who was personally wealthy, complains about the high cost of living in the White House:

THE WHITE HOUSE
Oct. 7, 1942

Memorandum for E.R.

In view of the new income tax law, it will, of course, result in such a cut in the net I receive from the Government that we shall have to take some steps to reduce the White House food bill, to which I pay $2,000 a month, or $24,000 a year. Next year the taxes on $75,000 [the president's salary] *will leave me only about $30,000 net and SOMETHING HAS TO BE DONE! I do not think I can contribute more than $1,500 a month—leaving a total of $18,000 for Mrs. Nesbitt* [the head of the White House kitchen— see below] *for the year.*

The only thing I can think of is to reduce the number of servants whom we feed. Because they have a Civil Service status we should, of course, see that they get employment elsewhere in the Government. We must remember, too, that I am away on an average of about ten days out of each month, not counting the more extended trips like the last, which I take at least once a year. When you are away my entertaining very rarely amounts to more than a dinner party of four or five people.

I do realize that the cost of food has gone up. However, I would suggest that something drastic be done about the size of the portions served.

For instance, for my luncheons I have pleaded—when it is an egg dish—for only one egg apiece, yet four eggs for two people constantly appear. In the same way in the evenings, vegetables and meat keep coming up to the Study when night after night more than half of the dish goes back to the pantry. I know of no instance where anybody has taken a second help—except occasionally when I do—and it would be much better if I did not take a second help anyway.

There is a backstory to this letter. Henrietta Nesbitt, the head of the White House kitchen, commonly known as the cook although she supervised rather than did the actual cooking, was notorious for the terrible meals she concocted. Supposedly, she once served a formal state dinner sweet potato casserole with marshmallows. When the King and Queen of England visited, she made them hot dogs. Creamed dishes were another favorite of hers—but not of the president's.

At the beginning of their life in the White House, FDR put Eleanor in charge of all domestic affairs. She hired Mrs. Nesbitt to supervise the kitchen. Nobody knew why, because Mrs. Nesbitt had no experience as a chef or kitchen manager in any professional venue. Some speculated it was because both women were members of the League of Women Voters in Hyde Park, the Roosevelts' home. Others saw a darker motive: Mrs. Nesbitt was Eleanor's revenge for her husband's infidelity.

Whenever the president announced a preference, Mrs. Nesbitt would ignore it. He made known his dislike for broccoli, but it constantly appeared on his plate. If he asked for coffee, she served iced tea.

Her incompetence wasn't confined to Roosevelt's administration. Mrs. Nesbitt finally met her match in Bess Truman. They locked horns when Bess asked that brussels sprouts not be served, and the next day there they were again. Mrs. Nesbitt explained that the kitchen had a large stock of the offending vegetable, and they had to use it up. Later, the woman's club Bess belonged to asked her to bring a stick of butter to the next meeting. Butter was still scarce from wartime rationing, however, and Mrs. Nesbitt refused the First Lady's request. Bess spoke to Harry, who, as you know if you have read Harry's letters, would do anything for her. So, Mrs. Nesbitt lost her job at last. Somewhere, FDR must have smiled.

Harry S. Truman to
Bess Wallace Truman

In the spring of 1933, nine-year-old Margaret Truman, the only child of Harry and Bess, became ill. A doctor advised them to take her to Mississippi, where the warm gulf air would help her. Harry was serving as a judge (thanks to the support of the local Democratic Party machine) and could not accompany them. He was relieved to receive a letter from Bess reporting that Margaret was improving:

Good Friday night, April 14, 1933

My Dear Bess,

. . . I feel so much better about our daughter that it is almost as if a hundred-pound weight has been lifted from my head. Make her follow sun and diet as she should and by the time I come back down there, she ought to be as big and beautiful as her mamma. The weather has been terrible up here, snowed all day yesterday and rained today. The wind in the north and very cold. Paper says clear tomorrow. Hope you all have a good time and don't worry about anything up here. Everything is all right. I love you and miss you terribly, but if our child gets all right, I can stand it.

Lovingly,

Harry

Harry died in 1972, age eighty-nine. Bess set aside a letter he had written on their thirty-eighth wedding anniversary. Every morning, she would read it before going downstairs for breakfast. It contained a list of the major events in their lives from 1920 to 1938. It was signed, "Your no account partner who loves you more than ever!" Her own death came when she was ninety-seven, in October 1982.

Dwight D. Eisenhower to
Mary "Mamie" Geneva Doud Eisenhower

The first time General Eisenhower's name was publicly linked with Kay Summersby's was early in 1943. *Life* magazine published an article pointing out that the young and pretty member of the British Mechanised Transport Corps had arrived in Algiers to be Eisenhower's personal driver, a position she had previously held at his London headquarters. This article did not escape the attention of Mamie, who wrote to her husband and asked about the implied relationship. Here is Eisenhower's reply:

ALGIERS—Tuesday, March 2, 1943

. . . So Life says my old London driver came down! So she did—but the big reason she wanted to serve in this theater is that she is terribly in love with a young American Colonel and is to be married to him come June—assuming both are alive. I doubt that Life told that. But I tell you only so that if anyone is banal and foolish enough to lift an eyebrow at an old duffer such as I am in connection with Waacs [Women's Auxiliary Army Corps]—Red Cross workers—nurses and drivers—you will know that I've no emotional involvement and will have none. Ordinarily I don't try to think of all the details surrounding my existence when I write to you—they are all unimportant compared to the real things I like to talk to you about. And, by the way, my own driver is a Sergeant Drye!

[The editor of Eisenhower's letters, his son John S. D. Eisenhower, did not include signatures.]

The rumor of a romantic liaison between Eisenhower and Summersby continued after the war. Summersby wrote two memoirs. In the first one, she did not mention any romance between her and Eisenhower.

In the second, written after his death and shortly before her own, she claimed that there was an attachment that led to "stolen kisses" but was never "consummated."

President Truman claimed to his biographer Merle Miller that General George C. Marshall, chief of staff of the US Army during the war, told him that Eisenhower had asked Marshall for permission to divorce Mamie and marry Summersby, but Marshall refused, threatening to run Eisenhower "out of the Army" and prevent him from "ever drawing a peaceful breath." Truman said he personally destroyed the correspondence between the men. Many historians discount this story, pointing out that Truman resented the fact that Eisenhower never invited him to the White House when Eisenhower was president. The historian Robert H. Ferrell reviewed the tapes of Miller's interviews with Truman and found no mention of Summersby.

In addition, letters between Eisenhower and General Marshall were discovered in 1977. They revealed that at war's end, Eisenhower did in fact ask his commander for permission to bring a woman to Europe to join him—but it was his wife, Mamie. Marshall turned down the request, saying it would look like favoritism, since other high-ranking officers were not permitted to bring their wives to their headquarters.

Twenty-seven written messages from Eisenhower to Summersby, allegedly from her estate, were offered for auction in 1991. The text of one reads:

How about lunch, tea & dinner today? If yes: Who else do you want, if any? At which time? How are you?

Compare that to a wartime letter from Eisenhower to his wife:

AMILCAR (TUNISIA), September 8, 1943

Here I am once more—writing in a forward post for news of the development of plans. This is the thing that is making an old man of me! You cannot imagine how much I think of you under

such circumstances, and make up pipe dreams of what we'll do
after the war. Sometimes I think of travel, but then that seems to
involve too much effort. I usually end up in some scene where the
predominant note is laziness, soft climate, and utter contentment.
Often I think of this war as a terrible nightmare, and when I can
finally wake up you and I will be so thankful we'll just sneak
away from everybody and say how lucky we are!
. . . Lots of love my darling—you're always in my thoughts.

After the war Eisenhower was elected the thirty-fourth president of the
United States for two terms. At his first inauguration, after he took the
oath of office, he turned and kissed Mamie. It was the first time any
president had shown such public affection at the ceremony. He and
Mamie didn't "sneak away" until 1961, when they moved to their farm
in Gettysburg, Pennsylvania.

Gerald R. Ford to
Elizabeth Ann Bloomer "Betty" Ford

In 1947, Betty Bloomer's friends set her up on a blind date with Gerald
R. Ford, a World War II veteran and lawyer. She tried to turn down the
date, because she was going through a painful divorce. Finally, Betty
agreed to meet Gerry at a bar. As she recalled, "The next time I looked
at my watch, an hour had passed."

Gerry proposed in February 1948, and though she accepted, they
had to wait until the fall to marry because he was running for a seat
in Congress. Gerry's sister had warned Betty, "With Gerry, you'll never
have to worry about other women. Your cross will be his work."

With Betty taking care of what would eventually be their four children, Gerry's political star rose steadily. He was elected the Republican
minority leader of the House in 1965 and held that position until the
scandals of the Nixon administration resulted in Ford's becoming vice

Gerald and Betty Ford celebrate Ford's victory at the Republican National Convention in 1976, when he defeated Ronald Reagan for the party's presidential nomination. After the election in November, Betty had a less pleasant job—Gerry had lost his voice, so she gave a gracious concession speech declaring Jimmy Carter the victor.

president and then the nation's thirty-eighth president when Nixon resigned. He is the only person ever to become president without being elected either president or vice president.

Soon afterward, Betty was diagnosed with breast cancer. Rather than hide it, she decided to publicly urge other women to have early examinations to discover whether they had the disease. Her action saved the lives of many women who might not otherwise have had themselves examined.

Her husband wrote her this short letter:

Dearest Mom!
   No written words can adequately express our deep, deep love. We know how great you are and we, the children and Dad, will try to be as strong as you.

*Our Faith in you and God will sustain us. Our total love
for you is everlasting. We will be at your side with love for a
wonderful Mom.*
XXXX
Jerry

Betty Ford's treatment for cancer was successful, and she lived for another thirty-seven years. The Ford children have not made any other
examples of their parents' correspondence available.

George H. W. Bush to Barbara Pierce Bush

During the summer of 1988, George H. W. Bush, then vice president,
was expected to receive the Republican nomination for president. His
Democratic opponent (already nominated) was Governor Michael Du-
kakis of Massachusetts. By the beginning of August, Bush was eighteen
points behind in some polls, and was receiving a variety of advice from
people who claimed to know how he could improve his standing. One
suggestion was that he and his wife appear more affectionate, as Du-
kakis and his wife, Kitty, did. Bush attempts to explain this to Barbara.

8-8-88

Sweetie:
Please look at how Mike and Kitty do it.
Try to be closer in, more—well er romantic—on camera.
I am practicing the loving look, and the creeping hand.
Yours for better TV and more demonstrable affection.
Your sweetie-pie coo-coo.
Love 'ya
GB

George won the election and served as the forty-first president.

PART 4

Lovers

Introduction

Some of the letters in this part do not reflect the conventional defini-
tion of extramarital affairs, in that these relationships did not include
sexual relations. But George Washington's decades-long yearning for a
woman who was not his wife seemed to qualify as "extramarital," as did
Thomas Jefferson's passionate fling with Maria Cosway, even though it
occurred after the death of Jefferson's wife.

We also include here the reputed romance between President
James Buchanan and his longtime roommate (and vice president in a
previous administration) William Rufus DeVane King. Buchanan's letter to a woman in whose house King was staying holds some clues that
may or may not be persuasive to you.

If it's sex you're looking for, Warren G. Harding will meet your expectations. Just as presidents such as John F. Kennedy and Lyndon B.
Johnson were widely known to have had many sexual partners (Johnson, ever jealous of his predecessor, was said to have claimed to have
"had more women by accident than Kennedy did on purpose"), Harding was famous for his many affairs from his Ohio hometown to the
nation's capital. Fortunately (for us), his letters to his lover Caroline
"Carrie" Phillips were saved and recently revealed, so we can include a
selection of them here. Harding tried to keep his missives from being
offensively explicit by using code words for such things as body parts.
However, he left a key to the code. When he writes "Jerry," he is refer-
ring to his penis.

Another of Harding's mistresses Nan Britton was more faithful in
following Harding's instructions to burn his letters (according to her,
one of his letters ran to forty pages). She had idolized him from her
girlhood in Marion, Ohio, and had a picture of him, clipped from a
campaign poster, hanging on the wall of her bedroom. After he became
a senator, she wrote to ask him to help her find work, and he met her in

a New York hotel, where they kissed for the first time. She was eighteen. During the next two years, they met for kissing sessions until finally, in another New York hotel, in her words, "I became Mr. Harding's bride— as he called me—on that day."

Their affair continued while Harding was in the White House. Nan wrote of being led to his private office: "There were windows along one side of the room which looked out upon the green of the White House grounds *[where an armed guard walked back and forth, making Harding nervous about "prying eyes"].* . . . Whereupon he introduced me to the one place where, he said, he thought we might share kisses in safety. This was a small closet in the ante-room, evidently a place for hats and coats, but entirely empty most of the times we used it, for we repaired there many times in the course of my visits to the White House, and in the darkness of a space not more than five feet square, the President of the United States and his adoring sweetheart made love."

When Nan became pregnant, Harding provided financial support for her child, but after his death, his wife stopped the payments. Strapped for cash, Nan wrote a book about the affair titled *The President's Daughter,* but a smear campaign led by Harding's relatives convinced people that she was making the story up. However, in 2015, DNA testing proved that her daughter was Harding's child.

What impels men like Harding and others to be unfaithful to their wives? The answer may be simply that they can. But Harding, perhaps surprisingly, had thought about this question and declared it was love. Here is part of what he told Carrie Phillips:

"When a man loves with all his thoughts, loves as he walks, loves in his daily business, loves as he reads, loves at his work and loves at his play, when every song of his lips in some way, intimately or remotely, is associated with the one beloved, he is very much in love, and it must be the real thing. I grant you have reason to think I yield to the sex call. I do. I am ever wanting to kiss and fondle, to embrace and caress, to adore and possess. I can't help it. That is not spiritual, I grant, but very real."

Yet the very last letter in our book suggests otherwise.

George Washington to
Sally Cary Fairfax

As a teenager, George came to live with his older half brother, Lawrence, at Mount Vernon. Lawrence had recently married Anne Fairfax, the sister of George William Fairfax, who lived on a nearby plantation, Belvoir. George Fairfax also had a new bride, Sally Cary. Their home was the scene of frequent parties, to which the Washingtons were invited, along with many other upper-class Virginians who lived in the area.

Young George experienced a dazzling new world. His half brother and most of the other young men had gone to England for a formal education. After George's father died when he was ten, he learned mathematics, including trigonometry, preparing to become a surveyor. He

Lively portrait of Sally Fairfax was painted around the time that George Washington first met her. He sent her a shy letter of affection, which was rebuffed. As an old man, he remembered her fondly, and wrote again, recalling the happy memories he had of her.

had nothing to contribute to the sophisticated conversations at the parties at Belvoir. Noting his shyness, Sally Fairfax, who was two years older than George, took him under her wing. Sally was unusually well-read and lent George books from the extensive library at Belvoir.

Though George was not yet a licensed surveyor, he accompanied the trained men who were hired to survey the land belonging to the Fairfax family. Then, when George was twenty, his half brother died from tuberculosis. This changed George's status in life, because he was named to run the Mount Vernon plantation, and when Lawrence's wife died, he would inherit the property.

Lawrence had been commander of a group of Virginia militia, and the governor of the colony appointed George to take his place. At the time, France and Britain had been fighting over territory farther west, and since Virginia was still a British colony, George's military duties occasionally took him away from home. Sally was on his mind, as the following letter, sent to her from Fort Cumberland in June 1755, shows:

Dear Madam,
   When I had the happiness to see you last you express'd an inclination to be inform'd of my safe arrival in Camp . . . But at the same time [you] *desir'd it might be communicated in a Letter to somebody of your acquaintance.* [In other words, not sent directly to her.] *This I took as a gentle rebuke and a polite manner of forbidding my corresponding with you.* [He is implying that she may think a personal correspondence between a married woman and a single man was improper.] *If I am right in this, I hope you will excuse the present presumption. . . . If, on the contrary, these are fearful apprehensions only, how easy is it to remove my suspicions, enliven my spirits, and make me happier than the day is long, by honouring me with a correspondence which you did once partly promise to do. . . .*
   I am, Madam,
   Yr. most obedt. & most Hble. servt.
   G. Washington

Sally did in fact "honor" George by exchanging letters with him. He hid his true feelings by keeping the correspondence on a formal basis until, in 1758, he became engaged to Martha Custis, a widow with two children. This was indeed a good match for George, because Martha's husband had left her an estate that made her one of the wealthiest people in Virginia. As her new spouse, George would enter the highest rank of society. Apparently, Sally then discreetly broke off her correspondence with George, sending him only a brief note. The following letter was his response:

Camp at Fort Cumberland,
12th Sept, 1758

Dear Madam:

Yesterday I was honour'd with your short but very agreeable favour of the first Inst. How joyfully I catch at the happy occasion of renewing a correspondence which I fear'd was disrelish'd [disliked] *on your part. . . . In silence I now express my Joy. . . .* [He suggests that she must have broken off the correspondence because of his impending marriage to "Mrs. Custis," and continues:] *'Tis true I profess myself a votary to Love. I acknowledge that a Lady is in the case; and further, I confess that this Lady is known to you. Yes, Madam, as well as she is to one who is too sensible of her Charms to deny the Power whose influence he feels and must ever submit to. I feel the force of her amiable beauties in the recollection of a thousand tender passages that I could wish to obliterate . . . but Experience alas! sadly reminds me how impossible this is . . . You have drawn me, my dear Madam, or rather have I drawn myself, into an honest confession of a Simple Fact. Misconstrue not my meaning, 'tis obvious; doubt it not, nor expose it. The world has no business to know the object of my love, declared in this manner to—you, when I want to conceal it. One thing, above all things, in this World I wish to know, and only one person of your acquaintance can solve me that, or guess my meaning—but adieu to this till happier times, if ever I shall see them . . .*

Yr. most obedient
most obliged Hble. Servt.
G. Washington

Evidently Sally was a bit embarrassed by what she perceived as a declaration of love. Since she and George were certain to meet again in the
close-knit society in which they lived, she evidently sent him a letter in
which she pretended not to understand his meaning. This resulted in
the following reply:

> *Camp at Rays Town,*
> *25th Sept'r., 1758*
>
> *Dear Madam,*
> *Do we still misunderstand the true meaning of each other's*
> *Letters? I think it must appear so, tho' I would feign hope the*
> *contrary, as I cannot speak plainer without—but I'll say no more*
> *and leave you to guess the rest.*
> *Your most obedt. and obligd.*
> *G. Washington*

A little more than three months later, George did marry Martha Custis
and became a prominent member of Virginia society. He and Sally continued to be neighbors, but as far as anyone knows, they didn't write any
more letters to each other during those years.

When the colonial independence movement grew in strength,
Sally and her husband, George William Fairfax, departed for England, because he was a loyalist who opposed American independence. George Fairfax died in 1787, bitter at having lost his estate
and lands in America. It must have been particularly irksome to him
that the young man who once danced in his house had led the American army to victory over England. Sally Fairfax never returned to
America but lived on for many years, never mentioning Washington
in her letters. But he had not forgotten her, and in 1798, perhaps
sensing that death was not far away, he wrote her a final letter:

Mt. Vernon
16 May, 1798.

My Dear Madam:

Five and twenty years have nearly passed away since I have considered myself as the permanent resident at this place, or have been in a situation to indulge myself in a familiar intercourse with my friends by letter or otherwise. During this period so many important events have occurred and such changes in men and things have taken place as the compass of a letter would give you but an inadequate idea of. <u>None of which events, however, nor all of them together, have been able to eradicate from my mind the recollection of those happy moments, the happiest in my life, which I have enjoyed in your company.</u> [underlined in the original]

Worn out in a manner by the toils of my past labour, I am again seated under my vine and fig tree . . . and it is a matter of sore regret, when I cast my eyes toward Belvoir [the estate where she once lived], *which I often do, to reflect, the former inhabitants of it with whom we lived in such harmony and friendship no longer reside there and that the ruins can only be viewed as the memento of former pleasures . . .*

Thomas Jefferson to Maria Cosway

Thomas Jefferson's wife, Martha, died in 1782, nineteen years before he became the third president of the United States. On her deathbed, she told her husband that she "could not die happy" if she thought her daughters "were ever to have a stepmother brought in over them." Jefferson destroyed all correspondence between himself and Martha soon after her death. He kept his promise not to marry again—although that did not prevent him from having relations with Sally Hemings, one of his enslaved servants. She was in fact the half sister of Jefferson's wife, Martha; they each had the same father, who was a prosperous planter and slave trader. Sally Hemings had seven children by Jefferson; four of them survived to adulthood. He freed two of them during his lifetime and freed two others in his will. He did not free Sally Hemings.

In 1784, the Congress of Confederation government sent Jefferson to France on a diplomatic mission to negotiate commercial treaties with European countries. In Paris, he met Maria Cosway, seventeen years his junior. She was a talented artist of Anglo-Irish descent. They spent considerable time together, and even though she was married, a romantic relationship developed. As Jefferson explained when writing to her, the letters he sent and received were often opened by the French

Maria Cosway and Thomas Jefferson met in Paris during the summer of 1786. This picture is a print by Francesco Bartolozzi from a miniature painted by Maria's husband, Richard. A copy of the same picture was owned by Jefferson and today hangs in his home, Monticello.

authorities, so he was obliged to send them by private courier. Even so he felt he had to be discreet in what he wrote to her. So, there is no way of knowing how far their romance took them. But his feelings are evident. They carried on their correspondence even after she left Paris and returned to Italy, where she had been born.

> Paris, November 29, 1786
> . . . Heaven has submitted our being to some unkind laws. When those charming moments were present which I passed with you, they were clouded with the prospect that I was soon to lose you and now, when I pass the same moments in review, I recollect nothing but the agreeable passages, and they fill me with regret. Thus, present joys are damped by a consciousness that they are passing from us, and past ones are only the subjects of sorrow and regret. I am determined when you come next not to admit the idea that we are ever to part again. But are you to come again? I dread the answer to this question, and that my poor heart has been duped by the fondness of its wishes. What a triumph for the head! God bless you! May your days be many and filled with sunshine. May your heart blow with warm affections, and all of them be gratified! Write to me often. Write affectionately, and freely, as I do to you. Say many kind things, and say them without reserve. They will be food for my soul. Adieu my dear friend!

In a postscript, he explained that he could not sign the letter because he didn't have access to a messenger and had to send it through the post office and disguise the wax seal he used to close the envelope.

> Paris, December 24, 1786
> . . . I wish they had formed us like the birds of the air, able to fly where we please. I would have exchanged for this many of the boasted preeminencies of man. I was so unlucky when very young as to read the history of Fortunatus. He had a cap of such virtues that when he put it on his head, and wished himself anywhere, he was there. I have been all my life sighing for this cap. Yet if I had

it, I question if I should use it but once. I should wish myself with
you, and not wish myself away again. . . . I am always thinking
of you. If I cannot be with you in reality, I will in imagination.
But you say not a word of coming to Paris. Yet you were to come
in the spring, and here is winter. It is time therefore you should
be making your arrangements, packing your baggage etc. unless
you really mean to disappoint us. If you do, I am determined not
to suppose I am never to see you again. I will believe you intend
to go to America, to draw the Natural bridge, the Peaks of Otter
etc. that I shall meet you there, and visit with you all those grand
scenes. I had rather be deceived, than live without hope. It is so
sweet! It makes us ride so smoothly over the roughnesses of life.
When clambering a mountain, we always hope the hill we are on
is the last. But it is the next, and the next, and still the next.

Think of me much, and warmly. Place me in your breast with
those who you love most and comfort me with your letters. Addio
la mia cara ed amabile amica! ["Goodbye my dear sweet friend!"]
Th. Jefferson

Evidently here Jefferson is replying to a letter from Maria, in which
she complains about not hearing from him.

Paris, July 1, 1787
You conclude, Madam, from my long silence that I am gone to
the other world. Nothing else would have prevented my writing
to you so long. I have not thought of you the less. [He lists the
places in Italy where he has been traveling.] *Imagine to yourself,*
Madam, a castle and village hanging to a cloud in front. On one
hand a mountain cloven through to let pass a gurgling stream;
on the other a river, over which is thrown a magnificent bridge;
the whole formed into a basin, its sides shagged with rocks, olive
trees, vines, herds, etc. I insist on your painting it.

How do you do? How have you done? And when are you
coming here? If not at all, what did you ever come for? Only to
make people miserable at losing you. Consider that you are but 4

days from Paris. [She was in England.] *If you come* [here] *you will
see a new and beautiful country. Come then, my dear Madam,
and we will breakfast every day . . . and forget that are ever to
part again . . . I have the honor to be, dear Madam, your affectionate friend and servant,*
 Th: Jefferson

In the following letter Jefferson refers to a scene from Laurence Sterne's
novel *Tristram Shandy*, in which Maria, a beautiful young woman for-
saken by her lover, sits beneath a tree with her dog on a leash. Later,
Jefferson praises Maria Cosway's painting of dancers titled *The Hours
Crowning Love*, which, he claims, he has seen displayed all over Paris.

Paris, July 27, 1788
 *Hail, dear friend of mine! For I am never so happy as when
business, smoothing her magisterial brow, says, "I give you an
hour to converse with your friends." And with none do I converse
more fondly than with my good Maria: not her under the poplar,
with the dog and string at her girdle but the Maria who makes the
Hours her own, who teaches them to dance for us in so charming
a round, and lets us think of nothing but her who renders them
si gracieuses* [so pleasing]. *Your Hours, my dear friend, are no
longer your own. Everybody now demands them and were it
possible for me to want a memorandum of you, it is presented*
[to] *me in every street in Paris. Come then to see what triumph
time is giving you. Come and see everybody stopping to admire
the Hours, suspended against the walls of the Quai des Augustins,
the Boulevards, the Palais Royal etc. etc. with a "Maria Cosway
delint"* [drawn by Maria Cosway] *at the bottom. But you triumph
everywhere; so, if you come here, it will be, not to see your
triumphs but your friends, and to make them happy with your
presence. Indeed we wish much for you. Society here is become
more gloomy than usual. . . . We are told you are becoming more
recluse. This is a proof the more of your taste. A great deal of
love given to a few, is better than a little to many. . . . I remember*

*that under the hands of your Coeffeuse [hairdresser], you used
to amuse yourself with your pencil. Take then, some of these
days when fancy bites and the Coeffeuse is busy, a little visiting
card and crayon on it something for me. What shall it be? Cupid
leading the lion by a thread? Or Minerva clipping his wings? . . .
Or shall it be something better than all this, a sketch of your own
fancy? So that I have something from your hand, it will satisfy
me, and it will be the better if of your own imagination. I will put
a "Maria Cosway delint." at bottom, and stamp it on my visiting
cards, that our names may be together if our persons cannot.
Adieu, my dear friend, love me much, and love me always.*
   Yours affectionately,
   Th. Jefferson

Jefferson had just received a letter from Maria that began, "Is it possible
that I write another letter before I have an answer from my two last?
What can be the reason?" Here is Jefferson's reply:

Paris, July 30, 1788
   *Cease to chide me. It is hard to have been chained to a writing
table, drudging over business daily from morning to night ever
since my return to Paris. It will be a cruel exaggeration, if I am to
lose my friends into the bargain. The only letter of private friendship I wrote on my return, and before entering on business, was to
you. The first I wrote after getting through my budget was to you.
It had gone off on the morning of the last post, and in the evening
of the same day, yours of the 15th was brought here by I know not
whom, while I was out. I am incapable of forgetting or neglecting
you, dear friend, and I am sure if the comparison could be fairly
made of how much I think of you, or you of me, the former scale
would greatly preponderate. Of this I have no right to complain,
nor do I complain. You esteem me as much as I deserve. If I love
you more, it is because you deserve more. Of voluntary faults
to you I can never be guilty, and you are too good not to pardon
the involuntary. Chide me then no more; be to me what you have*

*been, and give me without measure the comfort of your friend-
ship. Adieu ma tres chere et excellente amie.* [Good-bye, my most
dear and excellent friend.]

Th.J.

Jefferson wrote the following letter just before he left for the United
States. Though they would continue to write letters to each other, the
couple never saw each other again.

Cowes, England

October 14, 1789

*I am here, my dear friend, waiting the arrival of a ship to take
my flight from this side of the Atlantic and as we think last of
those we love most, I profit of the latest moment to bid you a
short but affectionate adieu . . . My daughters are with me and
in good health. We have left a turbulent scene* [the French Revolution had broken out], *and I wish it may be tranquilized on my
return . . . Under present circumstances, aggravated as you will
read them in the English papers, we cannot hope to see you in
France. But a return of quiet and order . . . and the ensuing spring
might give us a meeting at Paris with the first swallow. So be it,
my dear friend, and adieu under the hope which springs naturally
out of what we wish. Once and again then farewell, remember me
and love me.*

James Buchanan to
Cornelia Van Ness Roosevelt

Since forty-six men have held the position of president of the United
States, it seems likely that one of them might have been gay. The con-
sensus of scholars is that among the presidents, that person is probably
James Buchanan, the fifteenth president. Though the proof is not iron-
clad, the argument that he was gay starts with the fact that Buchanan

was the only president who never married. It is true that he was once engaged to be married. His fiancée was Ann Coleman, the daughter of a wealthy steel manufacturer. She and Buchanan met in Lancaster, Pennsylvania, where he had a flourishing law practice. He was twenty-seven and she twenty-three—for a woman of that time a bit old to still be single. They became engaged in 1819, but the press of business affairs caused Buchanan to neglect her. When Ann heard that he had spent some time in a friend's house where there was another unmarried woman, she sent him an angry note breaking the engagement. Not long afterward, she caught a cold and may have taken an overdose of laudanum (as a cold remedy) and died. Buchanan asked her father for permission to attend her funeral but was denied.

Friends and political supporters attributed Buchanan's subsequent bachelorhood to his tragic love affair. In 1820, the year after Ann Coleman's death, he was elected to the US House of Representatives. This was the beginning of a long national political career. Andrew Jackson appointed him ambassador to Russia, and when he returned, he won election to the US Senate. That was in 1834, the year he and a Southern politician, William Rufus DeVane King, began to share quarters in a Washington boardinghouse. They would do so for the next ten years.

Buchanan and King, both lifelong bachelors, began to be seen together at social functions in the capital. People started to link them in other, more cutting ways. President Jackson referred to King as "Miss Nancy." Aaron Brown, a congressman from Tennessee, used similar nicknames for King—"Aunt Nancy" and "Miss Fancy"—and called King Buchanan's "wife" in a letter to Sarah Childress Polk, widow of the former president.

These may be explained merely as gibes employed in the rough-and-tumble of politics. When the two men wrote personal letters to each other, Buchanan cautioned King to burn his, and presumably needed no urging to do the same with King's letters. Except for the one quoted below, the few that survive contain no material that would throw a light on their personal relationship.

But when King's appointment as the American ambassador to France kept them apart for a longer period, Buchanan let his customary guard down. On his way to France, King stopped at the New York home of James Roosevelt, whose wife, Cornelia Van Ness Roosevelt, was a friend of Buchanan's. Buchanan wrote to her:

I envy Colonel King the pleasure of meeting you & would give any thing in reason to be of the party for a single week. I am solitary and alone, having no companion in the house with me. I have gone a wooing to several gentlemen, but have not succeeded with any one of them. I feel that it is not good for man to be alone, and should not be astonished to find myself married to some old maid who can nurse me when I am sick, provide good dinners for me when I am well, & not expect from me any very ardent or romantic affection.

James Buchanan was the only bachelor president. Rumors that he had a sexual relationship with William Rufus DeVane King abounded during his lifetime. Unfortunately nearly all of their correspondence was destroyed, either during the Civil War or by relatives.

From France, King wrote reports to his superior, Buchanan, who was secretary of state. He, too, could not resist a friendly aside, which was preserved because it was part of a business letter.

King wrote, "I am selfish enough to hope you will not be able to procure an associate, who will cause you to feel no regret at our separation. For myself, I shall feel lonely in the midst of Paris, for there I shall have no Friends with whom I can commune as with my own thoughts."

Buchanan's niece served as First Lady when he was in the White House. King, his friend and companion, had been elected vice president in the previous administration when Franklin Pierce became president, but King died within a few weeks of being sworn in.

Buchanan was elected the fifteenth president on the Democratic ticket in 1856. He tried to ward off the South's efforts to secede by following pro-slavery policies, but only failed to reconcile elements of both North and South. Some attributed his unsuccessful administration to his "feminine" traits. *The New York Times*, in an editorial on "Bachelor Presidents," blamed women for being "at the bottom of all great catastrophes . . . *[and]* so universal is the application of this grave truth . . . that we have always suspected some female influence in the aberrations, whims, contradictions, and tergiversations of Mr. Buchanan."

Woodrow Wilson to
Mary Allen Hulbert Peck

On a visit to Bermuda in 1907, fifty-year-old Woodrow Wilson, then president of Princeton University, met forty-five-year-old Mary Allen Hulbert Peck. Her first husband, Thomas Hulbert, had died in 1889. The following year she had married Thomas Dowse Peck, president of a woolen manufacturing company in Pittsfield, Massachusetts. Their marriage was unhappy and would lead to a divorce in 1912. She spent many winters in Bermuda, and her relationship with Wilson (then married to his first wife, Ellen Axson) gradually deepened through the years. The first Mrs. Wilson knew of her husband's close friendship with Mary Peck and sometimes accompanied him when he visited her, and even invited her to the White House after Wilson became president in 1913. However, she is thought to have burned many of the letters Mrs. Peck wrote to her husband and is known to have been disappointed when her husband visited Mrs. Peck without her. Given her devotion to her husband, it would have been surprising if she wasn't unhappy with the Wilson-Peck relationship. Many scholars have concluded, from Wilson's letters such as the ones below, that his relationship with Mary Peck was more than platonic.

Hamilton Hotel, Bermuda
18 February, 1910

Dearest Friend,

Why have you taken such complete possession of Bermuda? I cannot dissociate any part of it from you. I meet some memory of you at every turning, and am lonely wherever I go because you are not there! I fancied that I would presently get over my feeling of being in a place deserted, but I have been here now four days and the feeling has not lost its poignancy in the least. You must really come down to relieve me . . .

I called at Shoreby this afternoon, sat on the back piazza and had tea with them [Mr. and Mrs. Parrish, two mutual friends who owned the villa], *keeping up a gay front and talking like a man to whom his surroundings meant nothing, but beyond measure sad at heart. Mrs. P. sat in your hammock, Mr. P lounged in the long wicker lounge, I sat and thought one thing and said another. It was ghastly. I came away exhausted, and walked back around the harbour like one pursued, haunted. And so my letter ends as it began. This is a land without its presiding spirit. It is a dear, a blessed isle, and I love it; but I am orphaned in it. We talked of you this afternoon, but I changed the subject as quickly as possible. I could not stand it. And yet it was sweet to hear her talk of you with affection. I hope I do not make you sad, too, by this downhearted letter. It is really a way, a very deep and real way, of speaking my affection for an absent friend, whose beauty, charm, companionship, sympathy, quick comprehension, and largesse*

*of affection will always be the chief and most perfect thing that
Bermuda stands for in my thought. I am with her all the time in
thought while I am here. This is her isle, God bless her, and bring
her while she least expects it peace and happiness. I am, with
infinite tenderness,*
  Her devoted friend,
  Woodrow Wilson

The following letter was written just after Wilson received the Democratic Party's nomination for president. He was inundated with mail,
as he says, but still found time to write to Mary Hulbert, who had gotten
a divorce from Thomas Peck, her second husband, and in April 1912
left Bermuda. Afterward she settled in Nantucket, thus achieving the
"freedom" that Wilson refers to.

21 July 1912

My dearest Friend,
  *All week I have turned the hundreds of letters over that came in
by each post in the vain hope of finding a letter from you! I hope,
I hope you are not ill, that you are not blue,—that nothing but
what affects neither your health nor your happiness has prevented
your writing, but I cannot help being anxious. My thoughts turn
constantly to Nantucket, searching for my dear friend,—seeking
some glimpse of what she is doing or thinking. . . . I like to think
of you out there upon Nantucket island! You do not belong in
New England; you never did belong there; but you are not caged
now. You are free. You are like a splendid flower, native of
rich woods or the breezy mountain side. Transplanted to those
sands, to dominate them with a new note of life and colour. Or,
rather,—you are not like anything inanimate and rooted to the
spot,—you are like some free creature, some child of beauty and
free force, who might have been born in Greece or in Scandinavia,
or in the free West, where there are no types but untrammeled
people . . . . You are no longer in a cage. You can turn back to
where you left off when you were thrust in the cage, and can*

recover all the unspoiled elements that have been suppressed in you, or have asserted themselves only now and again because irrepressible or in rebellion. While I have reversed your story, I am now in a cage,—of a very different sort and yet a cage. . . . I try to discipline my spirit to it, but often I find myself beating my very head against the walls in a sort of despair. I love my freedom. It is the breath of life to me. Now that I have lost it and you have found it, do you not see that I must depend upon you to supply me with air for my lungs? . . . You must let me feel through you the fresh, untainted breath of the sea, which is shut off from me by the crowds on the lawn . . . Am I talking nonsense or poetry or—what? I am trying to release what is in my mind about you— and cannot find the words. I am trying to let you see what you really embody in my thoughts—a noble, sweet, free, unspoiled, inspiriting womanhood, for which nature found a fit form and a fit instrument of utterance. . . .

Your devoted friend
Woodrow Wilson

When Theodore Roosevelt ran against Wilson in the presidential election of 1916, an aide showed Roosevelt some letters that indicated Wilson was having an affair with Mrs. Peck. Roosevelt nixed making the letters public, saying no one could believe Wilson "cast so perfectly as the apothecary's clerk, could ever play Romeo."

After Ellen's death, Wilson married Edith Bolling Galt. She put a stop to his correspondence and meetings with Mary Peck.

Warren G. Harding to Carrie Phillips

Warren G. Harding was the twenty-ninth president of the United States, serving from 1921 until his death in 1923. Although Harding had married in 1891, when he was twenty-five, he didn't let it stop his continual philandering, both before and during his time in the White House.

(His father supposedly said, "It's a good thing Warren wasn't a girl. He'd be in the family way all the time.") Before his political career, he was the owner and editor of the Marion, Ohio, newspaper and had many opportunities to meet people. Among his friends and neighbors were James and Carrie Phillips. During the summer of 1905, Harding began an affair with Carrie, when James was recuperating from a nervous breakdown and Harding's wife, Florence (known as the Duchess for her haughty bearing), was suffering from a kidney ailment that would never be fully cured.

Fortunately for us, Warren was in the habit of writing letters to his lover, many of which were quite explicit in their descriptions of her

Carrie Phillips began an affair with Warren Harding while they were neighbors in Marion, Ohio. Warren's letters to Carrie are the most sexually explicit of any presidential love letters. She later used them to blackmail him.

charms. He requested that she destroy them, but she and her husband later used them to blackmail Harding when he was running for president in 1920.

Harding's letters to Carrie were hidden for many years until recently when they were made public by the Library of Congress. Today, more than a century after they were written, we can read Harding's lovestricken words—even when he indulges in verse to glorify his beloved.

[Jan. 28, 1912]

I love your poise
Of perfect thighs
When they hold me
in paradise. . . .
I love the rose
Your garden grows
Love seashell pink
That over it glows
I love to suck
Your breath away
I love to cling—
There long to stay . . .
I love you garb'd
But naked more
Love your beauty
To thus adore . . .
I love you when
You open eyes
And mouth and arms
And cradling thighs . . .
If I had you today, I'd kiss and
fondle you into my arms and
hold you there until you said,
'Warren, oh, Warren,' in a
benediction of blissful joy.

In the fall of 1911, Carrie Phillips visited Germany with her daughter. On her return, she spent New Year's Eve in Montreal with Harding. They apparently rang in the New Year by having sex at midnight, an experience so pleasurable that Harding often referred to it in his letters.

[Jan. 2, 1913]

I stopped play to have sandwiches and crack a bottle of wine, so I could dwell with my thoughts. You can guess where they centered—on the New Year's beginning a year before, when the bell rang the chorus while our hearts sang the rapture without words and we greeted the New Year from the hallowed heights of heaven. . . . When I got home I was too tired to sleep, but I rested, and you were summoned in finally. And you came—a vision vividly plain, a goddess in human form—and a perfect form— clad only in flowing hair, and you were joyously received, and Jerry came and insisted on staying while we all retrospected in the happiness of a Sunday in Richmond.
    Warren

When Harding mentions "Jerry," as in the preceding letter, and the following one, he is using a code word for his penis. Carrie's sex organ was dubbed "Mrs. Pouterson." The full code occupies several pages of notes.

[Sept. 15, 1913]

Honestly, I hurt with the insatiate longing, until I feel that there will never be any relief until I take a long, deep, wild draught on your lips and then bury my face on your pillowing breasts. Oh, Carrie! I want the solace you only can give. It is awful to hunger so and be so wholly denied. . . . Wouldn't you like to hear me ask if we only dared and answer, "We dare," while souls rejoicing sang the sweetest of choruses in the music room? Wouldn't you like to get sopping wet out on Superior—not the lake—for the joy of

fevered fondling and melting kisses? Wouldn't you like to make the
suspected occupant of the next room jealous of the joys he could
not know, as we did in morning communion at Richmond? . . .

Oh, Carrie mine! You can see I have yielded and written myself
into wild desire. I could beg. And Jerry came and will not go, says
he loves you, that you are the only, only love worthwhile in all this
world, and I must tell you so and a score or more of other fond
things he suggests, but I spare you. You must not be annoyed. He
is so utterly devoted that he only exists to give you all. I fear you
would find a fierce enthusiast today.

Warren

When Warren G. Harding died unexpectedly in San Francisco in 1923,
he was so popular with the American public that people lined up along
the tracks to see the railroad car carrying his body back to Washington.
Only later did the corrupt activities carried out by officials in his administration come to light, causing later historians to rate him one of the
lesser presidents.

Many of the letters Harding wrote to Carrie Phillips indicate that
he was a man who continually had sex on his mind. But occasionally he
wrote a letter like the following that indicated he was more complex
than that. The complete letter occupies twelve sheets of paper and was
written over four days.

[Sept. 21–24, 1913]

My Dear Carrie:
. . . There, I have replied to your note and answered every
suggestion therein, save one, which I reserved for the last. You
wonder about genuine love, and say it doesn't require propinquity
to keep it aflame. Perhaps not, but you will agree some day that
propinquity will work wonders. I am not sure whether you were
questioning the genuineness of my love or not. Of course I may
be mistaken about it myself, but if I am fooled, no man ever truly
loved. I have studied it a lot and scrutinized myself. If it isn't love,
it is an alarming case of permanent infatuation. When a man can

*think of no one else, worship nothing else and craves nothing else
than the one woman he adores, though he hasn't seen her in nine
or ten months, and she is four thousand miles away and can't
possibly be possessed, it seems more than infatuation. I often wish
it were less. I am so obsessed, but a mature reflection convinces
me that it is really big to know such a love, and then I am content.
When a man loves with all his thoughts, loves as he walks, loves
in his daily business, loves as he reads, loves at his work and loves
at his play, when every song of his lips in some way, intimately or
remotely, is associated with the one beloved, he is very much in
love, and it must be the real thing. I grant you have reason to think
I yield to the sex call. I do. I am ever wanting to kiss and fondle,
to embrace and caress, to adore and possess. I can't help it. That
is not spiritual, I grant, but very real. It may be only a symptom of
the greater love, or it may be a factor in the greater love's awak-
ening. I do not know. But this I do know, my greater admiration,
adoration, and worship has been inseparable from this experience. And it all endures . . .*

I send you my love, all yours, all the time, always
J.J.A.

[We haven't been able to decipher the meaning of these three
initials he used to close this letter, but they were underlined three
times. A curator at the Library of Congress suggested that one of
the Js might stand for the Jerry in Harding's private code.]

Harding's ardor for Carrie did not dim even after she began to blackmail him, as the following letter from Harding shows. Her threat to
expose him was made more powerful by the fact that she knew Harding
was preparing to run for president that same year.

Feb. 2, 1920

*Your proposal to destroy me, and yourself in doing so, will only
add to the ill we have already done. It doesn't seem like you to*

think of such a fatal course. I can't believe your purpose is to destroy me for paying the tribute so freely uttered and so often shown. . . .

Now to specific things. I can't secure you the larger competence [blackmail payment] *you have frequently mentioned. No use to talk about it. I can pay with life or reputation, but I can't command such a sum! To avoid disgrace in the public eye, to escape ruin in the eyes of those who have trusted me in public life—here I have never betrayed—will, if you demand it as the price, retire at the end of my term and never come back to* [Marion, Ohio] *to reside. . . . I'll pay this price to save my own disgrace and your own self-destruction to destroy me. That is one proposal, complete, final, and covers all.*

Here is another. If you think I can be more helpful by having a public position and influence, probably a situation to do some things worthwhile for myself and you and yours, I will pay you $5,000 per year, in March each year, so long as I am in that public service. It is not big, but it will add to your comfort and make you independent to a reasonable degree. It is most within my capacity. I wish it might be more, but we can only do that which is in his power. Destroy me, and I have no capacity, while the object of your dislike is capable of going on in her own account. . . .

Don't make me fool the public or my friends. If I must quit to pay the penalty, let me start at once on the plans which make it the least difficult. I can't just quit and be a yellow quitter, but I can plan and work it out in a fairly seemly way, so that no one knows but ourselves. Can't you send me a night letter, @ 143 Senate Offices. No fast telegram. In a night letter you can say: "We are writing. Go ahead with program with our best wishes. Think it will be fine." I'll construe that to mean go ahead, and do the best I can.

Warren

Harding was reaching the end of his six-year term as US Senator from Ohio and faced the loss of his seat if the letters were made public. However, his wife, Florence, known as the Duchess, decided to push his candidacy for president. It was well-known that the Duchess's ambitions were far greater than her husband's. A political cartoon, drawn after he became president, showed the couple with the caption "The President and Mr. Harding."

Fortunately for the Duchess, the Republican nominating convention of 1920 was deadlocked among three other candidates. The leaders of the party met in a suite in Chicago's Blackstone Hotel to hammer out a deal. This became known as the "smoke-filled room" where Harding's candidacy was decided on. Only after the delegates made Harding their choice did the party bigwigs find out about the letters that Carrie Phillips had. It was too late to withdraw the nomination, so the Republican Party and Harding's wealthy friend Ned McLean, owner of the *Washington Post*, paid Carrie $25,000 and a monthly stipend of $2,000 for her and her husband (who was perfectly happy to profit from his wife's infidelity) to go on a round-the-world trip until the presidential campaign was over. That fall Harding was elected the twenty-ninth president of the United States.

Franklin Delano Roosevelt to Lucy Mercer Rutherfurd

After Eleanor discovered her husband's love affair with Lucy Mercer, he promised he would never again see or communicate with Lucy. But he did not keep his word. They wrote each other letters even after she married Winthrop Rutherfurd. FDR sent her invitations to his inaugural ceremonies as president. And later, when she visited her sister in Washington, DC, a limousine would take her to the White House, and an usher would escort her to the president's private quarters, where they were left undisturbed until she was ready to leave. Lucy's niece recalled these comings and goings and was told not to tell anyone about them.

Operators at the White House switchboard were told to put through to the president any calls from a Mrs. Paul Johnson—later revealed by

Secret Service agents to be a code name for Lucy Mercer. Even the Roosevelts' daughter, Anna, was a conspirator to the ongoing romance. When Eleanor was away, Franklin asked Anna to arrange intimate dinners for him and Lucy in the White House.

Lucy once wrote Roosevelt a letter in which she fantasized about living together in "a small house" where one could grow vegetables and flowers. "I know one should be proud, very proud of your greatness instead of wishing for the soft life, of joy—and the world shut out." But she recognized that fate had taken them down different paths, and that "the fate of all that is good" was in his "capable hands."

Recently, the FDR Presidential Library in Hyde Park, New York, acquired four letters that Roosevelt wrote to Lucy in the 1920s. They don't show a romantic relationship, but they do show that Roosevelt broke his promise to his wife. In the letter below, he enthusiastically describes his latest attempt to "cure" himself of the paralysis that afflicted him ever since he contracted polio (also known as infantile paralysis) in 1921.

[Stationery: Franklin D. Roosevelt, Hyde Park, Dutchess County, New York]

May 22nd [1926]

Dear Lucy

I think you may be interested to know of my latest venture—I have bought Georgia Warm Springs, on the "installment plan"! and am busily engaged in its development—The chief feature is of course the spring itself which I am convinced has great possibilities for the treatment of infantile paralysis—They have never had any doctor there in the past, & now the orthopedic association will supervise an experimental period there this summer with about thirty patients—If the report is favorable we shall get facilities and take care of a lot more cases—and as there now are over 100,000 children & others who need treatment it might do much good.

My own legs continued to [improve?] *there this year and on June 16 I go to Marion Mass* [a coastal town in Massachusetts

Lucy Mercer is shown here at the time of her romance with Franklin D. Roosevelt, when he was assistant secretary of the navy. She was with him in Warm Springs when he died, having commissioned an artist to paint his portrait.

where a doctor had convinced Roosevelt that swimming would help strengthen his legs] *to take further exercise, though I will be back in N.Y. once or twice to go to the office. Between now and the 16th I am in N.Y. trying to catch up for lost time. . . .*

I suppose you are back at Allamuchy [the Rutherfurds' New Jersey estate] *for the summer.*

Very sincerely yours
Franklin D. Roosevelt

P.S. A very belated "Many many happy returns of the day." [Her birthday was April 26.]

Even though Franklin and Lucy's relationship had to be largely clandestine, it continued even after she married a wealthy man and had a child with him. It survived throughout Roosevelt's lifetime. On the day he died, he was in a cottage at his beloved Palm Springs, and Lucy was there, too. She had brought an artist who was working on a portrait of Roosevelt. When FDR collapsed from a stroke and it was evident that he would die, she and her companions had to leave hurriedly to avoid reporters who would soon appear—followed by Eleanor.

John F. Kennedy to Mary Pinchot Meyer

John F. Kennedy had many lovers, even after he became the thirty-fifth president of the United States in 1961. One of his most serious love affairs was with Mary Pinchot Meyer, an artist and the former wife of a top CIA official. Many people in Washington were aware of the dalliance, and the rumor that Mary kept a diary of her affair with Kennedy was worrisome to supporters of the president—and not just because he was unfaithful to his wife. Among other things, Mary is said to have persuaded him to try LSD with her. In October 1964, a year after Kennedy's assassination, Mary was killed while out jogging—a murder that remains unsolved. That same day, Kennedy's friend Benjamin Bradlee of the *Washington Post* (who was married to Mary's sister) and James Angleton of the CIA arrived separately at Mary's house. One of them is said to have found and stolen her diary, presumably to destroy it.

The following handwritten note by Kennedy to Mary was found in the files of his secretary Evelyn Lincoln after her death. It apparently was never sent.

Why don't you leave suburbia for once—come and see me— either here—or at the Cape next week or in Boston the 19th. I know it is unwise, irrational, and that you may hate it—on the other hand, you may not—and I will love it. You say that it is good for me not to get what I want. After all of these years—you should give me a more loving answer than that. Why don't you just say yes.

Acknowledgments

Our sincere thanks to Susan Eisenhower, for giving us permission to publish excerpts from her grandfather's letters.

Chris Banks, LBJ Presidential Library
Michal Becker, Shapell Manuscript Foundation
Katie Blizzard, University of Virginia Washington Project
Paul Carnahan, Vermont Historical Society
Scot Danforth, University of Tennessee Press
Stacy Davis, Gerald R. Ford Presidential Library
Hannah Elder, Massachusetts Historical Society
Allen Fisher, Personal Papers of Lyndon and Lady Bird Johnson
Andrew M. Foster, Virginia Museum of History and Culture
Sarah Galligan, New Hampshire Historical Society
Mark Holland and Judy Pocock, McKinley Presidential Library
Kate Holt, James K. Polk Memorial Association
Michael F. Holt, University of Virginia
Kathryn Johns-Masten, Penfield Library, State University of
    New York, Oswego
Brittany Knopf, Indiana State Library
Wendy Korwin, Ohio History Connection
Meghan Lee-Parker, Richard Nixon Presidential Library and Museum
Abigail Malangone, John F. Kennedy Presidential Library
Mary Kathryn Pastore Cryan, Wells College
Kristine Priddy, Southern Illinois University Press
Tiffany Raymond, Library Director, Louis Jefferson Long Library,
    Frances Folsom Cleveland Collection, Wells College
Dr. Ryan Semmes, Mississippi State University Library
Ann Sindelar, Western Reserve Historical Society
Cynthia Van Ness, Buffalo History Museum

Zachary Vickery, State University of New York at Oswego College
    Archives
Nadine Zimmerli, University of Virginia Press
Ryan Brubacher, Library of Congress Manuscript Division
Loretta Deaver, Library of Congress Manuscript Division
Patrick Kerwin, Library of Congress Manuscript Division
Bruce Kirby, Library of Congress Manuscript Division
Lara Szypszak, Library of Congress Manuscript Division
Kirsten Strigel Carter, Franklin Delano Roosevelt Library, Hyde Park
Patrick Fahy, Franklin Delano Roosevelt Library, Hyde Park
Mathew Hanson, Franklin Delano Roosevelt Library, Hyde Park
Sarah L. Navins, Franklin Delano Roosevelt Library, Hyde Park
Insaf M. Ali, and all the other members of the helpful staff at the
    Butler Library of Columbia University
The University Seminars of Columbia University
Our friend, Ed Stroligo, for his consistent technical help
Our daughter, Dr. Ellen Hoobler, without whose assistance we could
    not have completed this book, and Mandar, for supporting her
Our editor, Mindy Marqués, who liked what we were trying to do and
    helped us do it
Alyssa diPierro, Hana Park, and Brianna Scharfenberg at Simon &
    Schuster, for all their help
Our glorious agent, Eric Myers, without whom this book would never
    have been published
And heartfelt thanks to our friends and colleagues, too many to name
    here, whose suggestions and support have enriched this book.

Notes

INTRODUCTION

1 *"Do you think you can stand . . ."*: Arthur S. Link, ed., *The Papers of Woodrow Wilson*, vol. 8, *1892–1894* (Princeton: Princeton University Press, 1970), 459–60.

2 *"I have nothing to do with . . ."*: Betty Boyd Caroli, *First Ladies, From Martha Washington to Michelle Obama* (New York: Oxford University Press, 2010), 24.

2 *"a great deal of spice . . ."*: Betty Boyd Caroli, *First Ladies* (New York: Oxford University Press, 1987), 59

2 *"You can never appreciate . . ."*: Robert H. Ferrell, ed., *Dear Bess: The Letters from Harry to Bess Truman, 1910–1959* (New York: W. W. Norton, 1983), 523–24. Courtesy Harry S. Truman Library.

PART 1: ROMANCING

10 "As I am within a few Minutes . . .": "From George Washington to Martha Washington, 23 June 1775," *Founders Online*, National Archives, https://founders.archives.gov/documents/Washington/03-01-02-0013.

10 *"loved her husband madly"*: "Lafayette to Adrienne de Noailles de Lafayette, January 6, 1778," in Stanley J. Idzerda, ed., *Lafayette in the Age of the American Revolution* (Ithaca, NY: Cornell University Press, 1977), 1:225.

11 Octr. 4th, 1762: Margaret A. Hogan and C. James Taylor, eds., *My Dearest Friend: Letters of Abigail and John Adams* (Cambridge, MA: Belknap Press of Harvard University Press, 2007), 4.

12 Boston May 7th 1764, and Abigail's reply: Ibid., 18–20.

15 "To begin, he thinks so much . . .": David B. Mattern and Holly C. Shulman, eds., *The Selected Letters of Dolley Payne Madison* (Charlottesville: University of Virginia Press, 2003), 27–28.

15 Aug 18, 1794: Ibid., 28.

15 *"to tell you in short . . ."*: Ibid., 31.

16 "Mr. and Mrs. Madison would . . .": Quoted in Elizabeth Dowling Taylor, *A Slave in the White House* (New York: Palgrave Macmillan, 2012), 122.

17 June 2, 1796: The Adams Papers, 1639–1889 (Boston: Massachusetts Historical Society, 1954–1959), reel 381.

18–19 "*. . . you are I think . . .*" and "The Hague, April 13": The Adams Papers
        Digital Edition, ed. Sara Martin (Charlottesville: University of Virginia
        Press, Rotunda, 2008–2022).

20   May 12, 1797, and "Why my beloved": Adams Family Correspondence,
        vol. 12, March 1797–April 1798.

21   "*lustrous black eyes*": H. W. Brands, *Andrew Jackson: His Life and Times* (New
        York: Doubleday, 2005), 57.

22   May 9 1796: Sam B. Smith and Harriet Chappell Owsley, eds., *The Papers
        of Andrew Jackson*, vol. 1 (Knoxville: University of Tennessee Press, 1980),
        92–93.

23   December 5th 1812: Laura C. Holloway, *The Ladies of the White House*
        (Philadelphia: Bradley, Garretson, & Co., 1881), 369–72.

26   April 1, 1838: Roy P. Basler, ed., *The Collected Works of Abraham Lincoln*,
        vol. 1 (New Brunswick, NJ: Rutgers University Press, 1953), 117–19.

28   May 7, 1837: Ibid., 78–79.

30   Herndon's note to Jesse Weik: Douglas L. Wilson, "Keeping Lincoln's Se-
        crets," Part 2, *Atlantic Monthly* 285:5 (May 2000), 78–88.

30–1 Lincoln's answer to Speed: Daniel Mark Epstein, *The Lincolns: Portrait of a
        Marriage* (New York: Ballantine Books, 2008), 51.

31   June 4th, 1844: John T. Simon, ed., *The Papers of Ulysses S. Grant*, vol. 1,
        1837–1861 (Carbondale: Southern Illinois Press, 1967), 26.

32   August 31st 1844: Ibid., 35–36.

33   Sept. 14th 1845: Ibid., 53–55.

33   "*There is no date . . .*": *Ulysses S. Grant: Memoirs and Selected Letters* (New York:
        Library of America, 1990), 900–902.

35   Opening section for Rutherford B. Hayes: Charles Richard Williams, ed.,
        Diary and Letters of Rutherford Birchard Hayes, vol. 1, *1834–1860* (Columbus:
        Ohio State Archeological and Historical Society: 1922), 367–71.

36   June 22, 1851: Ibid., 379.

37   August 4, 1851: Ibid., 380.

39   February 27, 1853: Ibid., 444.

41   Nov. 16, 1854: John Shaw, ed., *Crete and James* (East Lansing: Michigan
        State University Press, 1984), 35–37.

43   December 13, 1885: Shapell Manuscript Foundation.

44   May 23, 1886: Shapell Manuscript Foundation.

47   August 15, 1880: Theodore Roosevelt Collection, Harvard College Li-
        brary; Theodore Roosevelt Digital Library, Dickinson State University.

48   October 17, 1880: Ibid.

49   November 5, 1881: Ibid.

52   April 19th, 1882: Library of Congress, William H. Taft Papers, series 2.

52   May 15th, 1883: Ibid.

52 November 3rd [1883?]: Ibid.

53 Feb. 19th, 1884: Ibid.

54 March 12, 1884: Ibid.

55 May 10th–June 20th, 1885: Library of Congress, William H. Taft Papers, series 2, no. 25.

56 May 31, 1885: Arthur S. Link, ed., *The Papers of Woodrow Wilson*, vol. 4, *1885* (Princeton, NJ: Princeton University Press, 1968), 676.

59 20 July, 1915: Arthur S. Link, ed., *The Papers of Woodrow Wilson*, vol. 33, *1915* (Princeton, NJ: Princeton University Press, 1980), 539–41.

62 4 Oct., 1915: Arthur S. Link, ed., *The Papers of Woodrow Wilson*, vol. 35, *1915–1916* (Princeton, NJ: Princeton University Press, 1980), 21–22.

65 [2-10-1905]: Vermont Historical Society, Coolidge Family Papers, 1802–1932, doc 392.7.

66 [2-14-1905]: Ibid.

66 [2-27-1905]: Ibid.

68 December 31, 1910: Robert H. Ferrell, ed., *Dear Bess: The Letters from Harry to Bess Truman, 1910–1959* (New York: W. W. Norton, 1983), 18. Courtesy Harry S. Truman Library.

69 April 12, 1911: Ibid., 27. Courtesy Harry S. Truman Library.

70 June 22, 1911: Ibid., 39. Courtesy Harry S. Truman Library.

71 July 12, 1911: Ibid., 40–41. Courtesy Harry S. Truman Library.

72 July 21, 1913: Ibid., 130. Courtesy Harry S. Truman Library.

72 November 4, 1913: Ibid., 141. Courtesy Harry S. Truman Library.

73 "Wish you were here, Jack": Thomas C. Reeves, *A Question of Character: A Life of John F. Kennedy* (New York: The Free Press, 1991), 113.

73 "he closed the door, firmly": Carl Anthony Sferrazza, *First Ladies: The Saga of the Presidents' Wives and Their Power, 1789–1961* (New York: William Morrow, 1990), 52.

74 "She hung onto him": Gil Troy, *Mr. and Mrs. President: From the Trumans to the Clintons*, 2nd ed. (Lawrence: University Press of Kansas, 1997), 128.

76 *[9/23/1934]*: Personal Papers of Lyndon and Lady Bird Johnson/LBJ Library.

77 *[9/26/1934]*: Personal Papers of Lyndon and Lady Bird Johnson/LBJ Library.

78 "he made sure . . .": Robert Caro, *Path to Power* (New York: Knopf, 1982), 302.

79 "You have to understand . . .": Paul F. Boller Jr., *Presidential Wives* (New York: Oxford University Press, 1988), 391–92.

80 "love at first sight . . . so much fun": Richard Nixon Foundation.

80 *[no date: Possibly March 16, 1938]*: Richard Nixon Foundation.

81 *[no date]* . . . "Dearest Heart": Richard Nixon Foundation.

81 *[no date]* . . . "Wednesday afternoon": Richard Nixon Foundation.

82 *"was going places . . . "*: *New York Times*, September 13, 1970.

82 *"You, darling"*: Anne Briscoe Pye and Nancy Shea, *The Navy Wife*, rev. ed. (New York: Harper and Brothers, 1945), 3–4.

84 "Rosalynn" (poem): Jimmy Carter, *Always a Reckoning and Other Poems* (New York: Crown, 1994).

85 [June 8, 1979]: George H. W. Bush, *All the Best, George Bush: My Life in Letters and Other Writings* (New York: Scribner, 2013), 280.

85 *"And so it was that Barack became a phone guy"*: Michelle Obama, *Becoming* (New York: Crown, 2018), 119.

86 "You're not only my wife . . .": Jason Choe and Grace Panetta, http://www.businessinsider.in, February 14, 2019.

PART 2: SEPARATION

92 *"I am now set down to . . ."*: "From George Washington to Martha Washington, 18 June 1775," *Founders Online*, National Archives, https://founders.archives.gov/documents/Washington/03-01-02-0003.

94 Sep. 30, 1764: Margaret A. Hogan and C. James Taylor, eds., *My Dearest Friend: Letters of Abigail and John Adams* (Cambridge, MA: Belknap Press of Harvard University Press, 2007), 22–24.

96 Decr. 2 1781: Ibid., 252–54.

98 July 26 1784: Ibid., 308–9.

98 "You will chide me . . .": L. H. Butterfield, Marc Friedlander and Mary Jo Klein, eds., *The Book of Abigail and John: Selected Letters of the Adams Family, 1762–1784* (Cambridge, MA: Harvard University Press, 1975), 397.

99 "To the memory of Martha Jefferson . . .": Founders Online, Epitaph for Martha Wayles Jefferson.

99 December 2d, 1799: David B. Mattern and Holly C. Shulman, eds., *The Selected Letters of Dolley Payne Madison* (Charlottesville: University of Virginia Press, 2003), 34–35.

101 "I arriv'd here this evening . . .": Harry Ammon, *James Monroe: The Quest for National Identity* (New York: McGraw-Hill, 1977), 64–65. April 13, 1787. Monroe Foundation, Fredericksburg, Virginia.

103 *"Do not, my beloved husband*. . .": Paul F. Boller Jr., *Presidential Wives* (New York: Oxford University Press, 1988), 69.

103 January 8, 1813: Harold D. Moser and Sharon MacPherson, eds., *The Papers of Andrew Jackson*, vol. 2, *1804–1813* (Knoxville: University of Tennessee Press, 1984), 353–55.

104–5 Rachel Jackson's letter and Andrew's reply: Harold D. Moser, David R. Hoth, Sharon MacPherson, and John H. Reinbold, eds., *The Papers of An-*

drew Jackson, vol. 3, *1814–1815* (Knoxville: University of Tennessee Press, 1991), 28–29, 34–35.

107 *"I wish that my husband's friends . . ."*: Carl Anthony Sferrazza, *First Ladies: The Saga of the Presidents' Wives and Their Power, 1789–1961* (New York: William Morrow, 1990), 120.

107 April 15th 1820: Library of Congress.

108 *"What lady should I choose?"*: *Tennessee Historical Quarterly* 11 (June 1952), 180.

109 June 9th 1843: Wayne Cutler, ed., *Correspondence of James K. Polk*, vol. 7, *1842–1843* (Nashville: Vanderbilt University Press, 1983), 315–16.

111 *"I love you, Sarah . . ."*: Chris Raymond, "Famous Last Words of U.S. Presidents," VeryWell Health, October 22, 2020.

112 May 22, 1847: Ray Franklin Nichols, *Franklin Pierce: Young Hickory of the Granite Hills* (Philadelphia: University of Pennsylvania Press, 1931), 149–50.

112 August 26, 1847: Library of Congress Manuscript Division, Franklin Pierce Papers, General Correspondence 1838–1868; 1838–1853; images 229–31.

115 June 12, 1848: Roy P. Basler, ed., *The Collected Works of Abraham Lincoln*, vol. 1 (New Brunswick, NJ: Rutgers University Press, 1963), 477–78.

115 *"How much I wish . . ."*: Jean H. Baker, "Mary Ann Todd Lincoln," in *American First Ladies*, ed. Lewis L. Gould (New York: Garland Publishing, 1996), 178.

117 March 27th 1863: LeRoy P. Graf and Ralph W. Haskins, eds., *The Papers of Andrew Johnson*, vol. 6 (Knoxville: University of Tennessee Press, 1983), 195–97.

119 March 3d 1846: John T. Simon, ed., *The Papers of Ulysses S. Grant*, vol. 1, *1837–1861* (Carbondale: Southern Illinois Press, 1967), 74–76.

120 May 11th 1846: Ibid., 84–87.

121 Oct. 3d 1846: *Ulysses S. Grant: Memoirs and Selected Letters* (New York: Library of America, 1990), 918–20.

123 July 13th 1853: John T. Simon, ed., *The Papers of Ulysses S. Grant*, vol. 1, *1837–1861* (Carbondale: Southern Illinois Press, 1967), 305–7.

124 June 10, 1861: Charles Richard Williams, ed., *Diary and Letters of Rutherford Birchard Hayes*, vol. 2, *1861–1865* (Columbus: The Ohio State Archeological and Historical Society, 1922), 23–24.

125 September 19, Thursday a.m. [1861]: Ibid., 95–97.

125 November 5, 1861: Ibid., 138–39.

126 September 4 [1864]: Ibid., 502–3.

127 March 12, 1865: Ibid., 566–67.

128 April 19, 1865: Ibid., 578–79.

129 30 August, 1867: Library of Congress, Chester A. Arthur Papers, series 1, General Correspondence and Related Manuscripts, 1843–1938, 70–77.

133 December 24, 1862: Library of Congress, Harrison MSS, vol. 4.

133 "I almost envy . . .": Library of Congress, Harrison MSS, vol. 4.

134 June 18th 1864: Library of Congress, Harrison MSS, vol. 5.

135 August 20, 1864: Library of Congress, Harrison MSS, vol. 5.

136 "Imagine my whispering . . .": Harry J. Sievers, *Benjamin Harrison, Hoosier Warrior, 1833–1865* (Chicago: Henry Regnery, 1952), 296.

137 "I received your precious letter . . .": McKinley Presidential Library & Museum, Canton, Ohio.

138 "My Precious Wife . . .": Ibid.

139 September 23rd, 1883: Theodore Roosevelt Collection, Harvard College Library, Digital Library, Dickinson State University.

141 Nov. 12th 1909: Ibid.

143 September 10, 1893: Arthur S. Link, ed., *The Papers of Woodrow Wilson*, vol. 8, *1892–1894* (Princeton, NJ: Princeton University Press, 1970), 365–66.

144 6 February, 1894: Ibid.

146 March 23 *[1919]*: Ohio Historical Society, Archives and Manuscripts Division, Warren G. Harding Papers, roll no. 242.

150 June 12, 1908: Elliott Roosevelt, ed., *F.D.R. His Personal Letters*, vol. 2, *1905–1928* (New York: Duell, Sloan and Pearce, 1948), 141–42.

151 July 1, 1911: Ibid., 163–64.

152 August 10, 1914: Ibid., 249–50.

154 July 14, 1917: Robert H. Ferrell, ed., *Dear Bess: The Letters from Harry to Bess Truman, 1910–1959* (New York: W. W. Norton, 1983), 225. Courtesy Harry S. Truman Library.

156 February 18, 1919: Ibid., 296. Courtesy Harry S. Truman Library.

157 June 28, *[1936]*: Ibid., 389–90. Courtesy Harry S. Truman Library.

159 August 18, 1944: Ibid., 509–10. Courtesy Harry S. Truman Library.

160 December 28, 1945: Ibid., 523–24. Courtesy Harry S. Truman Library.
     c. October 30, 1942: John S. D. Eisenhower, ed., *Letters to Mamie* (Garden City, NY: Doubleday, 1978), 50–52. Courtesy Susan Eisenhower.

163 December 30, 1942: Ibid., 74–75. Courtesy Susan Eisenhower.

165 "The stories and pictures . . .": Carl Anthony Sferrazza, *First Ladies: The Saga of the Presidents' Wives and Their Power, 1961–1990* (New York: William Morrow, 1991), 74.

165 December 12, 1943: George H. W. Bush, *All the Best, George Bush: My Life in Letters and Other Writings* (New York: Scribner, 2013), 38–39.

PART 3: ADVERSITY

172 *"Why would it bother me?"*: Carl Anthony Sferrazza, *First Ladies: The Saga of the Presidents' Wives and Their Power, 1961–1990* (New York: William Morrow, 1991), 293.

173 March 31 1776: Margaret A. Hogan and C. James Taylor, eds., *My Dearest Friend: Letters of Abigail and John Adams* (Cambridge, MA: Belknap Press of Harvard University Press, 2007), 110–11.

174 April 14, 1776: Ibid., 112–13.

175 July 10, 1777, and July 16: Ibid., 186, 188.

177 Oct. 31 *[1805]*, and James's reply: David B. Mattern and Holly C. Shulman, eds., *The Selected Letters of Dolley Payne Madison* (Charlottesville: University of Virginia Press, 2003), 69–70, 78.

178 *"Mr. and Mrs. Madison . . ."*: Thomas Fleming, *The Intimate Lives of the Founding Fathers* (New York: Smithsonian Books, 2009), 384.

179 "Mr. William's . . .": David B. Mattern and Holly C. Shulman, eds., *The Selected Letters of Dolley Payne Madison* (Charlottesville: University of Virginia Press, 2003), 192.

180 Tuesday, Augt. 23d. 1814: Ibid., 193–94.

181 Aug. 27, 10 OC.: Ibid., 194–95.

183 *August 23, 1814*: Harold D. Moser, David R. Hoth, Sharon MacPherson, and John H. Reinbold, eds., *The Papers of Andrew Jackson*, vol. 3, *1814–1815* (Knoxville: University of Tennessee Press, 1991), 117–18.

183 September 22nd 1814: Ibid., 145.

184 *"I try to summon up . . ."*: Carl Anthony Sferrazza, *First Ladies: The Saga of the Presidents' Wives and Their Power, 1789–1961* (New York: William Morrow, 1990), 114.

185 February 1, 1835: Lyon G. Tyler, *The Letters and Times of the Tylers*, vol. 1 (New York: Da Capo Press reprint of 1884 edition, 1970), 509–10.

188 *"What does he do . . ."*: Robert Seager II, *And Tyler Too* (New York: McGraw-Hill, 1963), 195.

190 April 16, 1861: Lyon G. Tyler, *The Letters and Times of the Tylers*, vol. 2 (New York: Da Capo Press reprint of 1896 edition, 1970), 640.

191 April 17, 1861: Ibid., 641–42.

193 April 1, 1850: Archives and Special Collections, Penfield Library, State University of New York, Oswego, New York.

195 *"never took any important step . . ."*: Betty Boyd Caroli, *First Ladies* (New York: Oxford University Press, 1987), 48.

196 *"For twenty-seven years . . ."*: Robert J. Scarry, *Millard Fillmore* (Jefferson, NC: McFarland & Co., 2001), 301.

197 "My precious child . . .": Franklin Pierce Papers, New Hampshire Historical Society, Concord, New Hampshire.

199 April 16, 1848: Roy P. Basler, ed., *The Collected Works of Abraham Lincoln*, vol. 1 (New Brunswick, NJ: Rutgers University Press, 1963), 466.

201 June 7th/64: *Ulysses S. Grant: Memoirs and Selected Letters* (New York: Library of America, 1990), 1056.

201 Grant meets Oscar Dunn, etc.: Nick Weldon, "Historic New Orleans Collection," January 18, 2021.

202 June 29th 1885: John Y. Simon, ed., *The Papers of Ulysses S. Grant*, vol. 31, *1883–1885* (Carbondale: Southern Illinois University Press, 2009), 387–88.

204 December 16, 1861: Charles Richard Williams, ed., *Diary and Letters of Rutherford Birchard Hayes*, vol. 2, *1861–1865* (Columbus: The Ohio State Archeological and Historical Society, 1922), 160.

204 December 23, 1861: Ibid., 166.

205 "a musket-ball passed . . .": Ibid., 353.

205 May 1, *[1864]*: Ibid., 455.

206 "*I know I am going . . .*": The Vintage News, May 20, 2022, thevintagenews .com.

206 Oct. 25, 1862: John Shaw, ed., *Crete and James* (East Lansing: Michigan State University Press, 1984), 167–68.

208 "*he took occasion . . . If Miss Booth . . .*": Ibid., 208.

208 Dec. 26, 1862: Ibid., 177–78.

210 Dec. 13, 1863: John Shaw, ed., *Crete and James* (East Lansing: Michigan State University Press, 1984), 195–96.

210 Feb. 14, 1864: Ibid., 202–3.

212 "Am in excellent shape . . .": H. W. Brands, ed., *The Selected Letters of Theodore Roosevelt* (New York: Cooper Square Press, 2001), 568.

213 *[probably June 17, 1885]*: Library of Congress, William H. Taft Papers, series 2, nos. 28–29.

215–16 May 16, 1911; May 17, 1911; July 14, 1911; July 27, 1912: Lewis L. Gould, ed., *My Dearest Nellie: The Letters of William Howard Taft to Helen Herron Taft, 1909–1912* (Lawrence: University of Kansas Press, 2011), 139, 141–42, 152–53, 245.

216 July 16, 1917: Elliott Roosevelt, ed., *F.D.R. His Personal Letters*, vol. 2, *1905–1928* (New York: Duell, Sloan and Pearce, 1948), 347.

217 *[July 25, 1917]*: Ibid., 352–53.

218 *[July 22, 1919]*: Ibid., 479.

219 *[October 1924]*: Ibid., 565–66.

220   Oct. 7, 1942: Elliott Roosevelt, ed., *F.D.R. His Personal Letters*, vol. 3, *1928–1945* (New York: Duell, Sloan and Pearce, 1950), 1352.

222   April 14, 1933: Robert H. Ferrell, ed., *Dear Bess: The Letters from Harry to Bess Truman, 1910–1959* (New York: W. W. Norton, 1983), 348. Courtesy Harry S. Truman Library.

222   "*Your no account partner . . .*": Paul F. Boller Jr., *Presidential Wives* (New York: Oxford University Press, 1988), 324.

223   March 2, 1943: John S. D. Eisenhower, ed., *Letters to Mamie* (Garden City, NY: Doubleday, 1978), 104–5. Courtesy Susan Eisenhower.

224   "How about lunch . . .": *New York Times,* June 6, 1991, A21.

224   September 8, 1943: John S. D. Eisenhower, ed., *Letters to Mamie* (Garden City, NY: Doubleday, 1978), 146–47.

226   "Dearest Mom . . .": Courtesy Gerald R. Ford Presidential Library.

227   8-8-88: George H. W. Bush, *All the Best, George Bush: My Life in Letters and Other Writings* (New York: Scribner, 2013), 394.

PART 4: LOVERS

231   "*had more women by accident . . .*": Robert Dallek, "Three New Revelations About LBJ," *Atlantic,* April 1998.

232   "*I became Mr. Harding's bride . . .*": Nan Britton, *The President's Daughter* (New York: Elizabeth Ann Guild, 1927), 49.

232   "*There were windows . . .*": Ibid., 172–73.

234   "Dear Madam": Wilson Miles Cary, *Sally Cary: A Long Hidden Romance of Washington's Life* (New York: Da Vinne Press, 1916), 31–32.

235   12th Sept, 1758: Ibid., 36–38.

236   25th Sept'r., 1758: Ibid., 40.

237   16 May, 1798: Ibid., 54–55.

237   "*could not die happy . . .*": Rev. Hamilton W. Pierson, ed., *Jefferson at Monticello* (New York, Michigan Historical Reprint Series, 1862), 106.

239   November 29, 1786: University of Virginia Library, Special Collections; John P. Kaminski, ed., *Jefferson in Love* (Madison, WI: Madison House, 1999), 75–76.

239   December 24, 1786: John P. Kaminski, ed., *Jefferson in Love* (Madison, WI: Madison House, 1999), 77–78,

240   July 1, 1787: Ibid., 88–89.

241   July 27, 1788: Ibid., 109–10.

242   July 30, 1788: Ibid., 111.

243   October 14, 1789: Ibid., 130.

244 "*Miss Nancy*" etc.: Thomas J. Balcerski, *Bosom Friends: The Intimate World of James Buchanan and William Rufus King* (New York: Oxford University Press, 2019), 9.

245 "I envy Colonel King . . .": Ibid., 9–10.

246 "*I am selfish enough . . .*": Ibid., 10.

246 "Bachelor Presidents": Betty Boyd Caroli, *First Ladies* (New York: Oxford University Press, 1987), 308.

247 18 February, 1910: Arthur S. Link, ed., *The Papers of Woodrow Wilson*, vol. 20, *1910* (Princeton, NJ: Princeton University Press, 1975), 138–41.

248 21 July 1912: Arthur S. Link, ed., *The Papers of Woodrow Wilson*, vol. 24, *1912*, (Princeton, NJ: Princeton University Press, 1977), 561–62.

249 "cast so perfectly . . .": Carl Anthony Sferrazza, *First Ladies: The Saga of the Presidents' Wives and Their Power, 1789–1961* (New York: William Morrow, 1990), 335.

251–55 *[Jan. 28, 1912], [Jan. 2, 1913], [Sept. 15, 1913], [Sept. 21–24, 1913]*, Feb. 2, 1920: Library of Congress.

257 "*I know one should be proud . . .*": Joseph E. Persico, *Franklin and Lucy* (New York: Random House, 2008), 264.

257 May 22nd *[1926]*: Courtesy Franklin D. Roosevelt Presidential Library.

259 "Why don't you leave suburbia . . .": RR Auction, June 23, 2016.

Bibliography

Adams, Charles Francis. *Familiar Letters of John Adams and His Wife Abigail Adams with a Memoir of Mrs. Adams.* Freeport, NY: Books for Libraries Press, 1970 reprint of 1875 edition.

Allgor, Catherine. *Dolley Madison: The Problem of National Unity.* Boulder, CO: Westvision Press, 2013.

Anthony, Carl Sferrazza. *First Ladies: The Saga of the Presidents' Wives and Their Power, 1789–1961.* New York: William Morrow, 1990.

———. *First Ladies: The Saga of the Presidents' Wives and Their Power, 1961–1990.* New York: William Morrow, 1991.

———. *America's First Families: An Inside View of 200 Years of Private Life in the White House.* New York: Simon & Schuster, 2000.

Balcerski, Thomas J. *Bosom Friends: The Intimate World of James Buchanan and William Rufus King.* New York: Oxford University Press, 2019.

Basler, Roy P., ed. *The Collected Works of Abraham Lincoln.* Vol. 1. New Brunswick, NJ: Rutgers University Press, 1953.

Beyer, Rick, and The History Channel. *The Greatest Presidential Stories Never Told.* New York: Harper Collins, 2007.

Bittinger, Cynthia D. *Grace Coolidge: Sudden Star.* New York: Nova History Publications, 2005.

Boles, John B. *Jefferson: Architect of American Liberty.* New York: Basic Books, 2017.

Boller, Paul F. Jr. *Presidential Wives.* New York: Oxford University Press, 1988.

Bradford, Sarah. *America's Queen: The Life of Jacqueline Kennedy Onassis.* New York: Vintage, 2000.

Brands, H. W., ed. *The Selected Letters of Theodore Roosevelt.* New York: Cooper Square Press, 2001.

Britton, Nan. *The President's Daughter.* New York: Elizabeth Ann Guild, 1927.

Bumgarner, John Reed. *Sarah Childress Polk: A Biography of the Remarkable First Lady.* Jefferson, NC: McFarland & Co., 1997.

Bush, George H. W. *All the Best, George Bush: My Life in Letters and Other Writings.* New York: Scribner, 2013.

Bush, Laura. *Spoken from the Heart.* New York: Scribner, 2010.

Bushnell, Mark. "Then Again: When Calvin Coolidge Wooed Grace Goodhue—A Story of Opposites Attracting." VTDigger, February 9, 2020, https://vtdigger.org/2020/02/09/then-again-when-calvin-coolidge -wooed-grace-goodhue-a-story-of-opposites-attracting/.

Butterfield, L. H., Marc Friedlander, and Mary Jo Klein, eds. *The Book of Abigail and John: Selected Letters of the Adams Family 1762–1784.* Cambridge, MA: Harvard University Press, 1975.

Caroli, Betty Boyd. *First Ladies.* New York: Oxford University Press, 1987.

———. *First Ladies from Martha Washington to Michelle Obama.* New York: Oxford University Press, 2010.

Carter, Jimmy. *A Full Life: Reflections at Ninety.* New York: Simon & Schuster, 2015.

Cary, Wilson Miles. *Sally Cary: A Long Hidden Romance of Washington's Life.* New York: Da Vinne Press, 1916.

Chafe, William H. *Bill and Hillary: The Politics of the Personal.* New York: Farrar, Straus and Giroux, 2012.

Chernow, Ron. Introduction to *My Dear Julia: The Wartime Letters of Ulysses S. Grant to His Wife.* New York: Library of America, 2018.

Coolidge, Grace. *Grace Coolidge: An Autobiography.* Edited by Lawrence E. Wikander and Robert H. Ferrell. Worland, NY: High Plains Publishing, 1992.

Cutler, Wayne, ed. *Correspondence of James K. Polk.* Vol. 5, *1839–1841.* Nashville: Vanderbilt University Press, 1979.

———. *Correspondence of James K. Polk.* Vol 6, *1842–1843.* Nashville: Vanderbilt University Press, 1983.

Dunlap, Annette. *Frank: The Story of Frances Folsom, America's Youngest First Lady.* Albany: State University of New York Press, 2004.

Eisenhower, John S. D., ed. and commentary. *Dwight D. Eisenhower: Letters to Mamie.* Garden City, NY: Doubleday, 1978.

Eisenhower, Susan. *Mrs. Ike.* New York: Farrar, Straus and Giroux, 1996.

Engel, Jeffrey, and Thomas D. Knock. *When Life Strikes the President.* New York: Oxford University Press, 2017.

Epstein, Daniel Mark. *The Lincolns: Portrait of a Marriage.* New York: Ballantine Books, 2008.

Ferrell, Robert H., ed. *Dear Bess: The Letters from Harry to Bess Truman 1910–1959.* New York: W. W. Norton, 1983.

Finkelman, Paul. *Millard Fillmore.* New York: Times Books, 2011.

Fleming, Thomas. *The Intimate Lives of the Founding Fathers.* New York: Smithsonian Books, 2009.

Foster, Thomas A. *Sex and the Founding Fathers.* Philadelphia: Temple University Press, 2014.

Gawalt, Gerard W. *My Dear President: Letters Between Presidents and Their Wives.* New York: Black Dog and Leventhal, 2005.

Gilbert, Robert E. *The Tormented President.* Westport, CT: Praeger, 2003.

Godbold, E. Stanley Jr. *Jimmy and Rosalynn Carter: The Georgia Years, 1924–1974.* New York: Oxford University Press, 2010.

Gordon-Reed, Annette. *The Hemingses of Monticello: An American Story.* New York: W. W. Norton, 2009.

Gould, Lewis L., ed. *American First Ladies: Their Lives and Their Legacy.* New York: Garland Publishing, 1996.

———. *My Dearest Nellie: The Letters of William Howard Taft and Helen Herron Taft, 1909–1912.* Lawrence: University Press of Kansas, 2011.

Graff, Garret M. *Watergate: A New History.* New York: Avid Reader Press, 2022.

Graham, Judith S., Beth Luey, Margaret A. Hogan, and C. James Taylor, eds. *Diary and Autobiographical Writings of Louisa Catherine Adams.* Vol. 1, *1778–1815.* Cambridge, MA: Belknap Press of Harvard University Press, 2013.

Grant, Ulysses S. *Memoirs and Selected Letters, 1839–1865.* New York: Library of America, 1990.

Greenberg, Amy S. *Lady First: The World of First Lady Sarah Polk.* New York: Knopf, 2019.

Heffron, Margery. *Louisa Catherine: The Other Mrs. Adams.* Edited by David L. Michelmore. New Haven, CT: Yale University Press, 2014.

Herman, Eleanor. *Sex with Presidents.* New York: William Morrow, 2020.

Hogan, Margaret A., and C. James Taylor, eds. *My Dearest Friend: Letter of Abigail and John Adams.* Cambridge, MA: Belknap Press of Harvard University Press, 2007.

Holloway, Laura C. *The Ladies of the White House: Or, In the Home of the Presidents.* Philadelphia: Bradley, 1881.

Holt, Michael F. *Franklin Pierce.* New York: Henry Holt and Company, 2010.

Hunt, Irma. *Dearest Madame: The Presidents' Mistresses.* New York: McGraw-Hill, 1978.

Hunter, Frederick. "Unraveling the Lincoln Courtship Conspiracy." *Christian Science Monitor,* November 14, 1989.

Kaminsky, John P. *Jefferson in Love: The Love Letters Between Thomas Jefferson and Maria Cosway.* Madison, WI: Madison House, 1999.

Kirkland, Mrs. C. M. *Memoirs of Washington.* New York: D. Appleton, 1857.

Lamb, Brian, Susan Swain, and C-Span. *The Presidents.* New York: Public Affairs, 2019.

Link, Arthur S., ed. *The Papers of Woodrow Wilson.* Vol. 4, *1885.* Princeton, NJ: Princeton University Press, 1968.

———. *The Papers of Woodrow Wilson.* Vol. 20, *1910.* Princeton, NJ: Princeton University Press, 1975.

———. *The Papers of Woodrow Wilson*. Vol. 24, *1912*. Princeton, NJ: Princeton University Press, 1977.

Mattern, David B., and Holly C. Shulman, eds. *The Selected Letters of Dolley Payne Madison*. Charlottesville: University of Virginia Press, 2003.

May, Gary. *John Tyler*. New York: Henry Holt, 2008.

McAdoo, Eleanor Wilson, ed. *The Priceless Gift: The Love Letters of Woodrow Wilson and Ellen Axson Wilson*. New York: McGraw-Hill, 1962.

McCullough, David. *John Adams*. New York: Simon & Schuster, 2001.

Minnigerode, Meade. *Seven American Ladies*. Freeport, NY: Books for Libraries Press, 1969 reprint of 1926 edition.

Morris, Roger. *Partners in Power: The Clintons and Their America*. New York: Henry Holt, 1996.

Moser, Harold D., and Sharon Macpherson, eds. *The Papers of Andrew Jackson*. Vol. 2, *1804–1813*. Knoxville: University of Tennessee Press, 1984.

Moser, Harold D., David R. Hoth, Sharon Macpherson, and John H. Reinbold, eds. *The Papers of Andrew Jackson*. Vol. 3, *1814–1815*. Knoxville: University of Tennessee Press, 1991.

Nichols, Roy Franklin. *Franklin Pierce: Young Hickory of the Granite Hills*. Philadelphia: University of Pennsylvania Press, 1931.

Obama, Michelle. *Becoming*. New York: Crown, 2018.

O'Brien, Cormac. *Secret Lives of the First Ladies*. Philadelphia, Quirk Books, 2005.

Persico, Joseph E. *Franklin and Lucy*. New York: Random House, 2008.

Reeves, Thomas C. *Gentleman Boss: The Life of Chester Alan Arthur*. New York: Knopf, 1975.

Robenalt, James David. *The Harding Affair: Love and Espionage During the Great War*. New York: Palgrave Macmillan, 2009.

Roosevelt, Elliott, ed. *F.D.R.: His Personal Letters*. Vol. 2, *1905–1928*. New York: Duell, Sloan and Pearce, 1948.

———. *F.D.R.: His Personal Letters*. Vol. 3, *1928–1945*. New York: Duell, Sloan and Pearce, 1950.

Scarry, Robert J. *Millard Fillmore*. Jefferson, NC: McFarland, 2001.

Seager, Robert II. *And Tyler Too*. New York: McGraw Hill, 1963.

Shaw, John, ed. *Crete and James: Personal Letters of Lucretia and James Garfield*. East Lansing: Michigan State University Press, 1994.

Sibley, Katherine A. S. *First Lady Florence Harding*. Lawrence: University Press of Kansas, 2009.

———. *Southern First Ladies*. Lawrence: University Press of Kansas, 2020.

Simon, John T., ed. *The Papers of Ulysses S. Grant*. Vol. 1, *1837–1861*. Carbondale: Southern Illinois University Press, 1967.

Smith, Sam B., and Harriet Chappell Owsley, eds. *The Papers of Andrew Jackson.* Vol. 1, *1770–1803.* Knoxville: University of Tennessee Press, 1980.

Taylor, Elizabeth Dowling. *A Slave in the White House.* New York: Palgrave Macmillan, 2012.

Taylor, Lloyd C. Jr. "A Wife for Mr. Pierce." *New England Quarterly* 28 (September 1955), 319–38.

Tribble, Edwin. *A President in Love: The Courtship Letters of Woodrow Wilson and Edith Bolling Galt.* Boston: Houghton Mifflin, 1981.

Troy, Gil. *Mr. and Mrs. President: From the Trumans to the Clintons.* 2nd ed. Lawrence: University Press of Kansas, 1997.

Tyler, Lyon G., ed. *The Letters and Times of the Tylers.* Vols. 1 and 2. New York: Da Capo Press, 1970.

Wikander, Lawrence E., and Robert H. Ferrell. *Grace Coolidge: An Autobiography.* Worland, WY: High Plains Publishing, 1992.

Williams, Charles Richard, ed. *Diary and Letters of Rutherford Birchard Hayes.* Vol. 1, *1834–1860.* Columbus: Ohio State Archaeological and Historical Society Press, 1922.

———. *Diary and Letters of Rutherford Birchard Hayes.* Vol. 2, *1861–1865.* Columbus: Ohio State Archaeological and Historical Society Press, 1922.

Wilson, Douglas L. "Keeping Lincoln's Secrets." Part 2. *Atlantic Monthly* 285:5 (May 2000), 78–88.

Woodward, Hobson, Sara Martin, Christopher F. Minty, Neal E. Millikan, Gwen Fries, Amanda M. Norton, and Sara Georgini, eds. *Adams Family Correspondence.* Vol. 15, *March 1801–October 1804.* Cambridge, MA: Belknap Press of Harvard University Press, 2021.

Image Credits

Index

Page number in *italics* refers to images.

About the Authors

DOROTHY AND THOMAS HOOBLER are the authors of more than one hundred books, including fiction and nonfiction for children and young adults. They have also written several works on historical topics for adults. Their work has been cited for excellence by the Library of Congress, the Society for School Librarians International, the National Council for the Social Studies, the National Council of Teachers of English, the International Reading Association, the Mystery Writers of America, the National Conference of Christians and Jews, Bank Street College, and the New York Public Library. They won an Edgar Award, from the Mystery Writers of America, for their YA novel set in eighteenth-century Japan.

DOROTHY E. HOOBLER earned her bachelor of arts degree with a major in history at Wells College. She has a master's degree in American history from New York University. She was an editor in the social studies school book department of Holt, Rinehart, and Winston before becoming a full-time writer.

THOMAS W. HOOBLER graduated with a major in English from the University of Notre Dame. He has a master's degree in education from Xavier University. He was a teacher at a private school in Cincinnati for several years. Before becoming a full-time freelance writer he was a school text editor for Globe Book Company and an editor on a trade magazine.